PHILOSOPHY
THE CLASSICS

Third edition

Nigel Warburton

Routledge
Taylor & Francis Group

LONDON AND NEW YORK

i

First edition published 1998

Second edition published 2001

Third edition first published 2006
by Routledge
2 Park Square, Milton Park, Abingdon, Oxon OX14 4RN

Simultaneously published in the USA and Canada
by Routledge
711 Third Avenue, New York, NY 10017 (8th Floor)

Routledge is an imprint of the Taylor & Francis Group, an informa business

© 1998, 2001, 2006 Nigel Warburton

Typeset in Aldus
by Florence Production Ltd, Stoodleigh, Devon

British Library Cataloguing in Publication Data
A catalogue record for this book is available from the British Library

Library of Congress Cataloging in Publication Data
A catalog record for this book has been requested

ISBN10: 0–415–35628–8 (hbk)
ISBN10: 0–415–35629–6 (pbk)
ISBN10: 0–203–00262–8 (ebk)

ISBN13: 978–0–415–35628–2 (hbk)
ISBN13: 978–0–415–35629–9 (pbk)
ISBN13: 978–0–203–00262–9 (ebk)

FOR ANNA

CONTENTS

ACKNOWLEDGEMENTS

I am grateful to everyone who commented on parts or all of this book, including Caroline Dawnay, Jonathan Hourigan, E. J. Lowe, Pauline Marsh, Derek Matravers, Tom Stoneham, Stephanie Warburton, Terence Wilkerson and several anonymous readers. I am particularly grateful to Michael Clark, whose close reading saved me from a number of errors, both philosophical and factual. My wife Anna also made many helpful suggestions which have greatly improved it.

Oxford, 1997

Note on the Second Edition
For this new edition I have added chapters on Boethius *The Consolation of Philosophy*, Machiavelli *The Prince*, Spinoza *Ethics*, and Rawls *A Theory of Justice*. I have also brought the reading lists up to date.

I am very grateful for useful comments from several anonymous publisher's readers on the new chapters. I also want to thank Tony Bruce and Muna Khogali at Routledge for their help with this new edition.

Oxford, 2000

Note on the Third Edition
There are three new chapters in this edition, those on Nietzsche's *Beyond Good and Evil*, Russell's *The Problems of Philosophy* and Sartre's *Existentialism and Humanism*. I have also made minor

changes to some of the suggested further reading. The chapter on Jean-Paul Sartre's *Existentialism and Humanism* draws on my article 'A student's guide to Jean-Paul Sartre's *Existentialism and Humanism*' which originally appeared in the magazine *Philosophy Now*. I am grateful for comments by Stephen Law and several publisher's readers on some of the new material here.

Nigel Warburton, Oxford, 2005

Email: n.warburton@open.ac.uk
Website: www.nigelwarburton.com

INTRODUCTION

This book consists of twenty-seven chapters, each focused on a single great philosophical book. The point is to introduce each book, bringing out its most important themes. The books dealt with here are worth reading today because they engage with philosophical problems that are still worth discussing, and because they continue to offer insights. Apart from that, many of them hold their own as great works of literature.

Ideally, reading this book should be a spur to your reading (or re-reading) the books it treats. But not everyone has the time or the energy to do that. At least I hope this will guide you to the books among the twenty-seven that you are likely to find most rewarding, and offer you some suggestions about how you might read them critically. I have tried to avoid recommending books which are unnecessarily obscure. This has led me to omit some acknowledged masterpieces, such as Hegel's *The Phenomenology of Spirit* and *Philosophy of Right* and Heidegger's *Being and Time*, for which I make no apology. At the end of each chapter I have given guidelines for further reading.

My choice of books is in some ways controversial, more for what I have left out than for what I have included, I suspect. What I have done is focused on books that I believe repay study today and which are amenable to the sort of treatment possible in three or four thousand words. This is a personal top twenty-seven; other philosophers, though their choices would certainly overlap with mine, would come up with a different top twenty-seven.

I have included brief chronologies, but haven't found space for any detailed historical background. My main aim is to introduce books rather than movements in the history of ideas. This doesn't mean that I am advocating a completely ahistorical reading of these texts. However, I do believe that the best way to approach them is, in the first instance, by getting an overview of their major themes and emphases. Those who want more contextual information can find it in the recommendations for further reading.

Don't be afraid to dip into chapters out of order. I have written each chapter to stand on its own without presupposing any knowledge of those which have gone before.

FURTHER READING

My two books, *Philosophy: The Basics* (London: Routledge, 4th edn, 2004) and *Thinking from A to Z* (London: Routledge, 2nd edn, 2000) complement this one. The first is a topic-based introduction to the central areas of philosophy; the second an alphabetically arranged introduction to critical thinking, the techniques of argument that are central to philosophical method. I have also edited a collection of readings, *Philosophy: Basic Readings* (London: Routledge, 2nd edn, 2004) and an introduction to study skills in philosophy: *Philosophy: The Essential Study Guide* (London: Routledge, 2004).

Other general books on philosophy which you might find useful include:

John Cottingham (ed.) *Western Philosophy: An Anthology* (Oxford: Blackwell, 1996).

Edward Craig (ed.) *The Shorter Routledge Encyclopedia of Philosophy* (London: Routledge, 2005).

Anthony Flew *A Dictionary of Philosophy* (London: Pan, 1979).

Ted Honderich (ed.) *The Oxford Companion to Philosophy* (Oxford: Oxford University Press, 1995).

Bryan Magee *The Great Philosophers* (Oxford: Oxford University Press, 1988).

Roger Scruton *A Short History of Modern Philosophy* (London: Routledge, 2nd edn, 1995).

J. O. Urmson and Jonathan Rée *The Concise Encyclopedia of Western Philosophy and Philosophers* (London: Routledge, new edn, 1989).

Mary Warnock (ed.) *Women Philosophers* (London: Dent, Everyman, 1995).

1

PLATO *THE REPUBLIC*

THE CAVE

Imagine a cave. Prisoners are chained facing its far wall. They've been kept there all their lives and their heads are held fixed so that they can't see anything except the wall of the cave. Behind them there is a fire and between the fire and their backs a road. Along the road various people walk casting their shadows on the cave wall; some of them carry models of animals which also cast shadows. The prisoners inside the cave only ever see shadows. They believe the shadows are the real things because they don't know any better. But in fact they never see real people.

Then one day one of the prisoners is released and allowed to look towards the fire. At first he is completely dazzled by the flames, but gradually he starts to discern the world around him. Then he is taken out of the cave into the full light of the sun, which again dazzles him. He slowly begins to realise the poverty of his former life: he had always been satisfied with the world of shadows when behind him lay the brightly lit real world in all its richness. Now as his eyes acclimatise to the daylight he sees what his fellow prisoners have missed and feels sorry for them. Eventually he becomes so used to the light that he can even look directly at the sun.

Then he is taken back to his seat in the cave. His eyes are no longer used to this shadowy existence. He can no longer make the fine discriminations between shadows that his fellow prisoners find easy. From their point of view his eyesight has been ruined by his journey out of the cave. He has seen the real world; they remain content with the world of superficial appearances and wouldn't leave the cave even if they could.

This parable of the prisoners in the cave occurs halfway through Plato's masterpiece, *The Republic*. It provides a memorable image of his theory of Forms, his account of the nature of reality. According to him the majority of humankind are, like the prisoners, content with a world of mere appearance. Only philosophers make the journey out of the cave and learn to experience things as they really are; only they can have genuine knowledge. The world of everyday perception is constantly changing and imperfect. But the world of the Forms to which philosophers have access is unchanging and perfect. It can't be perceived with the five senses: it is only by means of thought that anyone can experience the Forms.

PLATO AND SOCRATES

The life and death of his mentor, Socrates, was the main influence on Plato's philosophy. Socrates was a charismatic figure who attracted a crowd of wealthy young Athenians around him. He did not leave any writing but exerted his influence through his conversations in the marketplace. He claimed not to have any doctrine to teach, but rather, through a series of pointed questions, would demonstrate how little those he talked to really knew about such things as the nature of piety, justice, or morality. While Plato was still a young man, Socrates was sentenced to death for corrupting the youth of the city and failing to believe in its gods. Socrates drank hemlock, the conventional method of execution for Athenian citizens.

Plato gave Socrates a kind of afterlife in his dialogues. Yet the character called Socrates in Plato's work probably differs considerably in his views from the real Socrates. Plato wrote as if he were recording conversations which had actually occurred; but by the time he came to write *The Republic*, Plato's Socrates had become a mouthpiece for Plato's own views.

The Republic provides a mixture of Plato's two characteristic approaches to writing. In Book One, there is a conversation between

Socrates and some friends which could have been the first scene in a play: we are told something of the setting and the reactions of the different characters. But in later sections, although Plato continues to write in dialogue form, the thrust of exposition is in Socrates' voice, and the supporting cast simply agree with his pronouncements.

THRASYMACHUS AND GLAUCON

The main body of *The Republic* is a response to the challenges set by Thrasymachus and Glaucon. Thrasymachus maintains that what goes by the name of 'justice' is simply whatever happens to serve the interests of the strongest. Power is all that makes something right. Justice is simply a matter of obeying the self-serving rules set up by the strongest. At the level of individual behaviour, injustice pays much better than justice: those who help themselves to more than their fair share are happier than those who are just.

Glaucon takes this further, suggesting that those who behave justly only do so as a form of self-preservation. Anyone who, like the mythical character Gyges, found a ring that made them invisible would lose any incentive for behaving justly since they could guarantee getting away with any crime, seduction or deception. He imagines a situation in which a just man is thought by everyone else to be unjust. He is tortured and executed: his life seems to have nothing to be said in its favour. Compare this with the life of a cunning wicked man who manages to seem just while being completely unscrupulous whenever he can get away with it. He leads a happy life, it seems, and is considered a model of respectability even though beneath his disguise he is thoroughly evil. This suggests that justice doesn't pay, or at least that it doesn't always pay. It also suggests that if Socrates wants to defend the just life he will have to show that the situation described isn't the full story. In fact in the rest of the book Socrates attempts to do precisely that; he seeks to demonstrate that justice *does* pay, and that, besides, it is intrinsically worthwhile. It is good both for its consequences and in itself.

INDIVIDUAL AND STATE

Although *The Republic* is usually thought of as a work of political philosophy, and despite the fact that most of it is focused on the question of how Plato's utopian state should be run, the discussion of the state is only introduced as a way of getting clearer about individual morality. Plato's main concern is to answer the question 'What is justice and is it worth pursuing?' 'Justice' is a slightly strange word to use here, but it is the best translation of the Greek word *dikaiosunē*: it means, roughly, doing the right thing. Plato's main concern is the question of what is the best way for a human being to live. His reason for looking at the organisation of the state at all is his belief that the state is equivalent to the individual writ large; that the best way of proceeding is to study justice in the state and then transfer our findings to the individual. Just as someone who is short-sighted finds it easier to read large letters so it is easier to look at justice in the state than on the smaller scale of an individual life.

DIVISION OF LABOUR

Human beings cannot easily live alone. There are many advantages in co-operation and communal living. As soon as people group together it makes sense to divide work according to different people's skills: it is better for a tool maker to make tools all the year round and a farmer to farm than that the farmer stop his work to make new tools when the old ones wear out. The tool maker will be more skilled at tool making than the farmer. The same is true of all other professions which involve skill: skill requires practice.

As the state grows and work becomes more specialised, the need for a full-time army to defend the state from attack becomes apparent. The Guardians of the state must, according to Plato, be strong and courageous, like good guard dogs. But they must also have a philosophical temperament. A significant part of *The Republic* is taken up with Plato's training schedule for the Guardians.

RULERS, AUXILIARIES AND WORKERS

Plato divides his class of Guardians into two: Rulers and Auxiliaries. The Rulers are those who are to have the political power and who make all the important decisions; the Auxiliaries help the Rulers and provide defence against threats from outside. A third group, the Workers, will, as their name suggests, work, providing the necessities of life for all the citizens. Plato isn't much interested in the lives of the Workers: most of *The Republic* concentrates on the Guardians.

The Rulers are chosen as those who are most likely to devote their lives to doing what they judge to be in the best interests of the society. To weed out unsuitable candidates, Plato suggests that in the course of their education potential Rulers should be given various tests to see if they are likely to be bewitched by the pursuit of their own pleasure: their reactions to temptation will be closely monitored and only those who demonstrate complete devotion to the well-being of the community will be chosen to rule. They will be very few in number.

None of the Guardians will be allowed to own personal property, and even their children will be treated in common. In fact Plato provides a radical solution to the family: he wants to abolish it and replace it with state nurseries in which children are looked after unaware of who their parents are. This is supposed to increase loyalty to the state since children brought up in this way won't have confusing loyalties to family members.

Even sexual intercourse is regulated: citizens are only allowed to have sex at special festivals when they are paired off by lot – or at least, that's what the participants are led to believe. In fact the Rulers fix the outcome of the mating lottery so that only those of good breeding stock will be allowed to procreate. Thus Plato's republic has its own form of eugenics designed to produce strong and courageous children. At birth all children are taken away from their mothers to be reared by specially appointed officers. Children of inferior Guardians and any 'defective' offspring of the Workers are disposed of.

ROLE OF WOMEN

Not all of Plato's proposals in *The Republic* are as offensive as these plans for selective breeding and infanticide. Unlike most of his contemporaries, he thought that women should be given the same education as men, should be allowed to fight alongside them, and become Guardians if they showed aptitude. It is true that he still believed that men would surpass women at every activity. Even so, his proposals were radical at a time when married middle-class women were virtual prisoners in their own homes.

THE MYTH OF THE METALS

The success of the state depends upon its citizens' loyalty to the land and to each other. In order to assure this loyalty Plato suggests that all classes of society be encouraged to believe a myth about their origins. The 'magnificent myth' or 'noble lie', as it is sometimes translated, is as follows. Everyone sprang from the earth fully formed: memories of upbringing and education are just a dream. In fact all citizens are siblings since they are all the children of Mother Earth. This should make them loyal both to the land (their mother) and to each other (their brothers and sisters).

The myth has another aspect. God, when he created each individual, added metal to their composition. He added gold to the Rulers; silver to the Auxiliaries; and bronze and iron to the Workers. God instructed the Rulers to observe the mixture of metals in the characters of children. If a child with bronze in his or her composition is born of gold parents, then they must harden their hearts and consign him or her to the life of a Worker; if a Worker's child has gold or silver in him or her, then the child must be brought up as a Ruler or Auxiliary as appropriate. This myth is intended to produce not only loyalty, but contentment with your station in life. The class that you belong to is determined by factors outside your control.

THE JUST STATE AND THE JUST INDIVIDUAL

Because the ideal state he describes is perfect, Plato believes it must possess the qualities of wisdom, courage, self-discipline and justice. He takes it for granted that these are the four cardinal virtues of any perfect state. Wisdom is due to the Rulers' knowledge, which allows them to make wise decisions for the benefit of the state; courage is demonstrated by the Auxiliaries, whose training has made them brave and fearless in defence of the state; self-discipline arises from the harmony between the three classes, with the unruly desires of the majority being held in check by the wise decisions of the Rulers; and lastly, justice is evident in the state as a result of each person taking care of his or her own business in the sense of doing what he or she is naturally fitted for. Anyone who attempts social mobility is a potential threat to the state's stability.

The ideal state exhibits the four cardinal virtues because of its division into three classes and because of the harmonious balance between their assigned roles. Analogously, Plato insists, each individual consists of three parts, and the qualities of wisdom, courage, self-discipline and justice all depend on the harmonious interplay between these parts of the individual.

THE THREE PARTS OF THE SOUL

The word 'soul' suggests something more spiritual than is appropriate: although Plato believes in the immortality of the soul, what he writes about the three parts of the soul in *The Republic* doesn't turn on the soul being separable from the body, or even on its being something distinct from the body. His interest here is really in the psychology of motivation. The three parts of the soul he identifies are Reason, Spirit and Desire.

Reason corresponds to the role of the Rulers in the ideal state. Like the Rulers, Reason can plan for the good of the whole entity: unlike the other parts of the soul, it is not self-interested. Reason has the capacity to make plans about how best to achieve certain ends; but it also involves the love of truth.

Spirit is that part of the personality which provides emotional motivation for action in the form of anger, indignation and the like. When subject to the proper training Spirit is the source of bravery and courage. Spirit corresponds to the role of the Auxiliaries.

Desire is the pure appetite for particular things such as food, drink or sex. Desire can persist in direct opposition to Reason. Indeed the occurrence of conflicts between what people want and what they know is best for them is evidence Plato uses to support his distinction between the three parts of the soul. Desire corresponds to the role of the Workers.

The four virtues of wisdom, courage, self-discipline and justice can all be found in individuals as well as in states: Plato explains these virtues in terms of the parts of the soul. Someone who is wise makes decisions based on the dominance of Reason; someone who is brave gets the motivation to act in the face of danger from Spirit, which acts as the ally of Reason; someone who has self-discipline follows the dictates of Reason, keeping Desire under control. Most importantly, someone who is just acts so that all the parts of the soul are in harmony: each part functions in its appropriate role with Reason in command. So justice in the individual is a kind of psychic harmony. This is what makes it an intrinsically valuable condition.

PHILOSOPHER KINGS

Although Plato's pretext for discussing justice in the state is in order to illuminate questions about the individual, he is clearly also deeply concerned with the utopian republic he has created. He addresses the question of how such a political system could ever come about and concludes that the only hope is to rest power in the hands of philosophers. Plato defends this surprising suggestion with another parable. Imagine a ship whose owner is short-sighted, a bit deaf and more or less ignorant of seamanship. The crew quarrel about who should take the helm of the ship. None of them have devoted any time to the study of navigation and in fact they don't believe it can be taught. Factions compete to take control of the ship, and when they do they help themselves to the goods on board, turning the voyage into a kind of drunken pleasure cruise. None of them realise that a navigator needs to study the weather and the position of the stars. They think of anyone who acquires the relevant skills as a useless star-gazer.

The state in its present form is like the ship lurching around in the hands of the unskilled crew. Only in the hands of a skilled navigator will it be kept under control: and the philosopher, despised as he might be, is the only person in possession of the knowledge required to steer the state. Plato's theory of Forms explains why philosophers are particularly well-equipped to rule.

THE THEORY OF FORMS

The parable of the cave with which I began this chapter illustrates in a memorable way Plato's picture of the human condition. Most of humanity is content with mere appearance, the equivalent of the flickering shadows on the wall of the cave. Philosophers, however, since they love truth, seek knowledge of reality: they journey out of the cave and get access to the Forms.

The theory of Forms, although put forward by the character Socrates in *The Republic*, is generally recognised to be Plato's own contribution to philosophy. When people speak of Platonism they usually mean this aspect of his work. To understand what Plato meant by 'Form' it is easiest to consider one of his examples.

Many beds exist. Some are double, some single, some four-posted, and so on. Yet there is something they share which makes them all beds. What they share is a relation to an ideal bed, the *Form* of the bed. This Form actually exists: it is the only *real* bed. All other beds are imperfect copies of the Form of the bed. They belong to the world of appearance, not of reality. Consequently we can only have genuine knowledge of the Form of the bed: any information about actual beds is opinion, not knowledge. The everyday world we inhabit is constantly changing; the world of Forms is timeless and unchanging. Philosophers, with their love of wisdom, gain access to the world of Forms, and thus the possibility of knowledge, through thought; perception restricts us to the flux of the world of appearance.

Though he does not spell out precisely which things in the world have a corresponding Form, Plato does maintain that there is a Form of the Good. It is the Good which is the ultimate focus of philosophers' quest for knowledge. He uses the simile of the sun to explain this idea. The sun makes sight possible and is the source of growth; the Form of the Good allows the mind's eye to 'see' and understand the nature of reality. Without the illumination provided by the Form of the Good, we are condemned to live in a twilight world of appearance and opinion; in the light of the Good we can glean knowledge of how to live.

EXAMPLES OF INJUSTICE

Having shown that a just state is one in which the different classes fulfil their appropriate roles, and a just individual one in whom the different motivations are in harmony, Plato turns to some examples of injustice in the state and the individual. He considers four types of unjust state and their corresponding personality type. The four are timocracy, oligarchy, democracy and tyranny. A timocracy is a state, such as Sparta, which is dominated by a drive for military honour; in an oligarchy wealth is the sign of merit; a democracy is a state which is ruled by the people as a whole; in a tyranny the ruler has absolute power.

Again Plato exploits the alleged symmetry between the state and the individual. For instance, in his discussion of democracy he claims that state democracy ignores the principle of training to rule which he has shown to be so essential to the just state. The only prerequisite in a democratic ruler is that he professes to be the people's friend. The corresponding democratic individual, like the democratic state, entertains a wide variety of pleasures, not distinguishing those which are based on good desires from those which have their source in evil. The result is psychic disharmony: the democratic individual does not permit Reason to rule over inappropriate desires. Idle whims dominate; injustice is inevitable.

AGAINST ART

In his account of the Guardians' education Plato argues that various kinds of poetry should be censored. Any writing which gives a false impression of gods or heroes, or which when read out loud by students will lead to an over-identification with unjust characters, is to be banned. In Book Ten of *The Republic* he returns to the subject of art and its place in an ideal society. He concentrates on mimetic art, that is, art which is meant to represent reality. His conclusion is that such art should have no place in his republic. There are two main reasons for this. First, it can only ever be a copy of an appearance and so tends to distance us from the world of the Forms. Second, it appeals to the irrational part of our souls and so tends to disrupt the psychic harmony necessary for justice.

To explain the first sort of criticism Plato takes the example of a painter painting a bed. God made the Form of the bed; a carpenter made a shadowy copy of that Form; an artist painted a copy of the carpenter's copy, doing the equivalent of holding up a mirror to what was already an imperfect image of the one real bed. Consequently the artist obstructs rather than aids our knowledge of reality. The artist remains ignorant of the true nature of the bed and is content with copying the appearance of a particular bed. Plato takes poets to be doing more or less the same as the painter, and so extends his disapproval to the art of poetry.

The work of mimetic artists is nevertheless seductive, as Plato recognises. It does not appeal to reason, but to the lower parts of the soul, an effect exacerbated by artists' tendency to represent evil rather than good impulses. Mimetic artists can lead the unwary away from the path to knowledge. There is, then, no place for them in the republic.

CRITICISMS OF *THE REPUBLIC*

State/individual analogy

Plato's whole project in *The Republic* relies on there being a strong analogy between justice in the state and justice in an individual. If the analogy is weak, then any conclusions about justice for an individual derived from conclusions about the just state will be correspondingly weak. Plato treats it as obvious that his move from state to individual is a legitimate one. However, it is at least worth questioning whether or not this move is justified.

Only Rulers can be just

Furthermore, Plato's theory seems to have the consequence that only the Rulers can be just. After justice has been defined in terms of psychic harmony and each class in the republic in terms of their dominant source of motivation, it becomes clear that only those in whom Reason rules supreme will be capable of acting justly. The Rulers are the only class of people who are in this position. So it seems to follow that only the Rulers are capable of justice. Plato might not have seen this as a serious objection to his theory but rather as an illuminating consequence; for most readers today, however, it brings out the uncompromising elitism inherent in Plato's thought.

Equivocates about 'justice'

When Plato tells us that justice is really a kind of mental health in which the three parts of the soul function harmoniously he seems to have discarded the ordinary sense of 'justice'. He seems to have redefined the word arbitrarily to suit his purposes, or at the very least to have used it in two different senses. Why would anyone want to talk of 'justice' in this way?

Plato would no doubt respond to this criticism that his notion of justice *does* bring out what we ordinarily mean by justice. Plato's just individual won't steal or take more than his share because that would involve Reason's yielding to lower desires. However, this seems to leave open the possibility that some people whom we might be tempted to label 'just' on account of their behaviour would not pass Plato's test since their behaviour might stem from less than harmonious psychic functioning. They might simply have a desire to behave justly, but a very underdeveloped capacity to reason.

Involves deception

At several key points in his argument Plato advocates lying in order to preserve loyalty to the state and to fellow citizens. For instance, there is the so-called 'noble lie' of the myth of the metals; there is also the lie about the mating lottery. Many people find this unacceptable. An ideal state should not be founded on deception. Plato, however, seems unconcerned about this. His interest is in the end result and the best way to achieve it, not in moral questions about how this end result is achieved.

Theory of Forms is implausible

Plato's theory of Forms provides an important foundation for his arguments about the ideal republic. Yet it has little intuitive plausibility for most philosophers today. Perhaps hardest to stomach is the notion that the Forms actually exist and are the reality of which the observed world is simply a shadowy copy.

If we jettison the theory of Forms, then the metaphysical underpinning of many of Plato's proposals would be removed. For instance, without the notion that philosophers are particularly good at gaining knowledge of reality, there would be no obvious justification for putting them in charge of the ideal state. Nor would there be an obvious reason for banning the mimetic arts from the state.

Justifies totalitarianism

However, perhaps the most significant criticism of Plato's *Republic* is that it provides a recipe for totalitarianism. With its plan for eugenics, its 'noble lie', its outlawing of the family and its censorship of art, the state intrudes into every area of life. Individuals in Plato's world must be subservient to the requirements of the state and are expected to sacrifice every element of personal freedom to this end. Those of us who value individual liberty and freedom of choice find Plato's vision a decidedly unattractive one.

DATES

427 BC Plato born into an aristocratic Athenian family.
399 BC Socrates drinks hemlock.
399 BC–347 BC Plato writes more than twenty philosophical dialogues.
347 BC Plato dies.

GLOSSARY

Auxiliaries: Guardians who help the Rulers and provide defence from outside threats.

democracy: a state ruled by the people.

dikaiosunē: usually translated as 'justice', this has the sense of doing what is morally right.

Forms: sometimes known as Ideas. The world of Forms is the real world of perfect entities: the world of appearance which most of us occupy most of the time consists of imperfect copies of the Forms.

Guardians: the class of citizens who protect and rule the state. They consist of Rulers and Auxiliaries.

mimesis: imitation. This is the word Plato uses to describe what he takes to be the essence of artistic endeavour: mirroring nature.

oligarchy: a state ruled by a wealthy elite.

philosopher kings: the Rulers in Plato's ideal society. Philosophers were to be given this role because of their ability to perceive the Forms.

Rulers: the philosopher-kings who hold power in Plato's republic.

timocracy: a state in which military honour is all important.

totalitarian state: a state in which everything is controlled and there is little or no scope for individual freedom.

tyranny: a state ruled by a powerful leader.

utopian: presenting a vision of an ideal society.

FURTHER READING

Bernard Williams *Plato* (London: Phoenix, Great Philosophers series, 1998). This brief book provides the best available introduction to Plato's work and includes some discussion of *The Republic*.

Julia Annas *An Introduction to Plato's Republic* (Oxford: Clarendon Press, 1981) and Nicholas Pappas *Plato and The Republic* (London: Routledge, 1995) are both excellent commentaries.

Karl Popper *The Open Society and its Enemies* (London: Routledge, 1945) includes a convincing case against Plato's republic, arguing that it would be a totalitarian nightmare. This serves as an antidote to the widespread tendency among Plato scholars to give his political proposals a more sympathetic treatment than they deserve.

2

ARISTOTLE
NICOMACHEAN ETHICS

Aristotle was a practical man. Though taught by Plato, he rejected his teacher's idea that reality lay beyond the everyday world in the realm of the Forms. He did not believe in Plato's myth of the Cave. In Raphael's painting *The School of Athens* (1511), Plato points skywards to the Forms; Aristotle, in contrast, reaches forward into the world. His studies went far beyond what we now think of as philosophy: he was, for example, one of the first great biologists. In philosophy his interests were wide-ranging, taking in metaphysics, ethics, politics and aesthetics.

Despite the fact that his *Nicomachean Ethics* is only a collection of lecture notes, is uneven in style, obscure in places, and was certainly never intended for publication, it remains one of the most important works in the history of ethics. Here Aristotle asks one of the fundamental questions for all human beings, 'How should we live?', a question which was at the heart of ancient ethical discussions, but has been sadly neglected by twentieth-century philosophers. His answer, though complex, and in places bizarre, is important, not just as a landmark in the history of civilisation, but also as a significant influence on current philosophical debate.

The *Nicomachean Ethics* is a dense and complex work, and scholars quibble about its precise interpretation; nevertheless, the central themes are easy enough to follow. Some of the key terms

Aristotle used do not translate easily into English. In fact most philosophers who discuss Aristotle have found it more straight-forward to use transliterations of a number of the Greek words rather than rely on confusing English near equivalents. One of the most important of such terms is *eudaimonia*.

EUDAIMONIA: A HAPPY LIFE

Eudaimonia is often translated as 'happiness', but that can be very misleading. It is sometimes also translated as 'flourishing', which, although slightly awkward, has more appropriate connotations: it, for instance, suggests the analogy between the flourishing of plants and the flourishing of human beings. Aristotle believes that we all want *eudaimonia*, by which he means that we all want our lives to go well. A *eudaimon* life is a life that is successful. It is the kind of life that if we could achieve it we would all choose; the kind of life we would want for those we love. *Eudaimonia* is always pursued as an end, never a means to an end. We may seek money, for instance, because it provides a means to buy expensive clothes, and we may buy expensive clothes because we believe they will make us more attractive to people we want to attract; we want to attract these people because we believe that they have a capacity to make our lives go well. But it doesn't make any sense to ask why we want our lives to go well. *Eudaimonia* can't serve any other purpose: it is the place where this sort of chain of explanation finishes. It doesn't make sense to ask 'Why pursue *eudaimonia*?' since, for Aristotle, it is a concep-tual truth that this is what all human beings do. *Eudaimonia* is not the only thing pursued as an end in itself; we may, for instance, listen to music, or spend time with our children, not because we expect to get anything further out of these activities, but because these are the ways we want to while away our time on earth. However, in such cases, we pursue these things because we believe, rightly or wrongly, that they are ingredients in a *eudaimon* life.

One aim of the *Nicomachean Ethics* is to illuminate the pursuit of *eudaimonia*. If we know more about what it is that we are seeking and how it is characteristically achieved then we will be more likely to achieve it ourselves, even if ultimately, as Aristotle believed, our early training and current material circumstances will determine to a great extent our capacity to follow the right path. Aristotle, unlike many subsequent moral philosophers, was realistic about the influence of events beyond our control on the success of our lives. He thought that having a certain amount of money, reasonable looks, good ancestry and children were prerequisites for any genuinely *eudaimon* life. Without the benefit of such assets we may not be able to achieve the highest state of *eudaimonia*, but should tailor our actions to the particular circumstances we find ourselves in. For Aristotle living well is not a matter of applying general rules to specific cases so much as adapting our behaviour to the particular circumstances of our lives.

It is, Aristotle says, a mark of intelligence only to pursue the kind of precision appropriate to the field in which you are working. Judgements about how to live are only true for the most part. They don't hold for every individual in every circumstance, so there are no hard-and-fast rules. Ethics is not a precise subject like mathematics. A carpenter's interest in a right angle is a practical one; this is very different from a geometer's interest. It would be a mistake to treat ethics as anything but a practical subject with its own standards of generality. And, as a practical subject, it aims to show us how to become good people, not simply to provide us with a better theoretical understanding of what the good life amounts to.

Despite believing that we all do and should pursue *eudaimonia*, Aristotle was very far from being a hedonist in the sense of advocating a life of sensual indulgence. He thought that those who want nothing more than the pleasures of sex, eating and drinking lower themselves to the level of cattle. *Eudaimonia* is not a blissful mental state. It is rather an activity, a way of living, one which brings with it its own pleasures, but which cannot be assessed in particular actions. The whole life of an individual has to be taken into account before we can say for certain that that person achieved *eudaimonia*: as Aristotle memorably put it, one swallow doesn't make a summer, nor does one happy day guarantee a happy life. A tragedy towards the end of your life could put a completely different slant on the question of whether or not your life as a whole went well. There is, then, some truth to the idea that we can't call someone's life *eudaimon* until they are dead. Aristotle even considers the ways in which events after your death can affect the assessment of whether or not your life went well; his answer was that the fortunes of your descendants after your death *can* affect your *eudaimonia* to a limited extent.

THE FUNCTION OF A HUMAN BEING

Aristotle thought that human beings have a characteristic function or activity (an *ergon*). In other words, just as carpenters are recognisable by their characteristic activity (making things with wood), so human beings as a whole have a distinctive activity that makes us what we are. The word 'function' suggests that human beings were designed for a particular purpose, but this is not the connotation that Aristotle intends. He isn't claiming the existence of a wise deity responsible for the construction of the species, but rather drawing our attention to the distinctive powers that we have that make us what we are and not something else. This human *ergon* can't be bodily growth, since that is shared with plants. Bodily growth doesn't distinguish a human being from a geranium. Nor could it be capacity for perception, because other animals have that: horses, for instance. The *ergon* of human beings is rational activity; this is what is most central to our lives as human beings.

The *good* human being is someone who excels in this characteristic activity. Excellence at being human involves virtuous action. Aristotle's conclusion is that the good life for human beings is a life of rational virtuous activity. It is not enough to have the *potential* to act virtuously. The winners at the Olympic Games are chosen only from the competitors and not from those who might have run faster had they entered the events. Similarly, only those who *act* win the reward in life. And the reward in life is true happiness. Roses flourish in a well-manured soil, growing strongly and flowering profusely; human beings flourish when living lives of rational virtuous activity. Much of the *Nicomachean Ethics* is taken up with spelling out what such lives might be like, what sort of character you need in order to live the good life. Central to this is an analysis of the virtues and how they are acquired.

THE VIRTUES

A virtue is a feature of one's character: a disposition to act in a certain way in relevant circumstances. It is important to realise that the term 'virtue' used today has moral connotations: to call someone virtuous is to make a positive assessment of their moral character. But for Aristotle, the phrase translated as 'virtue', *ethikai aretai*, simply meant 'excellence of character' and had no moral implications in our sense of 'moral'. Being virtuous in his sense is simply possessing and acting upon excellences of character, some of which may be completely irrelevant to estimates of your moral worth. In fact some commentators have even questioned the extent to which the *Nicomachean Ethics* is a work of moral philosophy in the sense that we now understand 'moral'. Morality is usually thought to involve at least some concern for the interests of others: it wouldn't make sense to say (using the present-day understanding of 'morality') 'I have developed my own private morality which is entirely selfish.' Aristotle's main interest, however, was not in our concern for other people but in what it takes to make a success of your own life. In some ways the *Nicomachean Ethics* is like one of those practical manuals for self-development and greater personal efficiency that are so popular with managers today.

Aristotle describes several key virtues. Someone who is brave, for instance, is never so overcome with fear that he cannot act in the right way. A brave soldier will risk his own life to save his comrade and will not be reduced to inaction by fear; a brave dissident will stand up to government opposition and pronounce her beliefs even though this will mean certain imprisonment and possible torture or death. Someone who is generous will gladly give money or time to those who need it.

Aristotle distinguishes two types of virtue: the moral and the intellectual. Moral virtues, such as temperance, are acquired through early training and reinforced to become a matter of habit rather than conscious decision; intellectual virtues, such as intelligence, on the other hand, can be taught. The moral virtues are shaped by the non-rational elements of the individual; the intellectual virtues by the rational. Aristotle identifies a common structure to all the virtues: they fall between two extremes. This is the basis of his doctrine of the Golden Mean.

THE GOLDEN MEAN

It is easiest to understand Aristotle's notion of the Mean by considering some of his examples. The virtue of courage lies between two vices: a deficiency of courage is cowardice; an excess of it is rashness. The virtue of wittiness lies between the vices of boorishness and buffoonery; modesty between shyness and shamelessness. Notice that wittiness and modesty are not usually considered moral virtues, though courage might be.

A common misinterpretation of the Doctrine of the Mean is that it is a counsel of moderation. As the mean always lies between two extremes of behaviour, it seems that Aristotle is advocating moderation in all things. However, just because the mean is between over-reacting and under-reacting, it doesn't follow that the virtuous person always acts in a moderate way. For instance, if you were to see someone attacking a child, a moderate reaction would clearly be inappropriate. Aristotle's theory, however, would probably support aggressive intervention in such circumstances. Such behaviour would lie between the extremes of indifference and vengeful violence.

Virtuous action is always a mean of a kind that would be chosen by a person of practical wisdom, the *phronimos*. The *phronimos* is sensitive to the features of particular circumstances and an excellent judge of how to behave.

ACTION AND CULPABILITY

Aristotle is particularly interested in action rather than just behaviour. Human beings can be said to act rather than just behave since in many areas of our lives we have a capacity for choice; in contrast, an ant simply behaves because it cannot deliberate on what it might or might not do. We usually only hold individuals responsible for their actions: if they could not help doing what they did, then it would be strange to blame them. Aristotle distinguishes intentional actions from two other forms of behaviour: involuntary and non-voluntary.

Involuntary behaviour results from either compulsion or ignorance. For instance, if someone pushes you through a window, you aren't likely to be held responsible for breaking the glass, particularly if you didn't want to break it. If you accidentally ate a toadstool, through ignorance, thinking it was a mushroom, this too would be involuntary. You might well regret the outcome in both cases, but in neither case do you have any direct control over what happens. These things happen against your will and you would not have done them if you could have prevented yourself from doing them. But some forced actions are different in that they still allow you to make a kind of choice. For instance, if the only way of saving a ship in a gale is to jettison the cargo, then when the captain orders this to be done it may seem that his action is voluntary in that he chooses to perform it. However, in another sense, it is forced by the extreme circumstances. In a different context the act of throwing your cargo overboard would be blameworthy, but in the particular circumstances it is forced by events.

Aristotle considers, and rejects, the idea that you could be forced by desire for pleasure to behave in certain ways; for instance, that your lust might *compel* you to become a serial seducer, and so remove your responsibility for your actions. If you take this line, then, as Aristotle points out, consistency demands that you shouldn't be praised for your good actions, since, if they arise from desire, they are equally outside your control.

Non-voluntary or non-intentional behaviour differs from involuntary or unintentional in that you do not regret it. Regret of the consequences of unintentional behaviour shows that if you had had full control you would not have done what you did: you would not have let yourself be pushed through the window; or if you had had full knowledge you would never have eaten a toadstool. It is only external factors which led you to do what you did. If I tread on your toe without intending to, but don't regret my action, then my action was non-voluntary.

AKRASIA: WEAKNESS OF WILL

Akrasia is usually translated as 'incontinence', a term which to most modern readers suggests a specific and often embarrassing loss of bodily self-control; but Aristotle meant something more general by the word. It is the familiar situation when you know what you should do, what would make your life more successful, yet you stubbornly choose what you know to be the worse option. Unlike incontinence in the medical sense, it is a *voluntary* action. For instance, you might know that marital infidelity will undermine your *eudaimonia*. Yet, faced with an attractive and willing adulterer, you may be overcome by your desire for immediate pleasure and succumb to temptation even though you are well aware that adultery will harm your prospects of *eudaimonia* and even though you, like all human beings, seek *eudaimonia*. You choose what you know to be worse for you. Aristotle, influenced by Plato, sees a problem in the idea that you might really know what would be the best course of action yet not choose it. For Plato, if you really know the Good, that is, have knowledge of the Form, then you automatically act in accordance with it. According to Plato, genuine *akrasia* cannot exist: any apparent instance of it must really be a case of ignorance of the Good. In contrast Aristotle maintains that the phenomenon of *akrasia* does actually occur. Those who suffer from it know in a general way that certain types of action are not good for them, and won't make them flourish. They may even pay lip service to the idea that what they are doing in a particular case is wrong; but when they do this they don't really feel it, but are simply reciting learnt lines. They are overcome by their appetite and they succumb to the temptation of immediate pleasures rather than acting in a way that is conducive to long-term flourishing. Even though they know at some level what is good for them, they don't choose it because they don't make the inference from the general principle to the particular case.

THE CONTEMPLATIVE LIFE

Towards the end of the *Nicomachean Ethics* Aristotle describes the kind of activity which he considers the most important ingredient in a good life: theoretical or contemplative activity. Despite devoting most of his book to questions of practical virtue with an emphasis on the kinds of action which would bring about flourishing, he reveals that reflecting on what you know is the supreme activity possible for human beings. His reasoning is as follows. Since the characteristic activity of human beings is rational activity, and since the excellence of anything at all arises from its fulfilment of its distinctive function, then it must be true that human excellence is achieved in rational activity. However, only gods would be able to sustain a life of uninterrupted philosophical contemplation; for human beings such contemplation is a vital ingredient, but can't constitute the whole of the good life. Nevertheless, it is the highest form of activity open to us.

CRITICISMS OF THE *NICOMACHEAN ETHICS*

Human nature

The whole of Aristotle's discussion of human excellence and character is based on the idea that there is such a thing as human nature and that what is most central to our humanity is our rational capacity. There are various ways in which Aristotle's assumptions about human nature can be challenged.

One radical approach is to deny that there is anything which merits the name 'human nature'. This is the view of some existential philosophers, such as Jean-Paul Sartre, who think that any attempt to declare in advance what human beings must be is doomed to failure, since we create ourselves by our choices rather than conform to some pre-existing template.

A second way of challenging this aspect of Aristotle's approach is to criticise the particular account of human nature he gives and from which he derives the rest of his conclusions. Is a capacity for rational activity *really* what separates us from other animals? Why this and not our capacity to kill each other using weapons? Or perhaps our capacity to play musical instruments?

Incommensurability of values

For Aristotle there is one supreme form of life, the life of contemplation, which can be measured against other forms of life and found superior. But is this obviously so? Some philosophers have argued that many of the things which human beings value are simply incommensurable, that is, there is absolutely no way in which they can be compared, no form of measurement which would allow us to judge them comparatively. On this view, the contemplative life might be one valuable approach to living; but the life of the active participant in daily affairs might be another. There is no place from which we can sit back and judge the comparative merits of the two lives and no common currency of value in which they can be measured.

Egoistical

A further criticism of Aristotle's ethics is that it only provides a recipe for an individual's *eudaimonia* and shows no concern for the well-being of other people. It is an egoistical approach teaching its readers how to pursue their own best interests.

One response to this sort of criticism is that it simply fails to appreciate what the ancient Greeks understood by ethics. Individual character development was precisely the focus of Greek ethics.

Another response is that the virtues Aristotle champions are, for the most part, precisely those needed by individuals if a society is to flourish.

Virtues seem arbitrary

From our perspective, the particular portfolio of virtues that Aristotle put together in the *Nicomachean Ethics* can be seen as a product of his environment. Aristotle did not challenge the status quo, but rather enshrined the pre-existing values of his society in the form of a philosophical treatise. For instance, he thought slavery an acceptable practice. His is a defence of the values esteemed by the nobility of ancient Athens. Yet he presents these values as if they were obviously part, not just of an ancient Athenian's nature, but of human nature itself. He treats them as universal features of the human condition, albeit adaptable to particular circumstances.

However, the choices and omissions of virtues and vices appear arbitrary to many readers. Why, for instance, has he nothing to say about sympathy or altruism? His account of virtuous activity looks parochial. And if it is parochial, its relevance to present-day moral theorising must be diminished.

Elitism

Furthermore, Aristotle's theory is unashamedly elitist in several ways. First, there is no sense that *eudaimonia* is available to everyone: you need good looks, children, a moderate income and a certain amount of good luck. Unlike many moral theories, with Aristotle's there is no presumption that you can achieve the highest state by will power alone. External factors determine whether or not you lead a good life. Second, if we are to take seriously the suggestion that the good life is a life dominated by philosophical contemplation, then it is clear that only those fortunate enough to have time on their hands to engage in this sort of thought can lead a supremely good life.

Aristotle would not have been bothered by the charge of elitism. However, it is an important feature of his theory and needs to be made explicit. Many present-day readers will feel that in its elitist elements the theory fails to capture something important about the nature of morality.

Vagueness

Perhaps the most telling criticism of a theory explicitly intended to help us become better people is its vagueness about precisely how we are to behave. The doctrine of the Mean doesn't provide much in the way of guidance. To say that we should act as the *phronimos* would act is uninformative unless we happen to have a *phronimos* with us to ask what he would do in the circumstances. Even within the theory there seems to be a conflict: are we supposed to commit ourselves to a life of virtuous action (the view which Aristotle expresses through large sections of the *Nicomachean Ethics*), or are we supposed to aim at one which includes substantial philosophical contemplation, the way of life endorsed towards the end of the book? Scholars try to reconcile these apparently opposed views, but it cannot be denied that Aristotle conspicuously fails to provide clear guidelines about how to live.

DATES

384 BC   Aristotle born in Stagira.
             Student of Plato in Athens.
             Tutor to Alexander the Great.
             Publishes on numerous topics including politics, tragedy and biology.
322 BC   Dies in Chalcis.

GLOSSARY

akrasia: weakness of will: knowing what is best, but still choosing to do something else. Aristotle, unlike Plato, believes that weakness of will does genuinely occur.

egoism: concern only with your own interests. The opposite of altruism.

ergon: the characteristic function of anything.

eudaimonia: happiness. For Aristotle this wasn't a transient blissful mental state, but rather flourishing over the course of a whole life.

Golden Mean: Aristotle's doctrine that right action lies between two extremes.

incommensurability: the impossibility of comparing two things because of the lack of a common currency in which comparison can be made.

incontinence: *akrasia,* or weakness of will.

phronimos: the man of practical wisdom or prudence who is sensitive to particular circumstances and is a good judge of what to do.

virtue: a disposition to behave in a way that will make you a good person.

FURTHER READING

J. L. Ackrill *Aristotle the Philosopher* (Oxford: Oxford University Press, 1981) is a good general introduction to Aristotle's philosophy.

J. O. Urmson *Aristotle's Ethics* (Oxford: Blackwell, 1988) is a clear and very useful commentary on the *Nicomachean Ethics*.

Amelie O. Rorty (ed.) *Essays on Aristotle's Ethics* (Berkeley: University of California Press, 1980) is an excellent anthology of articles on this book.

3

BOETHIUS *THE CONSOLATION OF PHILOSOPHY*

As *The Consolation of Philosophy* opens, Ancius Manlius Severinus Boethius is in a prison cell bemoaning his condition. He wants to die. He has nothing to hope for. Fortune, who gave him his wealth and freedom, has now taken both away. Then, as he is giving vent to his sorrow in the form of a poem, he becomes aware of a woman standing over him. Her height seems to fluctuate from average size to immeasurably tall. Her dress is embroidered at the bottom of the hem with the Greek letter *pi*; at the top is the letter *theta*; in between them is embroidered a ladder. Her dress is torn in places; she carries some books and a sceptre. This woman is Philosophy personified. The letter *pi* stands for practical philosophy (including ethics); the letter *theta* stands for contemplative philosophy (metaphysics and science).

Philosophy rebukes Boethius for forsaking her. Through her dialogue with Boethius she offers him the consolation he is seeking. Although he has been unjustly condemned to death and has lost his great wealth, reputation, and the comforts of freedom, she points out the inner strength that she, Philosophy, can give him. She diagnoses his despair and provides soothing medicine in the form of reason. Philosophy in this form is a kind of self-help, a consolation to the mind. Boethius sometimes refers to Philosophy as his nurse.

As far as we can tell, *The Consolation of Philosophy* was written in around 524, while Boethius was imprisoned in Pavia, awaiting execution for an alleged act of treason against the Gothic emperor Theodoric. This was a dramatic fall from eminence: Boethius had been one of the most respected and honoured members of Theodoric's government. Boethius was subsequently tortured and bludgeoned to death, an ignominious way to die that a citizen of his standing might have hoped to have avoided.

Although he published other books on a wide range of subjects, including music, and translated a substantial part of Aristotle's works into Latin, it is for *The Consolation of Philosophy*, his last work, that he is now remembered. It is a compelling book written in a mixture of prose, poetry and dialogue. During the medieval and Renaissance periods it was one of the most widely read books; Chaucer translated it, as did Elizabeth I. Its philosophical content is not wholly original, but the manner in which the ideas are communicated makes it an entertaining as well as a stimulating book to read.

PHILOSOPHY

Philosophy, personified as a woman, as we have seen, comes to visit Boethius in his prison cell. But what did Boethius mean by Philosophy? He was a Neo-Platonist, that is, his view of philosophy was deeply influenced by Plato's. In particular, he followed Plato in believing that philosophical contemplation takes us away from the misleading world of appearances to a true experience of reality. He repeatedly uses the image of the shadowy world of appearances which is contrasted with the light of truth. This is an allusion to Plato's image of the Sun as the symbol of the Form of the Good in the parable of the cave that Plato uses in *The Republic*.

Philosophy teaches Boethius – or rather reminds him – that as a philosopher he should be immune from the effects of good or bad fortune. The fact that Philosophy jogs Boethius' memory is probably meant, again, as an allusion to a doctrine of Plato's: the view that knowledge is a kind of recollection.

CHANCE AND HAPPINESS

A true philosopher is impervious to chance. The wheel of Fortune inevitably turns, and those who are at the top find themselves very soon at the bottom. That is the nature of Fortune: to be fickle. In fact, Philosophy tells him, it is when she is adverse that Fortune best serves humanity. Good fortune dupes us, because it gives us the illusion of true happiness; but when Fortune takes off her mask and shows us how treacherous she can be, that is when we learn most. Adversity teaches us the frailty of the sorts of happiness that wealth, fame and pleasure can inspire. It teaches us which of our friends are true friends.

Boethius had indeed been blessed with good fortune: his two sons were made consuls on the same day as a public demonstration of gratitude for his contribution to the running of the state. His imprisonment, though, takes his happiness away. Philosophy tells him that he is being foolish: true happiness can't be found in anything that is governed by chance such as wealth or fame. It must come from within. Here Boethius is influenced by aspects of Stoicism, a philosophy which emphasises the need for equanimity in the face of external trouble. For a Stoic, happiness comes from inner resources and is immune to the effects of chance and misfortune.

EVIL AND REWARD

Boethius laments the fact that there doesn't seem to be justice in the world. Evil people often flourish, while the good and virtuous suffer. In response Philosophy claims that it is the virtuous who are truly rewarded since they have the power to attain the ultimate end, genuine happiness, through their pursuit of the good. The evil only appear to flourish: in fact by abandoning their reason they become subhuman and are more deserving of pity and remedial treatment than of retributive punishment.

GOD AND FREE WILL

Having reminded Boethius that true happiness, which everyone seeks, comes from philosophical contemplation, not from fame, fortune or pleasure, and that, despite appearances, the wicked cannot genuinely flourish, Philosophy engages him in debate about God and human free will. Here the book becomes a serious philosophical dialogue in the style of Plato's dialogues. Boethius takes on the role of questioner, and Philosophy explains the nature of God to him, leading him with the aid of reason away from mere appearances to a world of purity and light.

Much of the discussion focuses on the question of how humans could have free will, the capacity for genuine choice over what they do, and yet at the same time there could be a God who knows in advance precisely what they will in fact do. Without free will there cannot be rational action; yet if God can see what we are going to do, it is not at all clear in what sense we are genuinely free to exercise choice.

Philosophy's answer to this conundrum in part turns on the distinction between predestination and foreknowledge. Those who believe in predestination argue that God has brought it about that certain events will inevitably happen in the future; foreknowledge is simply *knowing* in advance what will happen. Philosophy argues that God's knowing that certain choices will be made does not *cause* those things to happen – human beings can still make choices. So divine foreknowledge is compatible with genuine choice for humans since knowing what will happen does not predestine it to happen.

And yet it might seem that if God knows in advance what we will choose, our apparent choice is an illusion, not really free will, but the fantasy of it. Philosophy's response to this line of criticism is that our idea of foreknowledge erroneously, but understandably, rests on human experience of time. But God is not like us in important respects. In particular God is outside time and lives in an eternal present. Because God stands outside time, His foreknowledge is comparable to our knowledge of the present: past, present and future are all as one to Him. Our perception of what is happening now doesn't *make* what is happening happen. Nor then does God's foreknowledge wipe out the possibility of genuine free choice about what we do. Our mistake is to think of God's relation to time as like our own. God is aware of everything that has happened, is happening, and will happen.

Philosophy ends the book by exhorting Boethius to virtue since he is living in the sight of a judge who, from a position outside time sees and knows everything. Thus in *The Consolation of Philosophy* Boethius' intellectual journey retraces the path of the philosopher in Plato's *Republic*. Boethius leaves behind the shadowy world of appearances – the equivalent of the flickering shadows on the wall of the cave – and achieves knowledge of the Form of the Good and ultimately of God.

CRITICISM OF *THE CONSOLATION OF PHILOSOPHY*

Rationalisation?

Boethius' celebration of everything that is insulated from the effects of chance might be seen as a rationalisation. Given that he was in prison and facing torture and almost certain execution, with no hope of retrieving his former wealth and public esteem, is it surprising that he should celebrate rational activity above all else? Nothing else significant is left to him. Perhaps his rejection of wealth and fame as significant elements in a life that goes well, is just the self-serving argument of a desperate man.

Even if it is true that Boethius saw the overriding value of rational deliberation because little else was left to him, as this criticism suggests, it doesn't follow that he was wrong. The truth of the matter is independent of his motivation for believing it. An alternative interpretation is that Boethius was jolted from his complacency by having everything he had thought valuable to him removed. Only then could he come to understand (or rather recollect) Philosophy's powerful message; only then could he return to the austere vision of self-sufficient happiness that Philosophy teaches. This interpretation is supported in the text by Philosophy's insistence that adversity can draw people back to the true way of goodness, whereas the external trappings of success can lure them into believing that they have achieved true happiness.

So, even if Boethius' motivation for believing what Philosophy taught him was suspect, it does not follow that her message is in error. What would be devastating to Philosophy's doctrine, however, would be the discovery that in fact wealth, fame and other worldly goods are an essential part of happiness. Aristotle, for example, believed that a certain amount of wealth, and having children of one's own, were important ingredients in happiness. If he was right, then Boethius' attempt to gain true consolation from philosophy alone was destined to failure.

DATES

c. 480   born in Rome.
c. 524   writes *The Consolation of Philosophy* and is executed.

GLOSSARY

foreknowledge: knowing in advance what will happen.

free will: the ability to make genuine choices; this is usually contrasted with determinism, which is the view that all our thoughts and actions are caused in such a way that we have no choice about what to think or do.

Neo-Platonism: a modified version of Plato's philosophy.

Stoicism: the Ancient Greek school of philosophy which emphasised that honour and wealth should not be pursued for their own sake and that happiness can be achieved by elimination of the passions.

FURTHER READING

V.E. Watts' introduction to his translation of *The Consolation of Philosophy* (London: Penguin, 1969) gives a clear account of Boethius' life and writing.

C.S. Lewis *The Discarded Image* (Cambridge: Cambridge University Press, 1964) includes an interesting discussion of *The Consolation of Philosophy*.

NICCOLÒ MACHIAVELLI
THE PRINCE

Most readers of *The Prince* expect it to be a self-help manual for the ruthless. But the book is far subtler than that. Although Niccolò Machiavelli does advocate dissimulation and cruelty at times, he reserves his praise for those who know how and when to use force and guile. He explains how a strong and effective ruler can best serve the interests of the state. His advice is not meant for just anyone: it is advice for princes – rulers whose actions determine the fate of their subjects. Such people, he suggests should not be squeamish. They need to act swiftly and effectively to do what is best. And what is best for the state may be to ignore conventional morality.

Machiavelli had a successful career as a statesman in his native Florence. In 1513, however, he was accused of plotting against the powerful Medici family. He was imprisoned, tortured, and then sent into exile just outside the city. It seems that he wrote *The Prince* in order to demonstrate his suitability as an adviser to new princes. It was a kind of calling card intended to help him re-enter the fray of political life. In this respect it failed. He did not get the position he hoped for. First published in 1532, shortly after Machiavelli's death, *The Prince* has always been a controversial book. Today it is frequently cited in discussions of the alleged inevitability of 'dirty hands' in politics and the adjective 'machiavellian' is used, misleadingly, to describe cunning pursuit of self-interest.

ae Prince is written in the genre of 'mirrors for princes' – short .acts advising and inspiring rulers. These were popular in the Renaissance. Typically they would counsel such virtues as courage and compassion. In complete contrast, Machiavelli's advice was that a successful prince needs to learn how not to be good, to take swift and sometimes cruel action when this is necessary. A successful prince will only honour his word when it suits him to do so, though it usually pays him to *appear* honest. He needs to act like a fox in order to recognise and avoid the traps others set for him, but also, sometimes as a lion to frighten off the wolves that surround him. The message is that a prince needs to know how to act like a beast: a challenge to the humanistic tradition in which princes were expected to act as moral exemplars to their people.

HUMAN NATURE

Machiavelli has a low view of human nature. Based on his own observation, and his knowledge of Florentine history and classical texts, he declares that people behave in predictably bad ways. They are fickle, they lie, they shun danger, and they are greedy. In these circumstances, a prince needs to use fear to achieve effective rule: being loved isn't a reliable source of power, since people break bonds of gratitude when it suits them to do so. If you have a choice it is best to be both loved and feared; but if you have to choose one above the other, choose to be feared.

Machiavelli is interested in how people actually behave rather than in how they ought to behave. His point is that unless a prince recognises how fickle human beings really are and always have been, he is likely to come to grief. It is no use trusting people to keep their promises if they are in fact likely to break them. And the prince should not feel bound to keep his promises in such circumstances: that would be foolhardy. Machiavelli argues that the successful prince should follow a very different code from that advocated by traditional morality, whether that comes from a classical or Christian source.

Appearance is everything for a prince. People react to superficial characteristics and rarely, if ever, perceive a prince as he really is. Consequently a prince must manipulate the way he appears, even if, behind the mask, he is something quite different.

VIRTÙ

The key concept in understanding *The Prince* is, in Italian, usually translated as 'prowess'. Although it comes from the Latin word for virtue (*virtus*), it has, for Machiavelli, a very different meaning. Throughout the book Machiavelli's aim is to explain how a prince can display this quality of *virtù*. *Virtù* is the ability to act swiftly and effectively to do whatever will secure the safety and continuing prosperity of the state. This may mean making false promises, murdering those who threaten you, even, where necessary, butchering your own supporters.

Virtù will increase his chances of success as a ruler, but even a *virtuoso* ruler (one who displays *virtù*) won't necessarily flourish. Machiavelli believes that half of our lives are governed by chance events over which we have no control: no matter how well-prepared he may be, a prince's projects can still be thwarted by misfortune. Fortune is like a river which floods its banks: once it is in full flood, there is nothing anyone can do to control it. But this doesn't stop us from taking action before the river floods, so that the damage caused will be less severe. Chance events usually cause most damage where no precautions have been taken. Machiavelli does, however, believe that fortune favours the young and the bold. In a disturbing metaphor, fortune is a woman who responds to the advances of an audacious young man who beats and coerces her. *Virtù* is the manly quality he uses to subdue her.

Machiavelli's model of a prince who demonstrated *virtù* was Cesare Borgia. His prowess involved tricking the Orsini into coming to Sinigaglia where he had them murdered. However, the move of Borgia's which Machiavelli seems to appreciate most was taken against one of his own employees. Once Borgia had taken control of Romagna he placed a cruel henchman, Remirro de Orco, in charge, who quickly pacified the region through violence. Borgia decided that such cruelties could grow intolerable, and in order to expunge the hatred that was beginning to be directed at him, Borgia had Remirro de Orco murdered, and his body left hacked in two halves in a public piazza. With this single brutal spectacle he kept the people of Romagna both appeased and stupefied. Machiavelli applauds Borgia's actions as skilful uses of cruelty. He contrasts Borgia's approach with that of the ruthless tyrant Agathocles who was little more than a thug and whose actions failed to display *virtù*.

of Syracuse by crime: he slaughtered the
...izens of Syracuse and simply seized power.
...his country, but did so with cruelty and inhu-
...li's eyes his actions should not be confused with
...,uished Borgia from Agathocles? Machiavelli is
not c... ...ar about what sets them apart; however, the most
plausible in... ...tation is this. They both used cruelty effectively
and economically. Borgia's actions, however, had they achieved their
end, would have brought about a situation that was in the common
interest (despite being almost certainly inspired by a lust for power).
Agathocles, in contrast, was a brutal tyrant whose actions left
Syracuse in a worse situation than before: his actions were nothing
more than criminal. Hence Borgia demonstrated *virtù*; Agathocles
did not.

The fact that Machiavelli condemns Agathocles' actions should
silence those who claim that Machiavelli simply approves of immorality. It is true that he approves of some actions which conventional
morality would label 'immoral', such as Borgia's treatment of
Remirro de Orco; and it is certainly true that he had no respect whatsoever for what we would now see as basic human rights. He even
seems to take delight in descriptions of bloodshed. However, there
are actions, such as those of Agathocles, of which he disapproves.

INTERPRETATIONS OF THE PRINCE

Satirical?

Some commentators have found Machiavelli's approach to politics
so extreme that they have assumed he must be satirising tyrannical
princes. Surely, they argue, he can't have seriously held up Cesare
Borgia as a model of a good prince. By ironically championing the
immoral actions of a ruthless prince, they claim, he was really criticising rather than endorsing that approach to statecraft. This seems
to have been Jean-Jacques Rousseau's view of *The Prince*.

There is very little evidence in support of such an interpretation
apart from the fact that in his later book, *Discourses on Livy*,
Machiavelli reveals his republican sympathies: a fact which might

lend support to the view that he was fundamentally op[p]
idea that Florence should be ruled by a prince. The consens[u]
ical opinion, however, is that Machiavelli was writing in ear[l]
The Prince, and this explains why the work is so challenging.

Amoral?

An alternative interpretation of *The Prince* is that Machiavelli
was giving instructions for those who wanted to retain power and
didn't care in the slightest about morality. On this interpretation
Machiavelli is amoral, completely outside morality, and simply
giving guidance to those who are prepared to act like psychopaths.
This interpretation is implausible. As the comparison of Cesare
Borgia and Agathocles shows, Machiavelli does not approve of
unlimited cruelty exercised for purely selfish motives and without
beneficial effect for the state. Nor is the book an uncritical 'how to'
manual. In Machiavelli's discussions cruelty always has a point, a
moral point: it is to prevent even more cruel actions being taken later
on; it is for the common good. *The Prince*, then, is far from an amoral
book. It may advocate policies which are immoral by conventional
standards, but these policies are themselves given moral and political justifications. It is, then, far more than a manual providing
techniques by which the unscrupulous can become powerful.

Machiavelli's originality

The historian of ideas, Isaiah Berlin (1909–1997) gives a far more
subtle picture of Machiavelli's contribution to political thought. On
his interpretation, Machiavelli's great originality and appeal lies in
the fact that he recognised the shortcomings of classical and Christian
morality when applied to the situation of a prince. A prince who
displays the traditional virtues, such as honesty and compassion,
is likely to play into the hands of his enemies, who are unlikely
to be so scrupulous. Berlin's point is that, far from being amoral,
Machiavelli, perhaps unwittingly, introduced the notion that there
could be more than one morality and that these moralities might not
be compatible with one another. It's not that one morality is the true
one and all others false. Rather there are genuinely incompatible
moralities that are each consistent from within.

ition known as value pluralism, the idea that
mpatible moral systems and no principles for
ystems (though some systems can be recog-
ers). He sees a precursor of his own views in

... hands in politics

One way in which Machiavelli's ideas still inform present day debate
is in the area of 'dirty hands' in politics, the idea that some sorts of
apparently immoral behaviour are an inevitable consequence of the
role of being a political leader. Machiavelli's account in *The Prince*
seems to imply that any effective ruler will, necessarily, have to learn
to be cruel, and, on occasion, to go directly against the dictates of
conventional morality. This is not to say that behaviour such as
telling lies or half-truths, breaking promises and so on, are for him
genuinely immoral when done by political leaders with the interests
of their people at heart. On Machiavelli's account princes must follow
a different, and (for them) a more appropriate moral code from the
rest of humanity.

CRITICISMS OF *THE PRINCE*

Advocates immorality

Machiavelli shows no respect for what we would now call human
rights. For him, individuals can be sacrificed (literally if appropriate)
in the interests of the state. State torture and murder are sometimes
necessary; indeed he suggests that a ruler who is reluctant to use
such methods swiftly and effectively when the occasion arises is in
some sense a bad prince, since his squeamishness will very likely
lead to more extensive bloodshed later.

Recent history has shown the dangers of unleashing tyrants on
unsuspecting populations. The consequences of giving such tyrants
an apparent intellectual justification for their behaviour are likely to
include intense suffering for at least some of their subjects. Given
the human capacity for self-deception, it is easy to imagine such
leaders telling themselves that what they are doing is really necessary if their country is to thrive. In fact this may be a self-serving

rationalisation of appalling violence and far too high a price to pay for political stability. Machiavelli's response to such a criticism would be that the effectiveness of such violence is always to be judged by its results: did the state become richer, more stable, more powerful, or didn't it? For him there are no other relevant considerations.

Too cynical

Machiavelli has a very low view of human motives. Perhaps he is wrong about this. Many people are far more optimistic about the potential of human beings to care about one another's plight than he is. If he is wrong about human fickleness, then rule by fear and clinically effective cruelty may not be necessary. If he is right, however, political leaders who unswervingly display the conventional virtues may be placing their people in jeopardy.

DATES

1469   born in Florence, Italy.
1513   tortured and sent into exile. Begins writing *The Prince*.
1527   dies, Florence.
1532   *The Prince* is published posthumously.

GLOSSARY

amoral: completely outside the moral realm.

fortune: chance or luck. Machiavelli believed that half of all human matters were governed by chance.

immoral: going against an established moral system. Immorality is always measured against moral ideals or principles.

virtù: the key concept for Machiavelli, usually translated as 'prowess'. Not to be confused with 'virtue' as it is conventionally understood. For Machiavelli a display of *virtù* might involve deception or a swift and effective use of bloodshed.

FURTHER READING

Quentin Skinner *A Very Short Introduction to Machiavelli* (Oxford: Oxford University Press, 2000) is essential reading for anyone interested in finding out more about Machiavelli's life and thought.

Isaiah Berlin's classic essay 'The Originality of Machiavelli' is reprinted in Isaiah Berlin, ed. Henry Hardy *The Proper Study of Mankind* (London: Pimlico, 1998).

Nigel Warburton, Derek Matravers and Jon Pike (eds) *Reading Political Philosophy: Machiavelli to Mill* (London: Routledge, 2001) includes a discussion of *The Prince*, and readings on Machiavelli by Skinner, Berlin and others.

Sebastian de Grazia *Machiavelli in Hell* (London: Macmillan, 1996) is a prize-winning biography of Machiavelli. Maurizio Viroli's more recent biography *Niccolò's Smile* (New York: Farrar, Straus and Giroux, 2000) provides a character portrait that relates Machiavelli's rich life to his thought.

RENÉ DESCARTES
MEDITATIONS

Descartes's *Meditations* is a book designed to make you think. It is written in the first person in what seems to be an autobiography of six days' thought. However, this is in fact a highly ingenious device for encouraging the reader to follow the twists of the argument. To read the book in the spirit in which it was written involves active engagement with its ideas, not just passive absorption. You are invited to become the 'I' in the text, moving through successive phases of doubt and enlightenment. As philosophical literature the *Meditations* remains unsurpassed and many of the ideas expressed in it have held sway over subsequent philosophers. Descartes is usually taken to be the father of modern philosophy.

In the *Meditations* Descartes sets out to establish what it is possible to know. Consequently, his principal concern in the book is with epistemology, the theory of knowledge. Establishing the limits of knowledge was not a merely academic exercise: he believed that if he could eliminate errors in his thinking and discover sound principles for acquiring true beliefs then this would provide a bedrock on which the edifice of scientific understanding of the world and our place within it could be built. The dominant view in France in 1640 when Descartes wrote his *Meditations* was that of the Catholic Church, which was in many ways hostile to science. Descartes was also struggling against a tradition of scholasticism in philosophy which tended to promote debating skills above the quest for truth. Returning to first principles and jettisoning received opinion was a radical move for Descartes to make in these circumstances.

Before he could begin the constructive stage of his work, Descartes believed that he needed, once in his lifetime, to rid himself of all his former beliefs since he was aware that many of them were false. He thought it sensible to rid himself of all his former beliefs in one go and then consider one by one prospective replacements for them rather than to attempt a piecemeal repair of his belief structure. In a reply to a critic of his work he explained this approach by means of an analogy: if you are worried about rotten apples in a barrel you will be well advised to tip out all the apples and examine each one before you replace it in the barrel. Only if you are certain that the apple you are considering is sound should you put it back in the barrel, since a single rotten apple could contaminate all the others. This analogy explains his method of radical doubt, often known as the Method of Cartesian Doubt ('Cartesian' being the adjective from 'Descartes').

CARTESIAN DOUBT

The Method of Doubt involves treating all your former beliefs as if they were false. You should only believe something if you are absolutely certain that it is true: the slightest doubt about its truth should be sufficient to reject it. The fact that you can doubt it doesn't prove that it *is* false; it may well turn out to be true. However, the merest suspicion that it might be false is enough to render it unsuitable as a foundation for the edifice of knowledge. That has to be built on indubitable knowledge. Obviously this method is not a practical one for day-to-day living, as Descartes himself recognised; he advocated it as a once in a lifetime exercise. The point of this method was that it might allow Descartes to discover some beliefs which were immune from doubt and which would thus serve as foundations for his reconstruction of knowledge on sound principles. At worst it would show him that everything could be doubted; that nothing was certain.

THE EVIDENCE OF THE SENSES

In the First Meditation Descartes introduces this Method of Doubt and applies it rigorously to his former beliefs, beginning with those he has acquired through the five senses. His senses have sometimes deceived him. For instance, he has made mistakes about what he could see in the distance. On the principle that it is wise never to trust what has once deceived you, he resolves not to trust the evidence of his senses. But, despite sometimes being deceived about objects in the distance, surely he couldn't be deceived about some facts acquired through the senses, such as that he is sitting in front of a fire in a dressing gown holding a piece of paper?

Descartes's response to this is that, on the contrary, he *might* be mistaken even about something so apparently certain as this. Since in the past he had dreamt that he was sitting by the fire when in fact he was lying in bed asleep, he can't be sure that he is not now dreaming. But even in dreams things such as heads, hands, eyes and so on appear, which must be likenesses of things in the real world. So surely we can be certain that these types of object exist. The existence of more abstract notions such as size, shape and extension (by which he means the quality of taking up space) seems even more certain. Whether you are asleep or awake, $2 + 3 = 5$ and a square never has more than four sides. These things do indeed seem certain. But Descartes shows all these to be only *apparent* certainties. To do so he uses the thought experiment of the evil demon.

THE EVIL DEMON

What if there is a powerful and malicious demon who constantly manipulates what you experience and understand? Every time you look at an object in the world what is really happening might be that the demon is producing an illusory experience which you take to be reality but which is really his creation. If you find this difficult to imagine, think of what would happen if someone plugged you into a very sophisticated virtual reality machine without your realising what was going on. Now every time you add 2 and 2 together it comes to 5. But how can you be sure that this isn't because the evil demon, or the operator of the virtual reality machine, is tricking you? Perhaps the demon has introduced a 'bug' into your calculations so that you always get the wrong result. This might sound far-fetched, but that doesn't affect Descartes's argument. All that is important is that it is *possible* that you are now being deceived. If you apply the Method of Cartesian Doubt, the slightest possibility that your belief is false provides sufficient doubt for you to reject it. In everyday life, of course, we need much stronger evidence of the falsity of a fundamental belief before we will so readily jettison it, and that is as it should be. But when we are searching for a belief which is immune from doubt, the thought experiment of the evil demon provides a very strong test. Any belief which can pass this test, which you are sure hasn't been misleadingly implanted by the demon, must be certain indeed.

At this stage in his *Meditations* Descartes is tempted to believe that absolutely everything can be doubted. However, in the Second Meditation his doubt is revealed as pre-emptive. That is, he is pushing sceptical arguments to their very limit so as to demonstrate that there are some beliefs about which it is not possible to be sceptical. Another way of putting this is that he sets out to beat the sceptics at their own game: giving the strongest form of sceptical argument he can imagine and then showing that it would not prevent him from establishing at least one certainty.

The certainty which he discovers, the turning point in his philosophy, has come to be known as the *Cogito*, from the Latin *Cogito ergo sum* ('I think, therefore I am'), although it doesn't occur in the *Meditations* in quite this form. In the *Meditations* he says '*I am, I exist*, is necessarily true, every time I express it or conceive of it in my mind.'

THE *COGITO*

Descartes's point is that even if the evil demon does actually exist and is constantly deceiving him, there is still something about which he cannot be tricked, namely his own existence. It is impossible for him, Descartes, to doubt his own existence; and Descartes believes that his readers, on reflection, will come to the same conclusion about their own existence. Any thought that you have indicates that you, the thinker, exist. This is true even if you are completely confused about the content of your thought. You might think you are standing on the top floor of the Empire State Building admiring the view when in fact you are waiting on a station platform in Sidcup, but that doesn't matter: as long as you are having a thought at all, then this shows that you must exist.

Notice that the 'I' that Descartes believes he has shown to exist whenever he is thinking is not to be identified with his body. At this stage he can still raise all his former doubts about whether or not his body actually exists, or exists in the form he thinks it does. Only thinking is inseparable from his existence. The most that he can show from the *Cogito* is that he is essentially a thinking thing.

CARTESIAN DUALISM

Descartes's belief that he can be more certain of the existence of himself as a thinking thing than as a body suggests a division between the mind and the body. The mind is the real Descartes (or whoever) whose body may or may not exist. The mind can outlive the body. This sharp separation between mind and body has come to be known as Cartesian Dualism. Descartes believes that mind and body, although in principle separable, interact, and consequently his view is sometimes also known as interactionism.

THE WAX EXAMPLE

Descartes describes a piece of wax taken from a honeycomb: it still has a faint taste of honey, smells of flowers, and is hard and cold. As he puts it close to the fire its taste and smell are lost and its colour, shape and size all change. It becomes liquid and hot to the touch. The point of this example is to demonstrate that although we might think that we get an understanding of what the wax is via our sensory experience of it, in fact all the information we get about the wax in this way can change. Yet it remains the same piece of wax despite the changes. Descartes's explanation of how this is possible is that understanding the essence of the wax, what it is that makes it this piece of wax and not another thing, involves a judgement which goes beyond sensory experience. And this judgement, which is a thought, once again demonstrates to Descartes the greater certainty he has about his own existence as a thinking thing than about the nature and existence of the material world. This example reveals Descartes's rationalism, that is, his belief that we can acquire knowledge of the nature of the world by reason alone, a view which contrasts sharply with empiricism, which in its strongest form is the view that all our knowledge of the world must be acquired via the senses.

GOD

The *Cogito* is the first step that Descartes takes towards rebuilding the edifice of knowledge that he demolished with his Method of Doubt. From this point onwards he is entirely constructive. Yet at first it seems that he won't be able to get beyond the conclusions that he exists just so long as he is thinking, and that he is in essence a thinking thing. Such a position would be little better than the whirlpool of doubt that he felt himself drawn into at the end of the First Meditation.

However, Descartes has a strategy to avoid getting trapped at the *Cogito*. He undertakes to prove God's existence and to prove that God would not deceive us. He uses two arguments to do this, the so-called Trademark Argument and the Ontological Argument, which appear in the Third and Fifth Meditations respectively. Both arguments are controversial, and were thought so even in his day.

The Trademark Argument

Descartes points out that he had an idea of God in his mind. This idea must have come from somewhere since something can't come from nothing. Moreover, he thinks that there must be as much reality in any effect as in its cause: in this case the idea is the effect and the cause presumed to be God. Although Descartes didn't use the analogy, it is as if God had left a trademark on his work revealing his existence. This is a variant of a traditional argument for God's existence known as the Cosmological Argument.

Descartes's idea of God was that of a benevolent being, and such a God would not want to deceive humankind in a systematic way. Deception is a mark of malice, not of benevolence. Consequently, Descartes concludes that God exists and is no deceiver. The result of this is that he has confidence that whatever he perceives clearly and distinctly must be true. God would not have created us in such a way that we would feel certain when misled. The notion that whatever he perceives clearly and distinctly must be true plays a crucial role in the constructive phase of Descartes's philosophy.

The Ontological Argument

In the Fifth Meditation Descartes presents a version of what is known as the Ontological Argument. This is an *a priori* argument for God's existence, which means that it is not based on any evidence acquired through the senses, but rather on analysis of the concept of God. The interior angles of a triangle add up to 180 degrees. This conclusion follows logically from the concept of 'triangle'. It is an aspect of the essence of a triangle that the sum of its interior angles is 180 degrees. Similarly, according to Descartes, it follows from the concept of God as a supremely perfect being that he exists. It is part of God's essence that he exists. If God didn't exist, then he wouldn't be a supremely perfect being: existence is, according to Descartes, one of his perfections. So it follows from the concept of God alone that he necessarily exists.

BEYOND DOUBT

Once Descartes has established to his satisfaction that God exists and is not a deceiver, he begins to reconstruct the material world. He still has to explain the fact that his senses at least on occasion deceive him, and address the question of whether he can ever be sure that he is not dreaming. He can be sure that he, that is, his mind, is intimately attached to a particular body (his own), since God would not deceive him about the existence of something which he perceives so clearly and distinctly. But what about the material world which he seems to see, touch, taste, smell and hear?

His commonsense beliefs about the world are all derived from his ideas. When he sees a tower in the distance, for example, and perceives it as round, he has an idea of the round tower. Before reflecting on it, he assumes that objects in the world exist and resemble the ideas they cause. However, the case of optical illusions makes clear that he can have an idea of an object which gives the object different properties from those it actually possesses. The tower, for example, may in fact be square. Descartes's conclusion by the Sixth Meditation is that the existence of a God who is no deceiver guarantees that there are objects in the material world but that it would be foolish simply to accept all the evidence of the senses since they obviously do deceive on occasion. A benevolent God would not, however, have created us in such a way that we were systematically deceived about the existence of objects. Moreover, he has certainly provided us with the means to make accurate judgements about the nature of the world. But it does not follow that the objects in the world are exactly like our ideas of them. We can make mistakes about qualities such as the size, shape and colour of things. Ultimately if we want to understand what the world is really like we need to resort to a mathematical and geometrical analysis of it.

In the sceptical phase of the *Meditations* one of the most powerful arguments Descartes used was that we might be dreaming and unable to recognise that we were doing so. In the Sixth Meditation he declares that we do have at least two ways of telling dreams from waking life. Memory can never connect dreams up one with another as it can in waking life: the different stages of our life fit into a coherent pattern of memory, whereas our dream life does not cohere in the same way. The second way of telling a dream from waking life is that strange phenomena occur in dreams that do not occur in normal life: for instance, if someone were to vanish into air before my eyes as I was talking to him then I would have a very strong suspicion that I was dreaming.

CRITICISMS OF *MEDITATIONS*

Does he call everything into doubt?

Although the Method of Doubt seems to raise doubts about everything that could possibly be doubted, this is not the case. Descartes relies on the accuracy of his memory, for instance, never doubting that he has dreamt in the past, or that his senses have deceived him on occasion; he does not doubt that the meanings he associates with particular words are the same as they were when he last used them.

However, this is not a serious problem for Descartes. Cartesian Doubt remains a strong form of scepticism: he only undertook to doubt what it was possible for him to doubt. Stronger forms of scepticism might have undermined his power to do philosophy at all.

Criticism of the *Cogito*

One criticism sometimes made of Descartes's *Cogito*, particularly when it is given in the form 'I think, therefore I am', is that it assumes the truth of the general statement 'All thoughts have thinkers', an assumption which Descartes never attempts to establish or make explicit. This criticism is based on the assumption that

Descartes was presenting the conclusion 'I am' as the result of a logically valid inference of the following kind:

All thoughts have thinkers
There are thoughts now
So the thinker of these thoughts must exist.

However, this criticism does not affect the *Cogito* as presented in the *Meditations* since there is no suggestion there that there is a logical inference; rather Descartes seems to be advocating introspection on the part of the reader and challenging him or her to doubt the truth of the assertion 'I am, I exist.'

Cartesian Circle

Once Descartes has established his own existence as a thinking thing by means of the *Cogito*, the whole of his reconstructive project depends upon two foundations: the existence of a benevolent God and the fact that whatever we believe clearly and distinctly is true. Both are in themselves contentious. However, there is a more fundamental charge which is often raised against Descartes's strategy, namely that when he argues for the existence of God he relies on the notion of clear and distinct ideas; and when he argues for the doctrine of clear and distinct ideas he presupposes the existence of God. In other words he argues in a circle. Both the Trademark and the Ontological Arguments for God's existence presuppose an idea of God that Descartes knows to be accurate because he perceives it clearly and distinctly: without the idea of God neither argument could begin. On the other hand, the doctrine of clear and distinct ideas being true relies entirely on the supposition that a benevolent God exists and so would not allow us to be systematically deceived. So the argument is circular.

Some of Descartes's contemporaries noted this problem at the heart of Descartes's project; it has come to be known as the Cartesian Circle. It is a powerful criticism of the whole constructive enterprise in the *Meditations*, and there is no obvious way for Descartes to escape it, short of finding an alternative justification for his belief in God, or else an independent justification for his belief that whatever he perceives clearly and distinctly is true. Nevertheless, his sceptical arguments and the *Cogito* retain all their force even if the charge of circularity holds.

Criticisms of arguments for God's existence

Even if Descartes could somehow escape the charge of circularity, the two arguments that he uses to establish God's existence are notoriously vulnerable to criticism.

First, both arguments rely on the assumption that we all have within us an idea of God which is not simply derived from early indoctrination. This assumption can be challenged.

Second, the Trademark Argument relies on a further assumption, namely that there must be at least as much reality in the cause of something as is present in the effect. This assumption is needed for Descartes to move from the reality of his idea of God to the reality of God. But this assumption too can be challenged. For example, today's scientists can explain how life evolved from inanimate matter: we don't find it obvious that life can only be caused by living things.

The more common form of the Cosmological Argument is in fact more convincing than Descartes's version: it involves the attempt to understand not just the origin of an idea, but of the whole universe and everything in it. It answers the question 'Why is there something rather than nothing?' rather than the narrower question Descartes asked, 'Where does my idea of God come from?'

The Ontological Argument is particularly unconvincing as a proof of God's existence. It seems like a logical trick, an attempt to define God into existence. The most serious criticism of it is that it assumes that existence is just another property, like being all-powerful, or benevolent, rather than what it is: the condition of having these properties at all. A further problem with the Ontological Argument is that it seems to allow us to conjure into existence all kinds of entities. For instance, I have in my mind an idea of the perfect philosopher; but it seems absurd to say that because I have an idea of such a philosopher that philosopher must therefore exist on the grounds that (arguably) a non-existent philosopher could not be perfect.

Dualism is a mistake

Descartes's mind/body dualism finds few supporters amongst present-day philosophers. One of the most serious problems it raises is that of explaining how interaction between an immaterial mind and a physical body is possible. Descartes was aware of the difficulty and even went so far as to identify a place in the brain, the pineal gland, where he thought mind/body interaction took place. But locating where it occurs does not solve the difficulty of how something that is non-physical can bring about changes in the physical world.

Generally, some form of monism, that is, a theory which says that there is only one kind of substance (the physical), rather than a dualistic theory (which says there are two sorts of substance), seems to raise fewer difficulties, even though the task of explaining the nature of human consciousness remains an intractable one.

DATES

1596   born in La Haye (now named Descartes), France.
1641   publishes *Meditations*.
1649   moves to Stockholm, Sweden to teach Queen Christina.
1650   dies in Stockholm.

GLOSSARY

a priori: knowable independently of sense-perception.

Cartesian: the adjective from 'Descartes'.

Cartesian Circle: the name sometimes given to a particular difficulty with Descartes's system. Clear and distinct ideas are reliable sources of knowledge because they are vouchsafed by a benevolent God who is no deceiver; but God's existence is only proved by relying on the knowledge given from clear and distinct ideas. So Descartes is caught in a vicious circle.

Cartesian Doubt: Descartes's sceptical method in which, for the purposes of his argument, he treats as if false any belief about which he is not absolutely certain.

Cogito: Latin for 'I think'; short for 'Cogito ergo sum', which is usually translated as 'I think, therefore I am.' However, since according to Descartes at this stage of his argument I can only be sure of my existence while I am actually thinking, it is probably better translated as 'I am thinking, therefore I exist.'

Cosmological Argument: an argument which purports to demonstrate God's existence. It usually takes the form: there must have been a first cause of everything that exists; that uncaused cause was God.

dualism: the view that there are two sorts of fundamentally different substances in the world: mind or soul and body or matter.

empiricism: the view that knowledge of the world comes from sensory input rather than being innate and discoverable by reason alone.

epistemology: the branch of philosophy that deals with knowledge and its justification.

interactionism: the view that mind and body interact with each other: events in the mind bring about events in the body and vice versa.

monism: the view that there is only one type of substance in the universe (a view incompatible with dualism).

Ontological Argument: an argument which purports to prove God's existence on the basis of the definition of God as a perfect being. A perfect being which didn't exist wouldn't be totally perfect; so God must exist.

rationalism: a philosophical approach which contrasts with empiricism. Rationalists believe that important truths about the nature of reality can be deduced by reason alone, without the need for observation.

scepticism: philosophical doubt.

Trademark Argument: an argument that Descartes uses to attempt to prove God's existence. We have an idea of God in our minds. But where did this idea come from? It must have been implanted there by God as a kind of trademark.

FURTHER READING

Bernard Williams' interview 'Descartes', in Bryan Magee *The Great Philosophers* (Oxford: Oxford University Press, 1988), gives a brief yet illuminating overview of Descartes's thought. This interview is reprinted in my anthology *Philosophy: Basic Readings* (London: Routledge, 2nd edn, 2004).

John Cottingham *Descartes* (Oxford: Blackwell, 1986) provides a more detailed, yet accessible, introduction to Descartes's philosophical work.

For information about Descartes' life, see Stephen Gaukroger *Descartes: An Intellectual Biography* (Oxford: Clarendon, 1995) and Anthony Grayling *Descartes* (London: Free Press, 2005).

THOMAS HOBBES
LEVIATHAN

The frontispiece of Thomas Hobbes' *Leviathan* is one of the few memorable pictorial representations of a philosophical idea. A huge man, whose body is composed of thousands of smaller people, towers above the well-ordered city below. The church spire is dwarfed by this giant who wears a crown and wields a sword in one hand, a sceptre in the other. This is the great Leviathan, the 'mortal god' described by Hobbes. The Leviathan, which appears in the Old Testament as a sea monster, is Hobbes' image for the powerful sovereign who represents the people and is in a sense their embodiment: the multitude united in the form of an artificially created giant.

In *Leviathan* Hobbes diagnoses the general causes of strife and conflict and identifies a cure. The central arguments of the book address the question of why it is reasonable for individuals to consent to be ruled by a powerful sovereign (which could be either a single figure or an assembly). Peace can only be achieved if everyone accepts a social contract. Hobbes' discussion of these issues is at the heart of *Leviathan*, but the book touches on numerous other topics from psychology to religion. In fact more than half of *Leviathan* is devoted to detailed discussion of religion and Christian scripture: the half that is seldom read today. Here I focus on the main theme of the book, the contract which free individuals make to give up some of their natural freedom in return for protection from each other and from outside attack. Hobbes begins his account of this contract with an analysis of what life would be like if no society or commonwealth existed.

THE STATE OF NATURE

Rather than describing actual societies, Hobbes breaks society down into its most basic elements: individuals fighting for their survival in a world of limited resources. He invites the reader to imagine the conditions of life in a state of nature, the condition in which we would find ourselves if all state protection were removed. In this imagined world there would be no right or wrong since there would be no laws, there being no supreme power to impose them. Nor would there be any property: everyone would be entitled to whatever they could acquire and hold on to. For Hobbes morality and justice are the creations of particular societies. There are no absolute values which hold independently of particular societies. Right, wrong, justice, injustice are values determined by the sovereign powers within a state, rather than somehow discovered pre-existing in the world. So, in the state of nature there would be no morality whatsoever.

Hobbes' account of the state of nature is a thought experiment designed to clarify the limits of political obligation. If you find the state of nature unattractive, then you have an excellent reason for doing whatever it takes to avoid ending up in it. The state of nature is a state of perpetual war of every individual against everyone else. Since there is no powerful law-giver or law-keeper, no co-operation between individuals is possible. Without such power no one need keep any promises they make since it is always in their interest to break the promises when it suits them. Assuming that you have a strong desire to survive, it is simple prudence to break agreements when it suits you in the state of nature. If you don't seize what you need when you can get away with it, you run the risk of someone else stealing what little you have. In this situation of direct competition for meagre resources essential for survival, it makes sense to mount pre-emptive attacks against anyone who you think might pose a threat to your safety. This is the most effective strategy for survival. Even if there isn't any fighting going on, Hobbes says, this is still a state of war, since there is the constant threat of violence breaking out.

In a state of nature there can be no human projects which require co-operation, such as extensive agriculture or architecture. Even the weakest can potentially kill the strongest, so no one is safe, and everyone is a possible threat. Hobbes memorably described life in the state of nature as 'solitary, poor, nasty, brutish, and short'. If you are faced with the possibility of such a life, giving up some of your freedom seems a small price to pay for peace and safety. Hobbes explains what individuals in a state of nature must do to escape their unattractive predicament. Fear of a violent death and desire for the benefits of peace provide strong motives for doing so.

In the state of nature everyone has a natural right to selfpreservation, and they continue to have this right even after other rights have been given up in the social contract. Hobbes contrasts this natural right with natural laws. A right identifies something which you are free to do should you so wish, but are not obliged to do; a law compels you to follow its dictates.

LAWS OF NATURE

Even in the state of nature there are laws of nature: these are laws which follow from the use of reason. They are not like the present-day law against drink-driving: Hobbes used the term 'civil law' to refer to this kind of proscription (the content of civil laws is determined by the sovereign or by people acting on his behalf). Laws of nature, in contrast, are principles that any rational person is bound by. In the state of nature everyone has a right to everything. The inevitable consequence of this is, as we have seen, lack of security and a state of constant war. The law of nature which reason gives in these circumstances is *Seek peace wherever possible*. A second law of nature is *When others are prepared to do the same, give up the rights you have in the state of nature and be content with as much freedom in relation to others as you would grant them in relation to you* (this is a version of the religious prescription to *Do as you would be done by*). Hobbes constructs quite a long list of laws of nature, the consequence of which is that, provided that others are prepared to do likewise, it is rational for anyone in the state of nature to give up their unlimited freedom in return for security.

THE SOCIAL CONTRACT

The rational course of action is to make a social contract, yielding freedoms to a powerful sovereign. The sovereign must be powerful enough to be able to enforce any promises made, because, as Hobbes points out, 'covenants without the sword, are but words, and of no strength to secure a man at all'. The sovereign's power guarantees that the people will do what they have undertaken to do. The result is peace.

It is true that some animals, such as bees and ants, appear to live in societies which run smoothly without the need for any coercive direction from above. Hobbes points out that the human situation is very different from that of bees and ants. Human beings are constantly in competition for honour and dignity, which leads to envy and hatred and eventually war; ants and bees have no sense of honour and dignity. Human beings have the power of reason, which equips them to find fault with the way they are governed, and this gradually brings about civil unrest; ants and bees have no such power of reason. Human beings only form societies by means of covenants; ants and bees have a natural agreement with each other. Consequently human beings need the threat of force to guarantee that they will not break their promises, even though ants and bees don't.

For Hobbes the social contract is a contract made with other individuals in a state of nature to give up your natural rights in exchange for protection. This contract need not have historical reality: Hobbes is not claiming that at a certain point in the history of each state, everyone suddenly agreed that fighting wasn't worth the energy and that it would make more sense to co-operate. Rather he provides a way of understanding, justifying and changing political systems. One way of reading *Leviathan* is to take Hobbes to be saying that if the existing conditions of an implicit contract were to be removed, then we would find ourselves in a state of nature with its war of everyone against everyone. If Hobbes' argument is sound, and his portrayal of the state of nature accurate, then *Leviathan* provides compelling reasons for maintaining peace under the rule of a powerful sovereign.

THE SOVEREIGN

The sovereign, whether an individual or an assembly, becomes an artificial person. Once the wills of all have been bound together by contract then the sovereign is the living embodiment of .... Although Hobbes allows for the possibility of a sovereign assembly (that is, a group such as a parliament rather than an all-powerful individual), his sympathies are with a strong monarchy. However, he had little respect for the then widely held view known as the divine right of kings, according to which God approved of succession to the throne and gave sacred rights to royal heirs.

The social contract does not remove the natural right of self-protection that individuals have in the state of nature. Hobbes went so far as to say that everyone has a natural right to save themselves, even if attacked by people acting on behalf of the sovereign. The condemned man on the way to his execution, even if he had agreed to abide by the law, and had had a fair trial, would not act unjustly if he resisted the soldiers charged with taking him to the scaffold. However, no one has the right to intervene to help someone else in such circumstances. You can only struggle to save your own skin.

THE PRISONERS' DILEMMA

Some present-day commentators on Hobbes' work point out the similarity between his discussion of the state of nature and what is known as the prisoners' dilemma, an imaginary situation designed to illustrate certain problems about co-operation with other people. Imagine that you and your partner in crime have been caught, but not red-handed; you are being interrogated in separate cells. You don't know what your partner has or hasn't owned up to.

The situation is this: if neither of you confesses, then both will go free, because the police don't have enough evidence to convict you. At first thought this seems the best course of action. However, the catch is that if you remain silent and your partner confesses and thereby incriminates you, he will be rewarded for his collaboration and also set free, whereas you will get a long prison sentence. You too can have a reward if you confess but he doesn't. If it turns out that you both confess, you both get a short sentence. In this situation, whatever your partner in crime does, it makes sense for you to confess (assuming that you want to maximise your own benefit). This is because if he doesn't confess, you stand to get the reward as well as being released; and if he does confess, then it is far better for you to go to prison for a short while than end up there for a long time because he has incriminated you. So if you are both out to maximise your rewards and minimise your sentences, you will both confess. Unfortunately this produces a worse outcome for each of you than if you had both remained silent.

Hobbes' state of nature is similar in that, in it, it always makes sense for you (and everyone else) to break a contract when you stand to gain from it. Keeping the contract is risky: the worst scenario occurs if you keep the contract and someone else breaks it. If the other person keeps it, then you will most likely profit by breaking it. If the other person breaks it, then you should cut your losses by breaking it too. So either way you should not keep your contract. There is, in this situation, no incentive for a rational individual intent on getting the best result for himor herself to keep any contract. This is why Hobbes has to introduce the notion of the sovereign, since without such a powerful enforcer of contracts, no one would have an incentive to keep any promise they made. The contract with others to concede your rights to the sovereign is different from other contracts in that if you break it then you will be punished for this, probably severely. So in this case you have a strong incentive to keep the basic social contract.

CRITICISMS OF *LEVIATHAN*

Mistaken view of human nature?

A frequent criticism of Hobbes' description of the state of nature is that it paints an unduly bleak picture of human nature outside the civilising influence of the state. Hobbes believes that at heart we are all egoists, constantly seeking to satisfy our desires. He is a strict materialist, believing that the whole universe and everything in it can be explained in terms of matter in motion. Human beings are like sophisticated machines. In contrast to his somewhat pessimistic view that it is inevitable that human beings will compete and fight when the veneer of civilisation is stripped away, some more optimistic philosophers have claimed that altruism is a relatively common human trait, and that co-operation between individuals is possible without the threat of force.

However, in Hobbes' defence, his theory does seem to describe the sorts of rivalries and aggression that hold between countries in international relations. If it weren't for mutual mistrust there would be no need to stockpile nuclear weapons. But if Hobbes' theory does apply between states as well as within them then the future is even bleaker, for it is unlikely that a sovereign powerful enough to enforce covenants made between states will emerge, and so we can expect a perpetual war of all against all (even if this is not a literal war, only a state of potential conflict).

Social parasites

A further criticism of Hobbes' account is that he doesn't provide any reasons for someone to abide by the social contract when they can get away with breaking it. Why should a pickpocket abide by civil laws against theft declared by the sovereign if he is sure he won't be caught? If, as Hobbes argues, force is needed to make people in the state of nature keep their covenants, then, presumably, the same people will need to be forced to keep civil laws. But no state can watch everyone all the time, not even one equipped with closed-circuit television cameras.

Hobbes would probably answer this criticism by maintaining that it is a law of nature that you should not accept the state's protection without accepting the obligation to keep the state's civil laws. However, this answer is not really adequate.

State of nature pure fiction

A fundamental criticism of Hobbes' methodology is that his state of nature is a meaningless fiction which bears no relation to history and is set up in such a way that it allows him to smuggle in his monarchist prejudices as if they were the conclusions of rational arguments.

On the first point, although he does think that some native Americans lived in a state approximating the state of nature, it is generally agreed that Hobbes doesn't intend his account to be anything more than hypothetical. He points out what life would be like if there were no sovereign power, or if a sovereign power were removed. However, as we have seen, his assumptions about what that state would actually be like can be challenged, as can the value of a thought experiment which is so unlike what actually happens.

On the question of smuggled prejudices, it is interest. Hobbes allows that the sovereign may be an assembly rathe. just a monarch. If Hobbes is simply revealing his monarc of prejudices, the inclusion of this possibility seems beside the point; unless, of course, Hobbes was rationally considering his own self-preservation (which would be consistent with his philosophical views about human nature), not wanting to commit himself in public to too extreme a form of monarchism.

Totalitarian?

Like Plato before him, Hobbes seems content to reduce citizens' freedom considerably in his ideal state. For instance, he thinks censorship by the sovereign entirely acceptable, and indeed desirable: no book should be published before its doctrines have been examined and assessed for their tendency to promote peace. The commonwealth is an intolerant place, and individuals' consciences are not to be taken seriously. It is for the sovereign to declare what is right or wrong, and the individual should not attempt to make such judgements. Many of us would find this aspect of Hobbes' alternative to the state of nature particularly unattractive. Even though Hobbes set limits on the power of the sovereign to do whatever he or she likes, these limits are not sufficiently stringent to prevent the commonwealth becoming a totalitarian state with all that that involves.

Hobbes' probable response to this sort of criticism is given in one of his section headings: *sovereign power not so hurtful as the want of it*. Yet, at a certain point even the rigours of the state of nature would seem preferable to life under some totalitarian regimes. Some might opt for a solitary, poor, nasty, brutish and short life in preference to one of virtual enslavement.

DATES

1588	born in Malmesbury, Wiltshire.
1641	writes objections to Descartes's *Meditations*.
1651	publishes *Leviathan*.
1679	dies in Hardwick, Derbyshire.

GLOSSARY

civil laws: rules created by human beings (contrasted with natural laws).

commonwealth: a group of individuals joined together by a social contract to form a political body.

divine right of kings: the notion that the succession of rulers through birth is God's will.

Leviathan: an Old Testament sea monster, taken by Hobbes as a metaphor for the great body of the state composed of all its members joined together by a social contract.

natural laws: rules which are given by reason and which hold even in the state of nature. Any rational person is bound by them. They include the law: *seek peace wherever possible.*

prisoners' dilemma: a type of thought experiment designed to bring out important features of situations of co-operation and conflict. It involves the notion of two prisoners in separate cells each calculating whether or not it is rational to reveal the other's guilt.

rights of nature: basic rights, which entitle you to act according to them if you so wish. An example of a right of nature is the right to self-preservation, which we all have in virtue of being human and which can't be overridden by socially constructed laws.

social contract: an agreement to give up some freedoms in return for protection by a sovereign. The social contract permits the move from a state of nature to a civil society.

sovereign: a powerful individual or group of individuals acting as one person who provides protection for members of society in return for their giving up some of the freedoms they have in a state of nature. The sovereign enforces contracts made between members of the society.

state of nature: a hypothetical situation in which we would find ourselves if society broke down. It is a state of perpetual war with every individual ready to attack every other.

FURTHER READING

Richard Tuck *Hobbes* (Oxford: Oxford University Press, Past Masters series, 1989) is excellent. Tuck sets Hobbes in his historical context and demonstrates his importance as a philosopher. He also provides a useful overview of the wide range of interpretations that have been made of Hobbes' political theory.

Richard Peters *Hobbes* (Harmondsworth: Penguin, 1956) is a well-written and interesting account of Hobbes' thought, including his work on science and religion.

A. P. Martinich *A Hobbes Dictionary* (Oxford: Blackwell, 1995) is a useful reference book which includes a short biography of Hobbes.

BARUCH DE SPINOZA
ETHICS

Baruch de Spinoza's *Ethics* is a strange book. It bristles with all the jargon of Euclidian geometry: definitions, axioms, numbered propositions, corollaries and scholia. Yet, if you get beyond this intimidating technical apparatus, you will find a fascinating and, in places, profound attempt to understand our place in the universe.

The full title of the book is *Ethics Demonstrated in a Geometrical Manner*. Why, you might ask, would anyone attempt to write a philosophical treatise in the form of a geometry textbook? One answer is that Spinoza was impressed by the way in which Euclid deduced his conclusions logically from the various explicit assumptions that he made. The conclusions followed inexorably from the premises and were derived with transparency and elegance. Spinoza's conclusions spell out what the true implications of various definitions are. If you accept his premises, then you must accept his conclusions, provided that his reasoning is good.

Despite the jargon of geometry with which this book is liberally sprinkled, Spinoza's arguments never quite achieve the purity of those found in geometrical treatises. Within the pages of this difficult book, however, are philosophical and psychological insights of great power.

Spinoza is usually described as a rationalist. He believed that knowledge about our place in the universe could be achieved by the power of reason alone. In this his emphasis was very different from empiricists who believed that the basic source of knowledge is experience and observation. Spinoza believed not only that reason could discover the nature of the universe, but also that this was because the universe was arranged in a rational order. The structure of the universe is no accident; it is necessarily as it is. Sense experience, which is imperfect, could never give us an adequate understanding of the universe. This is not to say that Spinoza denigrated scientific research: he earned his living as a lens-grinder, work which depended on the science of optics. The lenses he made would have been used in microscopes and telescopes, instruments used to increase scientific knowledge.

THE TITLE

It is accurate, as we have seen, to describe this book as '*Demonstrated in a Geometrical Manner*'. However, not all of the contents of the book discuss what we would now think of as *ethics*. Much of the first part of the book is about substance and God, which turn out to be the same thing. We would now classify this discussion as metaphysics. Spinoza's theme is the universe and our place in it – the nature of reality. For him metaphysics and ethics were not separable. The nature of reality determines how we ought to live.

GOD AND PANTHEISM

In the early sections of *Ethics* Spinoza sets out to prove from his definition of substance that there can only be one substance (a position known as monism) and that this substance is God. The consequence of this is that everything that exists is somehow in God. God didn't create nature, He *is* nature. Spinoza writes of 'God or Nature', apparently equating the two. Thought and extension (the occupying of physical space) are simply two of God's infinite attributes, the two attributes that we have access to. Spinoza's argument for this position is complex. His conclusion that everything is somehow in God is often taken to be a species of pantheism. More subtle interpreters stress that Spinoza is only saying that all God's attributes are expressed in the world, not that God is nothing more than the world. So if Spinoza is a pantheist, his is not the crude pantheism which declares that the world simply is identical with God.

Whatever the correct interpretation of Spinoza's theological position, it is evident that it was very far from Christian and Jewish orthodoxy about the nature of God. Of Portuguese descent, Spinoza was born in Amsterdam in 1632 and raised as a Jew. He was excommunicated in 1656 because he had abandoned orthodox Jewish beliefs. It is easy to see why he could only have his *Ethics* published posthumously and why some of his contemporaries were convinced that he had ceased to believe in God at all.

MIND AND BODY

Spinoza had an interesting solution to the mind/body problem, the problem of explaining the relationship between the mental and the physical aspects of our existence. He knew his contemporary Descartes' work well and even published a book about his philosophy. Much of Spinoza's philosophy specifically opposes Descartes' views. Unlike Descartes, who argued that mind and body were entirely distinct, Spinoza maintained that the mental and the physical were inseparable aspects of the same thing. The mind is the same thing as the body. We can conceive this thing as either physical or mental. Mind is not itself a substance but rather a mode of substance. Mind and body do not interact in the way that Descartes described: they are just two aspects of the same thing. A consequence of this view, that Spinoza accepts, is that all physical things can have mental aspects.

FREEDOM AND HUMAN BONDAGE

The idea of freedom lies at the heart of Spinoza's moral teaching. Yet he denies that we can ever be free from chains of cause and effect. All our actions, and everything that happens in the universe, are determined by prior causes. You picked up this book and are reading it, but on Spinoza's account your decision was determined by prior decisions, physical events and so on. Your decision did not arise spontaneously from nowhere, even if it felt that way. Only God can be truly free in the sense that God's actions do not have prior causes.

So in the sense of being outside of the chain of cause and effect, there is no hope of human freedom. Yet Spinoza does argue that we can save ourselves from enslavement to the passions. This will make us free in the only sense in which we can be free, which is acting from internal rather than external causes. Moral action is acting for oneself rather than being in the grip of passions. The passions are forces which push us one way or another leaving us as helpless victims. When we can liberate ourselves from the passivity of being the vehicles of such passions and come to understand our actions we become free.

Human bondage is the condition of those who are ignorant of the causes of their actions. People in this condition are moved by external causes alone: they are incapable of acting freely in the sense just described. They are like stones pushed around by forces they don't comprehend. It is only by forming an adequate idea of the causes of our behaviour that we can escape this bondage, and make the causes of our action internal rather than external. Once we recognise the causes of an emotion it ceases to hold us in its grip as a passion. The *Ethics* is designed in part to teach the reader to attain this kind of agency, to become more fully human.

In this respect, then, Spinoza's thought recommends a kind of psychotherapy. To achieve freedom from the passions we must understand the true causes of our actions. Yet this doesn't mean that free decisions cease to have causes. When understanding is achieved these causes are internalised. They are transformed by being understood. But the actions they give rise to remain determined. So Spinoza sees human free will in this particular sense as compatible with our actions being causally determined.

LOVE OF GOD

In the later sections of the *Ethics* Spinoza presents an almost mystical picture of the wise way to live. We should strive to make sense of ourselves and our place in the universe. That is the path to wisdom. It is also the path to joy as the mind becomes more active and attains a higher degree of perfection. Although Spinoza makes the intellectual love of God a central aspect of his philosophy, this is not the love of any personal God concerned with our well-being. Indeed, Spinoza's philosophy has no room for the God described in traditional Christianity and Judaism: Spinoza's God is as impersonal as the geometrical arguments he uses to deduce God's existence and scope.

CRITICISMS OF *ETHICS*

No need for God

Once Spinoza had dispensed with the idea of a personal God and had, as far as he was concerned, proved that the natural world somehow expressed God's attributes, he could have taken a further step and embraced an atheistic philosophy. The God he describes is so different from the God of orthodox Christianity and Judaism, that it scarcely merits the name 'God' at all. Indeed, some of Spinoza's contemporaries believed that his philosophy was tantamount to atheism. Yet he was convinced that he had proved God's existence, and that the good life was a life expressing love of God.

Denies genuine freedom

The picture of the human condition that Spinoza paints in the *Ethics* leaves no room for the spontaneity of uncaused choice that some philosophers, such as Jean-Paul Sartre, see as the essence of free will. The best that we can achieve is that our actions be brought about by internal rather than external causes according to Spinoza. And yet the bleaker account of human freedom that Spinoza provides is persuasive, and may be more accurate. Perhaps it is just wishful thinking to believe that we can make uncaused choices about what we think and do. Spinoza saw himself as exposing the delusion of free will.

Over-optimistic about reason

Spinoza, like many philosophers before and since, saw the human capacity for reason as the path to wisdom and happiness. The intellectual contemplation of God was for him the highest form of happiness possible and brought its own rewards. This sounds like the convenient conclusion of an intellectual who happened to find solace in his own thought. Perhaps he was over-optimistic about reason and its capacity to bring us happiness. And yet he is surely right that by coming to understand some of the causes of our states of mind we can gain greater control over our lives.

DATES

1632   born in Amsterdam.
1675   completes the *Ethics*.
1677   dies in The Hague. The *Ethics* is published posthumously.

GLOSSARY

monism: the view that there is only one type of substance in the world.

pantheism: the view that God is everything. It is debatable whether or not Spinoza really was a pantheist.

rationalism: the belief that knowledge can be acquired through the power of reasoning. This contrasts with the empiricists' view that knowledge comes from observation.

FURTHER READING

Roger Scruton *Spinoza* (London: Phoenix, Great Philosophers series, 1998) is a brief sympathetic treatment of the major themes of the *Ethics*. A slightly longer book by the same author is *Spinoza* (Oxford: Oxford University Press, Past Master series, 1986).

For a critical survey of interpretations of the *Ethics*, see Genevieve Lloyd *Spinoza and the Ethics* (London: Routledge, Philosophy Guidebook series, 1996).

Steven Nadler *Spinoza: A Life* (Cambridge: Cambridge University Press, 1999) and Margaret Gullan-Whur *Within Reason: A Life of Spinoza* (London: Pimlico, 2000) are two recent biographies.

8

JOHN LOCKE *AN ESSAY CONCERNING HUMAN UNDERSTANDING*

Is a newborn's mind a blank slate? Or do we come into the world armed with knowledge? John Locke addressed these questions in his *Essay Concerning Human Understanding*. His answer was that all our knowledge is derived ultimately from the information we receive from the five senses. We come into this world knowing nothing whatsoever. Experience teaches us everything we know. This view is usually known as empiricism, in contrast to innatism (the theory that some of our knowledge is inborn), and to rationalism (the contention that we can achieve knowledge of the world by the power of reason alone). There was lively debate about the origins of our knowledge when Locke was writing in the seventeenth century, and this has continued, in a somewhat altered form, to the present day.

Locke's *Essay*, published in 1689, soon became a philosophical bestseller. He produced four editions of it in his lifetime, and it had already reached its eleventh by 1735. It is a complex and wide-ranging work; its main focus is the origin and limits of human knowledge. What can we know? What is the relation between thought and reality? These are the perennial questions of the branch of philosophy called epistemology, or the theory of knowledge. Locke's answers to them had a lasting influence on the course of philosophy, and many great philosophers, including George Berkeley

(1685–1753) and Gottfried Leibniz (1646–1716) defined their own positions in relation to them.

Locke described his role as that of an 'underlabourer' clearing away conceptual confusions so that the scientists, or natural philosophers, as they were then known, could carry on their important work of adding to human knowledge. This slightly self-deprecatory remark shouldn't blind us to the difficulty of the task which Locke set himself, which was nothing less than to explain the origins and nature of human knowledge. This involved a rejection of a whole philosophical tradition built on the assumption that whatever was written by an authority such as Aristotle must be true. Locke took great pleasure in overthrowing received opinion and replacing it with reasoned hypothesis. His aim was to shed light on what had only until then been obscure. His motivation came from a love of truth, and the exhilaration of thinking for oneself about some of the most profound questions we can ask. He was under no illusion that his would be the last word on any of the topics he discussed. Nor was he particularly optimistic about human understanding in general: he believed that God had given us the wherewithal to achieve knowledge of God, of our moral duty and of whatever was necessary to get through life, but that, ultimately, the powers of reason were limited.

NO INNATE PRINCIPLES

Many seventeenth-century philosophers believed in the existence of God-given innate principles, that is, principles that every human being is born knowing. These might either be what Locke called speculative principles, such as the obviously true statement 'Whatever is, is'; or else practical principles, such as the moral claim 'Parents have a duty to look after their children' or 'Everyone ought to keep their promises.' Locke used a range of arguments to show that neither sort of principle was innate. Most of these arguments rely on his fundamental assumption that the contents of the human mind are *transparent* to itself: that is, if you are having a thought, then it must be possible for you to get access to the content of that thought. Locke does not believe that it makes sense to say that someone could be having a thought without their knowing what that thought was about. He rejects any notion of unconscious thoughts as nonsensical.

One argument he uses to support his claim that there are no innate principles is that it is obvious that there is not total agreement about what the supposedly innate principles might be. If we were all born knowing that, for example, 'We should keep our promises', then everyone would recognise this as a fundamental principle. But, as Locke points out, there is no such general agreement. Some people see no obligation whatsoever to keep their promises. Nor do children immediately recognise the principle as one that is binding on them; rather the principle is one that has to be taught and learnt. The same holds for any principle you care to examine, moral or otherwise.

Furthermore, we would expect the supposedly innate principles to be more evident in children than in adults because children will have been less affected by local customs and will have had less experience of the world. The innate principles should be clearly recognisable in them. But they aren't.

The notion that there are innate moral principles shared by all human beings is, for Locke, a complete non-starter since a glimpse at history reveals the immense diversity of moral principles that have been held by societies and individuals. It is simply implausible to think that this would result from identical principles implanted in everyone's mind.

These and other arguments lead Locke to reject the view that there are any innate principles. However, this leaves him with the task of explaining how it is that the human mind comes to be furnished with thoughts, beliefs and knowledge of the world. His answer is that all our ideas come from experience.

IDEAS

Locke uses the word 'idea' to mean whatever it is that anyone thinks about. When you look out of your window, what you see – a tree perhaps, or a sparrow – is not the tree or sparrow itself, but rather a representation of it, an idea, something like a picture in your head. What you see is not just a product of what is out there in the world, but is also in part a creation of your sensory system. But not all our ideas are received from immediate sensation of the world. Some of them are ideas of reflection, such as when we reason, or remember or will something.

Locke believes that all our ideas ultimately come from experience, so that the contents of our thoughts, even when we are reflecting rather than perceiving, all come from sensation. A child locked away from the world who had only had sensations of black and white would have no more idea of scarlet and green than he would of the taste of oysters or pineapple if he had never tried them.

Ideas can be combined in various ways, so that once we have the idea of scarlet and the idea of a coat, we can imagine a scarlet coat, even if we've never actually seen one. But the simpler ideas from which the complex ones are built all originate in perception by one or more of the five senses.

PRIMARY AND SECONDARY QUALITIES

When we say that a snowball is greyish-white and cold and round, what we mean is that it can produce in us ideas of these properties. Locke distinguishes primary and secondary qualities, giving a very different account of each.

Primary qualities are inseparable from objects. The primary qualities of a snowball would include its shape and solidity, but not its colour or its coldness. Here Locke was very much influenced by the science of his day, and in particular by the corpuscularian hypothesis put forward by Robert Boyle (1627–1691). Boyle suggested that all matter is composed of minute particles, or 'corpuscles', which are grouped together in various ways. A single corpuscle alone in the universe would still possess the primary qualities of shape, size and solidity. The ideas that we have of an object's primary qualities, Locke believes, resemble those qualities. So, for example, if a snowball has the primary qualities of roundness and a certain size, then the ideas we have of these features resemble these aspects of the actual snowball: they are accurate representations of these qualities.

Secondary qualities are powers to produce ideas. But secondary qualities do not resemble their objects; they are, rather, a consequence of the texture of corpuscles (i.e. the microstructure) out of which the objects are composed, the particular conditions under which they are perceived and the sensory system of the perceiver. Secondary qualities, unlike primary ones, aren't properties that the corpuscles themselves have independently of observers. Take colour, for instance: the snowball appears greyish-white. Colour is a secondary quality. What this means is that the actual snowball does not really have colour in the sense that it has shape and size. I have an idea of the snowball as greyish-white. However, under different lighting conditions it might appear to be a completely different colour, blue, for instance. But in this case the blueness would no more be in the snowball than is the greyish-whiteness. The colour of the snowball derives from the arrangement of the corpuscles from which it is composed; the primary qualities of the corpuscles give rise to my ideas of it. The same is true of the snowball's coldness, and its taste. These are not strictly properties found in the snowball but rather secondary qualities of the object dependent on its primary qualities.

Locke's discussion of primary and secondary qualities makes clear his realism: his unquestioned belief in the existence of real objects in the external world which give rise to our experience. This may just sound like common sense, but many philosophers then, before and since have been led to sceptical views about the nature of whatever it is that causes our experience.

PERSONAL IDENTITY

One part of Locke's *Essay* which has set the framework for most subsequent discussion on the topic and continues to exert an influence in the late twentieth century is the chapter 'Identity and Diversity'. This was only added to the work in the second edition. It contains a discussion of the problem of personal identity, the question of what it is that makes someone the same person after a period of time in which they may have changed quite significantly, both bodily and psychologically.

Locke's answer to this question involves a discussion of three separate but related questions: (1) What constitutes sameness of *substance*? (2) What makes someone at a later date the same *man*? and finally (3) What makes someone at a later date the same *person*?

We would say that we were dealing with the same substance if none of the particles of which an object is composed have changed or been removed. Clearly with a living organism this never occurs, since, at least at a microscopic level, parts are continually being lost and renewed. So sameness of physical substance won't be a useful criterion for determining personal identity over time, since no living human being ever maintains precisely the same physical constituents from moment to moment.

For Locke a 'man' is a particular biological organism, a member of the species we call *homo sapiens*. A man is like an oak tree or a horse in this respect. A huge spreading oak tree is still the same oak it was twenty years ago, despite having doubled in size and shed its leaves twenty times. It is not the same substance, but it is the same oak, in virtue of of the continued function of its living parts. In the same way, I am the same man I was ten years ago, despite both physical and psychological changes which anyone would be able to notice.

Part of Locke's originality on this topic lay in separating questions about the identity of a man from those of a man's *personal* identity. But what exactly is a person if it is not the same as a man? According to Locke, a person is 'a thinking intelligent being, that has reason and reflection, and can consider itself as itself, the same thinking thing in different times and places'. In other words, a person isn't simply a member of our species, since some human beings lack the power of reason and self-consciousness. Furthermore, in principle, some non-human creatures could be considered persons. Locke cites a report of a rational parrot that was able to answer quite detailed questions in a convincing way. He points out that we would be unlikely to call it a man, despite its intelligence: it would always be a rational parrot, but it might also be considered a person if it had the appropriate level of rationality and self-consciousness.

What, according to Locke, is the criterion of personal identity over time? Not simply bodily continuity, since that does not guarantee us that we are dealing with the same person. Rather personal identity stretches only so far as consciousness will stretch: memory and continuing recognition of being responsible for one's past actions are the conditions of personal identity. No matter how much I've changed physically, if I can remember my past actions as my own, then I am the same person that I was.

Locke illuminates this notion with a thought experiment. Imagine that one day a prince wakes up to find that he has all the memories of a cobbler, and none of his own. His body remains unchanged. On the same morning a cobbler wakes up to find that he has all the prince's memories. Locke maintains that, although the prince-bodied individual remains the same man, he is not the same person that he was when he went to sleep. It would not be fair to hold the prince-bodied person responsible for the prince's former actions, since he would not have any recollection of having performed them. This far-fetched example is intended to bring out the important difference between the terms 'man' and 'person'.

But where does this leave us with cases of memory loss? It would seem that on Locke's account we should never punish people for what they can't remember doing since in an important sense they would not be the same persons who committed the misdemeanours. 'Person' for Locke is a forensic term, by which he means that it is one which is particularly relevant to legal questions which relate to responsibility for one's actions. It would seem then that we should never punish a murderer who can't remember killing. Locke's view on this is that in cases of memory loss or alleged memory loss, we tend to assume that if we have identified the *man* who performed the actions, then this must be the same *person* who committed them. We punish drunks for their actions even if they claim not to be able to remember what they did. However, this is simply a result of the difficulty of anyone proving their ignorance of what they did. The law has to be practical and so rarely accepts memory loss as an excuse. However, Locke suggests, on the day of judgement, God will not hold anyone responsible for actions which they can't remember performing.

LANGUAGE

Locke is interested both in the nature of language and in its use in effective communication. Language, for him, is not simply a matter of making intelligible sounds: parrots (even non-rational ones) can do that. Rather, words are signs of ideas: they signify them. Because words are signs for ideas and all our ideas come from experience, all our language and thought using language is intimately connected with our experience.

By using words we can communicate our thoughts to others. But Locke believes that we do not necessarily all attach the same ideas to the same words. For instance, my particular associations for the word 'albatross' may be very different from yours on account of our different experience of individual albatrosses. You may have had no experience of an albatross, or only of a picture of one, and yet feel confident in using the word. The idea you have associated with the word would be very different from the idea held by someone who saw albatrosses on a daily basis. If you have no clear idea of an albatross you may just end up making sounds like a parrot that has been taught to mimic or a young child, signifying nothing. So although words are uttered in public, what they signify can still be private and idiosyncratic. This can be a source of confusion and misunderstanding.

There are far fewer nouns than there are things to which they refer. This is not surprising, since if there were a name for every particular thing it would be impossible to communicate effectively. We use the general term 'albatross' to refer to a whole species of bird. Locke maintains that we acquire such general words on the basis of abstracting from our particular experiences.

CRITICISMS OF *AN ESSAY CONCERNING HUMAN UNDERSTANDING*

Innate knowledge

Research by the linguist Noam Chomsky (1928–) has resurrected the debate about innate knowledge in the twentieth century. From close analysis of the sentences used by children when learning to speak he concluded that the best explanation for the universally shared grammatical structures of different languages and the patterns of children's grammatical mistakes was an innate framework for interpreting and using language that all children are born with, what he called a Language Acquisition Device. This view provides a serious challenge to Locke's belief that a newborn's mind is like a blank piece of paper waiting to be written on by experience. It is much closer to Gottfried Leibniz's belief that the mind is like a block of marble which has various fault-lines along which it is predisposed to break to reveal a well-designed sculpture.

Do ideas of primary qualities resemble their objects?

Locke's account of the distinction between primary and secondary qualities sounds plausible at first reading, and is lent support by the various sensory illusions that suggest that secondary qualities are qualities of objects as they appear to us, rather than actually being somehow in the objects themselves. However, as George Berkeley pointed out, Locke's claim that ideas of primary qualities resemble the objects themselves is unsupportable.

On Locke's account, objects as they really are are hidden behind a veil of perception. We only get direct access to ideas, not what those ideas are of. So for Locke to maintain that ideas of primary qualities resemble their objects is nonsensical. In order to ascertain whether one thing resembles another we need access to both of them. But on Locke's account of the mind, we only ever have access to one side: our own ideas. Berkeley went further than this, arguing that because, strictly speaking, we only have access to the contents of our own minds, we cannot even prove the existence of anything independent of the mind. Locke, in contrast, simply assumes that the mind could not produce our ideas without there being an external world.

Homunculus problem

Locke's account of ideas makes them very like pictures in the head. But this doesn't really explain much about the processes of thought, because in order to appreciate what a picture is of, it seems to require a little person (a homunculus) inside your head to interpret the pictures, and then one inside his head, and so on. This infinite series of ever smaller homunculi apparently implied by his account of the mind is clearly an unacceptable consequence. It suggests that there is something wrong with Locke's account.

Memory loss doesn't always sever personal identity

The philosopher Thomas Reid (1710–1796) countered Locke's claim that memory provides an adequate criterion of personal identity with the following example. Imagine a brave officer who was once flogged at school for stealing from an orchard. In his first campaign as a young soldier he succeeded in capturing a standard from the enemy. When he captured the standard he could remember that he had been flogged as a boy. Later, he was made a general. But by that time, although he could remember capturing the standard, he could no longer remember being flogged at school. The person who captured the standard is, on Locke's account, the same person who was flogged, because of the memory link. Similarly, the memory link makes the general the same person as the young officer who captured the standard. Logic seems to tell us that if the boy is the same person as the young officer, and the officer the same person as the old general, then the boy must be the same person as the old general. Locke, however, would have to deny this on the grounds that the old general can't remember being flogged, and so this link with the past is severed. Reid's point is that this is a logical absurdity, because Locke's account gives us two contradictory conclusions: both that the boy and the general are the same person, and that they are not. Any theory which leads to such an obvious contradiction must be false.

Locke's response to this sort of criticism would have to be that the boy and the general are the same *man* but not the same *person*, and that it would be wrong to hold the general responsible for what the boy did. Locke would have to deny that the pattern of overlapping memories described by Reid leads to the conclusion that the boy is the same person as the general.

DATES

1632   born in Wrington, Somerset.
1689   publishes *An Essay Concerning Human Understanding* and *Two Treatises of Government* (although the date printed on the books is 1690).
1704   dies in Oates, Essex.

GLOSSARY

corpuscularian hypothesis: Boyle's theory that all matter is composed of minute particles (corpuscles).

empiricism: the view that our knowledge is derived from our sensory experience.

epistemology: the branch of philosophy which investigates questions about knowledge and how it is achieved.

homunculus: a little person. Locke's theory of the mind seems to have the consequence that there would have to be a homunculus inside the head interpreting ideas (and one inside that homunculus's head, and so on).

idea: for Locke, any thought whatsoever, including a perception. The seventeenth-century use of 'idea' was much broader than ours.

innatism: the view that our knowledge, or at least a substantial part of it, is inborn.

personal identity: what makes someone the same person despite bodily or psychological changes.

primary qualities: properties of objects including shape and solidity, but not colour and coldness (which are secondary qualities). The ideas of primary qualities resemble those qualities (not so with secondary qualities). The corpuscles of which an object consists themselves have primary qualities but not secondary qualities.

rationalism: the belief that we can acquire knowledge simply through the exercise of our reason.

secondary qualities: powers to produce ideas. Secondary qualities are a product of the corpuscular texture of objects and the sensory faculties of the perceiver. Unlike ideas of primary qualities, ideas of secondary qualities do not resemble the qualities themselves. Secondary qualities include such qualities as colour and coldness.

FURTHER READING

Stephen Priest *The British Empiricists* (London: Penguin, 1990) is a clear, well-structured book. It includes a chapter on Locke.

E. J. Lowe *Locke on Human Understanding* (London: Routledge, 1995) provides a detailed examination of the main themes of Locke's *Essay*, bringing out the continuing relevance of much of his thought.

J. L. Mackie *Problems from Locke* (Oxford: Oxford University Press, 1976) is a series of essays on the most important topics raised in the *Essay*.

For information about Locke's life, see Maurice Cranston *John Locke: A Biography* (Oxford: Oxford University Press, 1985).

members of the community. By tacitly agreein~
of money, Locke believes, we have all accepted th
ity between individuals which almost inevitably

CIVIL SOCIETY

So far we have just looked at what Locke has to say about the state
of nature, a situation governed by God-given laws of nature. However, one of his main aims is to show how what he calls a civil society
or a commonwealth (he uses the terms interchangeably) can come
into being, and how the members of such a society stand to benefit
by its existence.

The principal motivation for leaving the state of nature is a need
for protection: protection of life, liberty and property, and especially
the last of these. Although in the state of nature everyone is entitled
to punish anyone who breaks a law of nature, inevitably self-interest
affects the partiality of those who are asked to judge their neighbours.
In order to guarantee a peaceful life it is necessary to move from the
state of nature into an organised society. This involves giving up some
of the rights you have in the state of nature. In particular it involves
waiving the right to mete out punishment for transgressions of the
laws of nature. By mutual agreement members of a society give up
this right because of the greater safety they stand to gain by doing so.
They put the power of making and enforcing laws in the hands of some
individual or group of people entrusted to act for the common good.

The only way in which individuals can give up some of the freedoms of the state of nature is by giving their consent. Locke writes
of the 'compact' that individuals make one with another, by which
he means the agreement or contract: it is his term for what is usually
known as the social contract. If this compact is entered into freely
and explicitly, it is what he calls an *express* agreement; when the
compact is simply implied by behaviour rather than explicitly agreed
on, it is a *tacit* agreement.

You might object that you weren't born into a state of nature, but
rather found yourself in the midst of an organised society with laws
and government already in place. How, then, can you have consented
to giving up some of your basic rights? The notion of government by consent might seem implausible, given that you have never
consciously consented to the present situation. Locke's response is

.yone who benefits from the protection of their property in ⌐il society, or enjoys the other benefits which such an organisa-⌐ion can bring, has thereby made a tacit agreement to give up some natural rights. Once the social compact has been made, the individual implicitly agrees to be bound by the decision of the majority.

However, this doesn't mean that individuals in civil society put themselves under an obligation to obey the dictates of arbitrary tyrants. The most controversial aspect of Locke's *Second Treatise* at the time of publication, and no doubt one of the reasons why he chose to publish it anonymously, was his view that it can sometimes be right for citizens to overthrow and replace their rulers.

REBELLION

The whole point of joining together to form a civil society is the protection of life, liberty and property. When a ruthless government or ruler oversteps its legitimate role and ceases to act for the public good in these respects, then, Locke argues, it is acceptable for the people to rise up and overthrow that government or ruler. The government or ruler is given a position of trust; when that trust is betrayed all obligation on the part of the people is dissolved. By failing to act for the public good the government or ruler forfeits the power which the people bestowed upon it by their social compact. This follows from Locke's belief that all legitimate government is government by consent. To the accusation that this sounds like an incitement to rebellion, Locke replies that it surely cannot be right to defer to robbers and pirates: the implication being that those who rule without the people's consent and act contrary to the common good are the equivalent of criminals and do not deserve to be obeyed. On Locke's account, no government or ruler has any right to absolute power over its citizens. The limits on power are the limits of serving the common good.

CRITICISMS OF *SECOND TREATISE* OF *GOVERNMENT*

Role of God

One obvious criticism of Locke's position is that it is heavily depen-dent on the existence of the Christian, or at least the Old Testament,

God. The notion of a law of nature, which is fundamental to his theory of government, is derived from orthodox Christian doctrine. Without God's existence we might expect the state of nature to be something much closer to the state of war of everyone against everyone described by Hobbes. Whilst atheism was a comparatively rare phenomenon when Locke wrote his *Treatises*, it is a common position today. Many people are convinced that there is no god, Christian or otherwise. For such atheists Locke's account will be unconvincing unless non-theological premises can be found for it.

No consensus about laws of nature

Even Christians might have worries about Locke's account of the laws of nature. These are supposed to be God-given and readily discoverable simply by reflecting on what it would be rational to do. But it is by no means obvious that such laws exist. Locke assumes that they exist and that they are easily discerned. Yet the range of incompatible principles of action that various philosophers have claimed to discover by reflection suggests that there is little agreement about what the supposed laws of nature actually dictate. If there are no laws of nature, or if there is serious confusion about what they are, then Locke's theory of government will founder.

Class bias?

Some of Locke's critics have singled out his discussion of property for special attention. They argue that it reveals him to have been concerned to justify the status quo in relation to land ownership, serving the interests of the property-owning classes at the expense of those who had nothing to sell but their labour. There is some textual support for this position, particularly when Locke comments that the land which has been worked by his servant becomes his (rather than his servant's). Indeed, despite his insistence that in the state of nature everyone is free and equal, the *Second Treatise* seems to be a justification for extreme inequalities of property ownership.

DATES

See previous chapter.

GLOSSARY

civil society: another term for 'commonwealth'.

commonwealth: a group of individuals who have, either explicitly or implicitly, given up some of their freedoms in return for protection by the state.

divine right of kings: the belief that monarchs have a God-given authority to rule.

laws of nature: God-given laws which apply to all human beings even in the state of nature.

licence: complete freedom to do as you desire with no constraints whatsoever.

social contract: an agreement to give up certain freedoms in return for state protection.

state of nature: the hypothetical state of humanity before any social contract has been made. The laws of nature supposedly apply even in the state of nature.

FURTHER READING

John Dunn *Locke* (Oxford: Oxford University Press, Past Masters series, 1984) is an excellent short introduction to Locke's life and work, focusing on his political thought. D. A. Lloyd Thomas *Locke on Government* (London: Routledge, 1995) provides a more detailed examination of Locke's *Second Treatise*.

Ian Hampsher-Monk 'John Locke', chapter 2 of *A History of Modern Political Thought* (Oxford: Blackwell, 1992), sets Locke's *Two Treatises of Government* in their historical context, as does Maurice Cranston's biography of Locke (see Further Reading, p. 84).

DAVID HUME *AN ENQUIRY CONCERNING HUMAN UNDERSTANDING*

Hume was a sceptic. But, unlike some ancient Greek sceptics, he did not advocate suspending judgement on every issue. He believed that nature had equipped us well for life, and that at a certain point instinct and feeling take over and philosophical doubts, rightly, seem absurd. Hume questioned the traditional view that human beings are essentially rational. He argued that the role of reason in human life is very limited, far more limited than most previous philosophers had supposed.

The rigour and originality of his work are startling, but particularly so in the light of the fact that he had worked out and published most of his philosophical ideas by the time he was 25 years old. His first book, *A Treatise of Human Nature*, received far less attention than he had hoped; he described it as having fallen 'dead-born from the press'. The *Enquiry Concerning Human Understanding* is a rewritten and extended version of the *Treatise* intended to make its content more accessible. He felt that readers had been put off by his style of expression, but was, for the most part, happy with the content of the *Treatise*. It is difficult to imagine a present-day philosopher going to such lengths for the sake of the reader.

Like Locke, Hume is usually described as an empiricist; like Locke he believes that the entire contents of the mind are ultimately derived from experience. Hume is an empiricist, not just in terms of his conclusions about the origins of our thoughts, but also in his methodology. Rather than attempting to deduce from first principles what human beings must be like, he relies on observation, usually in the form of introspection. His aim is to produce a coherent scientific view of humanity.

Many of his views on the mind and its relation to the world are influenced by Locke's *Essay Concerning Human Understanding*, but Hume took them a stage further. One aspect of his philosophy which is very similar to Locke's is his reliance on the theory of ideas. Hume, however, introduced several new terms. Where Locke just used the word 'idea', Hume talks of 'perceptions', 'impressions' and 'ideas'.

THE ORIGIN OF IDEAS

Hume uses the word 'perception' for any contents of experience: the equivalent of Locke's 'idea'. Perceptions occur when we are seeing, feeling, remembering, imagining and so on: a much wider range of mental activity than is covered by our present-day use of the word. For Hume perceptions are of two basic kinds: impressions and ideas.

Impressions are the experiences we get when we see, feel, love, hate, desire or will anything. Hume describes them as more 'lively' than ideas, by which he seems to mean that they are clearer and more detailed. Ideas are copies of impressions; they are the objects of our thought when we recollect our experience or exercise our imagination.

So, for example, I now have an idea of my pen moving across my page and of someone turning the pages of a book behind me in the library. I also have an impression of the texture of the paper underneath my hand. These sensory experiences are vivid: it would be difficult to convince me that I am simply remembering previous experiences, or that I am dreaming. Later, when I type these lines into my computer, I will no doubt think back to this moment and recollect my impressions. Then I will be having ideas rather than impressions, ideas which won't have the same vividness (or 'liveliness' in Hume's terminology) as do the present sensory impressions of which they are copies.

Hume recasts Locke's assertion that there are no innate ideas as *all our ideas are copies of impressions*. In other words, it is

9

JOHN LOCKE
SECOND TREATISE OF GOVERNMENT

We hold these truths to be self-evident, that all men are created
equal, that they are endowed by their Creator with certain
unalienable rights, that among these are life, liberty and the
pursuit of happiness . . . that whenever any government becomes
destructive of these ends, it is the right of the people to alter or
to abolish it.

These resounding lines from the American Declaration of Indepen-
dence of 1776 paraphrase the message at the heart of John Locke's
Second Treatise of Government, written almost a century earlier.
Locke published his *Two Treatises of Government* anonymously in
1689, but there is evidence that he wrote them in the early 1680s
when the idea that the people had a right to overthrow an unjust
government would have been considered radical treason and could
easily have incurred the death penalty. Much of the detail of
the *Two Treatises* is directed at the turbulent political events of the
1680s; but the *Second Treatise*, with its attempt to establish basic
human rights, has had an influence which extends well beyond the
concerns of the seventeenth century.

FIRST AND SECOND TREATISES

Of the *Two Treatises*, the second is by far the more interesting. The *First Treatise* is almost entirely negative: it is a critical attack on the ideas of Sir Robert Filmer. Filmer argued that the monarchy's power was God-given and had nothing whatsoever to do with the consent of the people, a view known as the divine right of kings. Adam, the first man, had been given authority over the whole earth by God; the authority of present-day rulers could then be traced back to this initial gift. The people's duty to obey their rulers was a duty to God since the rulers were there by God's will as a result of a subdivision of the world since the time of Adam. What the people wanted was beside the point. Everyone had an absolute duty to obey the monarch and this duty was, indirectly, a duty to obey God.

In the *First Treatise* Locke demolishes the detail of Filmer's argument; in the *Second Treatise* he outlines his positive account of government. The question that Locke addresses there is, 'What are the sources and limits of legitimate political authority?' Or, to put it in a more practical form, 'Why should we obey our rulers, and under what circumstances might we be justified in opposing them?'

THE STATE OF NATURE AND LAWS OF NATURE

In order to answer these questions, Locke, like many political philosophers before and since, imagined what life would be like in a state of nature, that is, in a world with no government-imposed laws and no organised society. This sort of thought experiment is not usually intended to give an account of what life was actually like at some particular point in time, but rather is a story invented to bring out the philosophical justifications for forming a society with a government and laws. Hobbes thought that in a state of nature we would be in a state of permanent war against each other, competing for scarce resources; Locke's state of nature, in contrast, is a far more attractive prospect. For Hobbes individuals in the state of nature would be driven by their appetites and desires, and for them prudence would dictate that they took pre-emptive action against any would-be competitors. Locke, however, believes that even in a state pre-existing any organised society human beings would be bound by what he calls the laws of nature, and that these prohibit harming others.

The laws of nature are God-given laws which any human being is capable of discovering by reflection. In Locke's state of nature individuals are both equal and free. There is no natural hierarchy that sets one human being higher than another: everyone counts the same as everyone else and is equal before God. Individuals are also free, but this liberty should not be confused with licence (freedom to do whatever you want). Your freedom, even in a state of nature, is limited by the self-evident God-given laws of nature which prohibit you from committing suicide (since God clearly intended you to live out your natural lifespan), and from harming other people (since God created us as equals not to be used by one another).

One reason why Locke's state of nature appears so much more congenial than Hobbes' brutal war of all against all is that Locke believes that the laws of nature can be enforced by any individual. This includes meting out punishment for breaking the laws of nature. Even outside society the God-given laws hold and are enforceable. If, for example, you were to attack me without good reason, then, since the law of nature forbids harming anyone without justification, I would be within my natural rights to punish you, both in order to get some kind of reparation and to restrain you from further violence. This right to punish extends to those who are not directly involved. Someone else might learn that you had attacked me, and choose to punish you accordingly. Obviously in the state of nature there would be a danger that individuals would be biased in the ways they upheld the laws of nature. They would tend to promote their own interests under the guise of applying the laws of nature. That is one of the reasons why joining together and forming a government is an improvement on the natural state, since a government can set up an independent judiciary.

PROPERTY

One of the fundamental rights that everyone in the state of nature has is a right to property. Locke sometimes uses the word 'property' to cover more than what we would understand by the word (land, buildings, personal belongings and so on). For Locke we also have a property in ourselves, that is, we own ourselves and have a right to do what we will provided that we don't harm others or take our own lives. Locke's account of the origin of property in the state of nature only deals with property in the familiar sense, and principally with land and the fruits of agriculture. Unfortunately he nowhere explains how it is that each of us has a property in ourselves.

How, then, do individuals acquire rightful claims on land, particularly in view of the religious doctrine that God handed the world over to Adam to be held in common by all humanity? The essence of Locke's answer is that human labour, which adds to the value of the land, gives a right of property in the state of nature, provided that no one else has a prior claim on the land. The labourer who 'mixes' his or her labour with the land is entitled to that land. Imagine someone in the state of nature who lives by foraging for nuts and seeds from wild trees and plants. If he collects a bag full of this meagre food, then it rightfully belongs to him in virtue of the work he has put into gathering the foodstuff. Similarly, someone who mixes her labour with the land, who digs, plants and reaps a harvest, has a rightful entitlement to the land and its crop. However, there are strict limits on the quantity of goods which can be acquired in this way: the limit set by the law of nature is that no one should take more than they can actually use. If the forager's nuts and seeds go mouldy before he gets round to consuming them, or the planter stores away crops which spoil, then they are both liable to punishment for transgressing the law of nature which limits an individual's property to what he or she can use. In effect, the forager or planter who takes too much encroaches on his or her neighbour's share.

MONEY

However, because of the inherent perishability of so many of the necessities of human existence, particularly food, human beings typically agree to give value to some less perishable objects such as gold or silver. By mutual consent, individuals in the state of nature undertake to exchange perishable goods for these non-perishable objects. Thus money is invented. And money transforms the possibilities of property-acquisition in the state of nature since it allows individuals to amass large amounts of property without risking spoilage. For example, a farmer can grow large amounts of corn and then exchange anything that he doesn't eat for money. Thus he acquires a valuable and lasting commodity which can be exchanged for the necessities of life as required. He also helps to feed other impossible for us to have an idea of something which we have not first experienced as an impression.

How, then, would Hume cope with my ability to imagine a golden mountain even though I have never seen one and so never had an impression of one? His answer relies on a distinction between simple and complex ideas. Simple ideas are all derived from simple impressions. They are ideas of such things as colours and shape, ideas which cannot be broken down into composite parts. Complex ideas are combinations of simple ideas. So, my idea of a golden mountain is just a complex idea composed of the simpler ideas of 'a mountain' and of 'golden'. And these simple ideas are ultimately derived from my experience of mountains and of golden things.

Support for the belief that all our ideas derive from earlier impressions comes from the suggestion that any of our ideas can on reflection be broken down into its component parts which can then be seen to have come from impressions. Further support for this account comes from the observation that a man who had been completely blind from birth would be incapable of having an idea of the colour red since he would have had no visual impression of the colour. Similarly, and more contentiously, Hume declares that someone who was selfish wouldn't be able to form an idea of feelings of generosity.

However, though Hume thinks that, for the most part, his refinement of Locke's theory of ideas will be able to explain the origin of any particular idea, he does nevertheless identify an exception to this principle. The exception is the missing shade of blue. Someone who has seen a wide range of shades of blue may never have had an impression of one particular shade. Despite this, he can form an idea of this missing shade of blue. According to Hume's theory this should be impossible since he will have had no simple impression to which the idea of the colour corresponds. However, he is not unduly worried about this apparent counterexample because it is so exceptional and hence he does not refine his basic principles in the light of it.

THE ASSOCIATION OF IDEAS

Hume suggests three types of link between ideas. These provide an explanation of how it is that we move from one thought to another. They are: resemblance, contiguity, and cause and effect.

If two things *resemble* each other, then our thought of one naturally leads us to thoughts of the other. So, for example, when I look at a picture of my daughter, my thoughts are naturally led to my daughter herself. If two things are *contiguous* in time or place, that is, if they occur close to one another, then, similarly, an idea of one will lead to an idea of the other. So, if I think about my kitchen, then my thought will move easily to the adjoining living room because they are close together. Lastly, if two things are related because one is the *cause* of the other, then thoughts about the cause will lead us to thoughts about the effect. For instance, if I have an idea of stubbing my toe, then, as this is the cause of pain, my thoughts will move easily to ideas of pain.

Armed with his distinction between ideas and impressions and the three principles of the association of ideas, Hume believes he can account for all the workings of our conscious minds.

CAUSATION

One billiard ball strikes another and causes it to move. That is what we see and that is how we describe it. But what does it mean to say that one thing *causes* another? This is a fundamental question for Hume since, as he points out, all our thinking about matters of fact involves arguing from known causes to expected effects, or from perceived effects to probable causes. For instance, if I found a watch on a desert island I would assume that the cause of its being there was that someone had once left it on the island. If I heard a voice speaking in the dark I would assume there was someone there. These are examples of reasoning from effects to their causes. When I see one billiard ball rolling towards another, I anticipate its effect when it makes contact, thus reasoning from cause to probable effect. Scientific reasoning too is based on reasoning about cause and effect.

Yet, rather than take the relations between cause and effect for granted, as we inevitably do most of the time, Hume questions where we get our idea of it from. No matter how many times I watch collisions of billiard balls, I will not be able to discern anything in the first ball that means that the second ball *must* move in a certain direction. Hume believes that the source of all our knowledge about causal relations is experience. Until we have observed two billiard balls colliding (or at least some similar event), we will have no idea about what will happen. Adam, the first man, wouldn't have been able to tell that the effect of submerging his head in water would be that he would drown. Until he had experience of water he would not have had any way of knowing its effects.

Once Adam learnt something about the effects of water, he would have predicted that it would continue to behave in the same way. This type of reasoning about the future based on past regularities is known as induction. Similar causes produce similar effects, and we cannot help assuming that in this respect the future will be like the past. However, it is at this point that the so-called problem of induction becomes apparent. Our justification for assuming that the future will be like the past is flimsy. Yet it is the basis of all our thought. I can't use the fact that the assumption of regularity in nature has served me well in the past as a justification of inductive reasoning about the future: that would be a viciously circular argument using induction to justify induction. The fact is that it is just a habit that human beings have, albeit one that, on the whole, serves us well. It is custom and habit that guide us through life, not our powers of reason.

Our knowledge of cause and effect, when closely examined, amounts to an assumption that if two things are constantly found together with one occurring prior to the other then we will call the first a cause of the second the effect. Beyond what Hume calls 'constant conjunction' and priority in time of cause to effect, there is no necessary connection between a cause and its effect. It's not that Hume wants us to abandon our trust in relations between causes and effects: that would be impossible for us anyway. Rather he is demonstrating how little our behaviour is dependent on reason, and how much on our inherited nature and habits.

FREE WILL

Traditionally human free will has been thought to be incompatible with all our actions being caused. If every human action is simply the effect of some prior cause, then our sense of having control over our actions is misleading. Free will on this view is just an illusion. And without free will there can be no room for moral responsibility and culpability: if all our actions are caused and are thus outside our control, it cannot be appropriate to praise or blame us for them.

Hume opposed this way of thinking, arguing both that all our actions are in some sense caused *and* that we have free will. This view is usually known as compatibilism. Hume's argument is somewhat sketchy. He stresses that human beings are just as much subject to natural laws as is physical matter. For instance, similar motives tend to produce similar actions: there is the same sort of constant conjunction of cause and effect found in the human world as in the material one. Someone who leaves a purse full of gold on the pavement at Charing Cross would no more expect to find it there when he returns than he would expect it to sprout wings and fly. There is a predictable regularity in human behaviour, and this is evident throughout history and in every nation. This regularity in human nature in no way undermines the possibility of each of us choosing what we will do. There is, then, for Hume no contradiction involved between our actions being predictable and their being freely chosen.

Hume considers the suggestion that his account of human behaviour has the consequence that either none of our actions are wrong, since they can be traced back to God as their cause; or else our evil actions ultimately spring from God. With a certain amount of irony Hume rejects both options as obviously absurd and suggests that the answer to this problem is beyond the scope of his philosophy. However, most of his readers would have appreciated that he was presenting a thinly concealed attack on the notion of God. If there is no God, or if God is not as the theologians describe him, then there may be no problem about attributing responsibility for evil human actions.

His scepticism about various arguments for the existence of God continues in two important chapters, one on the so-called Argument from Design, and the other on miracles. These chapters were not included in the *Treatise*. They were considered extremely controversial when published in the *Enquiry Concerning Human Understanding*, and the discussion of miracles was the subject of many pamphlets from enraged theologians. As the chapter on the Argument from Design overlaps substantially with the argument in his *Dialogues Concerning Natural Religion* (the subject of the next chapter in this book), I will not discuss it here.

MIRACLES

The basic principle that Hume asks us to accept is that a wise person will always proportion his or her belief to the evidence available on any issue. This uncontroversial principle is the starting point for his dismissal of the suggestion that we should believe sincere accounts by those who claim to have witnessed miracles.

Hume is very clear about what a miracle is. It is a transgression of a law of nature, and one which is usually presumed to have been caused by God. Miracles should not be confused with merely extraordinary occurrences. For example, it would be a miracle if I suddenly began to hover two feet above the ground with no support and nothing physically keeping me there. It would be merely extraordinary if I were to win the lottery. Hovering above the ground involves defying the established laws of physics; winning the lottery is no miracle (unless, perhaps, I were to win it without holding a ticket): it is just a relatively unlikely occurrence given the massive odds against its happening to me.

Many people claim to have witnessed miracles in the above sense. However, Hume argues that we should never believe their testimony unless it would be more miraculous that they were lying or deceived than that the miracle occurred. We should always believe the lesser miracle, and always prefer an explanation that relies on the merely extraordinary to one which is based on the occurrence of something miraculous. This is the sensible policy of someone who proportions belief to the available evidence.

Hume suggests that the evidence should always incline us to believe that no miracle has happened. This is because any law of nature has been confirmed by numerous observations of it holding. Given the principle of believing in proportion to the available evidence, Hume maintains that particular eye-witness testimony of miracles is insufficient evidence on which to base the view that a law of nature has been transgressed. His position is bolstered by facts of psychology such as that human beings get a great deal of pleasure from emotions of amazement and wonder, the kinds of emotions that are typically aroused by reports of miracles. This can be a stimulus to self-deception about whether what you are witnessing is a miracle or not. Most of those who claim to have witnessed miracles stand to gain a great deal: they are likely to be given special treatment and to be thought of as specially chosen by God. This can act as a strong incentive to deceive either others or themselves.

All these factors combine to make it much more likely in any particular case that a miracle didn't take place than that it did. Hume does not rule out the logical possibility of miracles occurring; but he does suggest that a wise person should never believe a report of one.

HUME'S FORK

Hume ends his *Enquiry* with a forceful condemnation of philosophical writing which does not meet up to his strict empirical principles. Of any book he asks two questions. The dichotomy set up by these two questions has come to be known as Hume's Fork. The two questions are: first, does it contain any abstract reasoning of the sort found in mathematics or geometry? If not, does it contain any factual statements of a kind that can be observed or tested? If neither, he declares, 'Commit it then to the flames; for it can contain nothing but sophistry and illusion.'

CRITICISMS OF *AN ENQUIRY CONCERNING HUMAN UNDERSTANDING*

Presupposes theory of ideas

Hume's philosophy, especially his account of induction, has been remarkably resilient in the face of criticism. However, one part of it which has been rejected by almost all present-day philosophers is the theory of ideas. Hume did not really argue for this account of the mind, but rather took it for granted and refined it. Yet, there are numerous difficulties which arise for this sort of representative theory, some of which were mentioned in the chapter on Locke's *Essay*, such as the homunculus problem.

The missing shade of blue presents a counterexample

As we have seen, Hume does consider the example of the missing shade of blue as a possible counterexample to his view that all our ideas come from prior impressions, but he dismisses it as an exceptional case. However, the same sort of example could be constructed for any of the five senses: the missing note in a musical scale, the missing taste between two known tastes, the missing texture, the missing smell that falls between two perfumes. This sort of example, if taken seriously, presents a greater threat to Hume's account of the mind than he seems to realise.

There are, however, at least two ways in which Hume might respond to this sort of criticism. First, he could simply deny the possibility of having an idea of the missing shade of blue (or any of its equivalents). He chose not to do this. Second, he might consider the idea of the missing shade a *complex* idea, perhaps a combination of the ideas of blue and of the relation of being lighter than. However, because of a commitment to the supposition that ideas of colours are always simple ideas, he chooses not to do this either.

DATES

1711   born in Edinburgh, Scotland.
1739–40   *Treatise of Human Nature* published.
1748   *Enquiry Concerning Human Understanding* published.
1776   dies in Edinburgh.
1779   *Dialogues Concerning Natural Religion* (see next chapter) published posthumously.

GLOSSARY

compatibilism: the belief that all our actions have prior causes and yet that we do genuinely have free will and not just an illusion of it.

constant conjunction: when two or more things are always found together.

contiguity: closeness, for example, in time or in space.

idea: a copy of an impression. Notice that Hume's use of this term is more restricted than Locke's.

impression: any direct perception, including of our own feelings. Impressions are, according to Hume, more vivid ('lively') than the ideas they give rise to.

induction: generalising on the basis of a limited range of cases. You use induction when you predict the future on the basis of what has happened in the past.

miracle: a transgression of a law of nature attributed to God's intervention.

perception: Hume's term for any thought, whether an impression or an idea.

scepticism: philosophical doubt.

FURTHER READING

John Passmore's interview with Bryan Magee in Bryan Magee *The Great Philosophers* (Oxford: Oxford University Press, 1988), provides a clear overview of some of Hume's central themes, as does the relevant chapter of Stephen Priest's *The British Empiricists* (Harmondsworth: Penguin, 1990).

Barry Stroud *Hume* (London: Routledge, Arguments of the Philosophers series, 1977) is a more advanced book that emphasises the constructive as well as sceptical aspects of Hume's philosophical project.

E. C. Mossner's biography *David Hume* (Oxford: Oxford University Press, 2nd edn, 1980) makes fascinating reading.

11

DAVID HUME *DIALOGUES CONCERNING NATURAL RELIGION*

Apart from Plato, very few philosophers have written successfully in dialogue form. David Hume is the most impressive exception. His *Dialogues Concerning Natural Religion* is a masterpiece both of philosophical argument and literary execution. Unlike Plato, who gave Socrates all the best lines, Hume shares the good arguments between the three main speakers, Demea, Cleanthes and Philo, though it is clear that his sympathies, on the whole, lie with the last of these. The effect is to draw the reader into the debate. The 'correct' view is not clearly labelled as such, and must be discovered through the cut and thrust of the dialogue, a technique he borrowed from the Latin author Cicero.

Hume did not publish this work in his lifetime: he feared persecution from the religious authorities. However, he took great pains to make sure that it was published posthumously. The central topic of the book is the Design Argument for the existence of the Christian God. The Design Argument was the mainstay of advocates of natural religion, that is, those who based their religious beliefs on scientific evidence. Natural religion was usually contrasted with revelation. Revelation was the supposed proof of God's existence and attributes provided by the Gospels, with their accounts of miracles performed by Christ, and in particular his resurrection. Hume had already mounted a sustained attack on the claims of revelation in his controversial essay 'Of Miracles', which appeared in his *An Enquiry Concerning Human Understanding* (discussed in the previous chapter). In the *Dialogues*, natural religion comes under fire, though in a more oblique way since the arguments are given by fictional characters rather than in Hume's own voice.

THE CHARACTERS

Although five characters are mentioned by name in the *Dialogues*, the debate is all carried by the three main speakers: Cleanthes, Demea and Philo. The whole conversation is reported by Pamphilus to his friend Hermippus, but neither of them joins in the philosophical discussion.

Each of the three main characters defends a recognisable position. Cleanthes believes in the Design Argument, the view that the apparent design in the universe proves the existence of God. He is, then, a defender of natural religion. Demea is a fideist: that is, he does not put his trust in reason, but makes a commitment of faith that God exists and that he has the attributes ascribed to him. However, he also believes that the so-called First Cause Argument provides conclusive proof of God's existence. Philo, whose arguments are, with one possible exception, the arguments that Hume himself would have been happy to use, is a mitigated sceptic. His principal role in the *Dialogues* is to criticise the positions put forward by the other two main characters and thereby demonstrate that reason can reveal nothing significant about God's attributes. In particular, his critique of the Design Argument and the conclusions which can be drawn from it is devastating. For most of the book it would be easy to take Philo to be an atheist. However, he does state that he thinks it is obvious that God exists and that the important questions are about which attributes he has. Whether or not this was an ironic touch added by Hume, to prevent the authorities banning the work as a defence of atheism, is unclear.

THE DESIGN ARGUMENT

Cleanthes puts forward the 'argument *a posteriori*' which is now better known as the Design Argument. *A posteriori* arguments are arguments from experience. This is the argument that we can prove the existence of an all-powerful, all-knowing, benevolent God by considering the natural world. If we look around us we find that every aspect of the natural world bears the marks of apparent design. It all fits together like a machine. For instance, the human eye is brilliantly suited to seeing; the lens, cornea and retina seem to have been thought up by a superior intelligence and the design and construction of the eye is more skilful than anything made by human hands. The conclusion that Cleanthes draws from this sort of observation is that the natural world must have been designed by an intelligent creator. This creator must have had an intelligence in proportion to the magnitude and grandeur of his work and so must have been God as traditionally conceived. In other words, Cleanthes draws an analogy between nature and human artifacts, and on the basis of this concludes not only that God exists, but that he is all-powerful, all-knowing and benevolent.

To lend further support to his argument, Cleanthes uses several memorable examples. If we were to hear a voice speaking intelligently in the dark we would certainly, and quite reasonably, conclude that there was somebody there. The articulate voice in the dark would be sufficient evidence for this conclusion. The works of nature provide, according to Cleanthes, at least as much evidence for God's existence as would an articulate voice speaking in the dark for the presence of a speaker.

Another example Cleanthes uses is the vegetating library. Imagine books were living things which could reproduce like plants. If we discovered a book with its markings (words arranged in a meaningful order), then we would treat this as conclusive proof of its having been written by an intelligent being. Even if books reproduced themselves, this would not detract from the evidence they present that they contain the traces of thought. Similarly, Cleanthes alleges, we can read intelligence and design in the works of nature. Only a blind dogmatist would deny the evidence that nature provides for God's existence and attributes. Or so Cleanthes believes. However, much of the *Dialogues* is taken up with Philo, and to a certain extent Demea, attacking Cleanthes' argument.

CRITICISMS OF THE DESIGN ARGUMENT

Weakness of analogy

One argument that Philo uses against the Design Argument is that it rests on a relatively weak analogy between the natural world, or parts of it, and human creations. Arguments from analogy rely on there being pronounced similarities between the two things being compared. If the similarities are relatively superficial, then any conclusion drawn on their basis will be weak and will require independent evidence or argument as support.

If we examine a house, then it is quite reasonable to conclude from its structure that it has been designed by a builder or an architect. This is because we have had experience of similar effects (other buildings) being brought about by this sort of cause (being designed by a builder or an architect). So far we are on firm ground when we use an argument from analogy. But when the entire universe is compared to something like a house the dissimilarity between the things compared is so striking that any conclusions based on the alleged analogy between the two can be nothing more than guesswork. Yet Cleanthes treats this sort of argument from analogy as conclusive evidence for God's existence and attributes.

Limitations on the conclusion

The basic principle that underlies the Design Argument is that similar effects are produced by similar causes. Because the parts and whole of the natural world resemble a machine in some respects, it is reasonable to conclude that they originate from the same sort of cause as does a machine, namely intelligent design. However, if this principle is applied rigorously, as Philo points out, Cleanthes would be forced into an extreme form of anthropomorphism (the tendency to attribute human characteristics to non-human things, in this case to God).

For instance, traditional theology teaches that God is perfect. But if we take the analogy between divine and human designers seriously, we can't be justified in claiming that God is perfect, since human designers, manifestly, are not perfect. In which case, even if the design argument does prove the existence of a creator, it is spectacularly uninformative about his attributes, which is the declared subject matter of the conversation between Cleanthes, Demea and Philo.

To take another example: traditional theology is monotheistic. However, most complicated large-scale human projects are achieved as a result of teams of designers and builders working together. If we make strict use of analogy when trying to explain the creation of the universe, then we will have to take seriously the suggestion that the universe was created by a team of gods.

Alternative explanations

Philo also suggests several alternative explanations of the apparent order and design in the world. Some of these are far-fetched, and deliberately so. His point is that if we scrutinise the evidence provided by the Design Argument it can't rule out these alternatives. There is at least as much evidence for them as there is that the Christian God is the source of order and design in the universe.

For instance, at one point Philo gets very close to suggesting a theory of evolution on the lines of natural selection. He conjectures that apparent design could have arisen from the fact that those animals not well adapted to the environment in which they find themselves simply die. Thus, he suggests, we should not be surprised to find animals well adapted to their surroundings. Since Darwin put forward his ideas about evolution, almost a century after Hume's *Dialogues*, most scientists have taken the theory of an impersonal natural selection as the best available explanation of the apparent design exhibited by animals and plants.

Another alternative explanation that Philo toys with is that of a gigantic spider spinning the universe from its abdomen. His point is that order and apparent design don't necessarily stem from an intelligent brain. Spiders spin webs with order and design, yet they spin from their abdomens. The analogy between a spider and a creator of the universe may seem absurd, Philo agrees. But if there were a planet inhabited solely by spiders, then it would seem the most natural explanation of order, as natural as it seems to us that all apparent design stems from human-like thought.

Evil

The most destructive criticism of the Design Argument is provided by the problem of evil. How could a benevolent God have designed a world in which there is so much suffering? Philo paints a picture of human life beset with pain. Cleanthes' response is that such pain might be the lesser of two evils. His claim is that the reason God designed a world with so much potential for pain and suffering built into it was that any alternative world would have been even worse. But, as Philo insists, an omnipotent God could have created a better world. Or at least that's how it seems to mere mortals. Philo identifies four principal causes of suffering, none of which seem necessary, but all of which are part of the human condition.

First, we are so constituted that pain as well as pleasure is in some cases needed to stir us into action. We seem to have been designed so that, for instance, the discomfort of extreme thirst gives us a strong incentive to find some water; whereas, Philo thinks, we could have been driven purely by the desire for pleasure of varying degrees. Second, the world, including the human world, strictly follows what he calls 'general laws'. These are the laws of physics. A direct result of this is that all sorts of calamities occur. Yet surely a good and omnipotent God could intervene to stop such events. A few minor adjustments (such as in the present century removing a few parts of Stalin's and Hitler's brains) would have produced a much better world with far less suffering in it. But God chose not to intervene. Third, nature equips us with the bare minimum that we need to survive. This makes us vulnerable to the slightest fluctuation in our circumstances. Philo suggests that a benevolent parent-like God would have provided more generously for us in such things as food and natural strength. Fourth, Philo points to the bad workmanship evident in the design of the universe, at least when it is seen from a human perspective. Thus we find that although rain is necessary to help plants grow and to give us drink, it frequently rains so hard that flooding results. This and numerous other 'design faults' lead Philo to the conclusion that the creator of the universe must have been indifferent to human suffering. Certainly the Design Argument does not provide sufficient evidence to warrant a belief in a *benevolent* creator.

THE FIRST CAUSE ARGUMENT

Although most of the discussion in the *Dialogues* focuses on the Design Argument, this is not the only alleged proof of God's existence and nature that is brought up. Demea is an ardent defender of what he calls the 'simple and sublime argument *a priori*', better known as the Cosmological or First Cause Argument. This is the argument which begins with the assumption that anything that exists must have had a prior cause which explains its existence. If we trace the chain of effects and causes back in time we must either keep on going in what is known as an infinite regress; or else we will find an uncaused cause, one that necessarily exists. Demea thinks the first option absurd, and so concludes that the necessarily existing uncaused cause is the first cause of everything and is God. Cleanthes' response includes the argument that if we are looking for a first cause of everything we needn't go back further than to the universe itself: there is no need to postulate a cause preceding that. Or, to put it another way, even if the First Cause Argument proves that there is a necessarily existing being, it does not prove that that being is God as traditionally conceived by Christians.

WAS HUME AN ATHEIST?

I have already mentioned the difficulty of unravelling precisely what Hume believed about religion on the basis of the *Dialogues*. Philo, despite being the character closest intellectually to Hume, is not simply a mouthpiece for the philosopher. Many of Hume's contemporaries took it for granted that he was an atheist, and no doubt if the *Dialogues* had been published during his lifetime it would have been treated as conclusive proof of this. However, Hume was genuinely shocked when he met unashamed atheists in Paris in the 1760s, though his views might have changed by the end of his life.

His official doctrine was mitigated scepticism: a moderate form of scepticism which takes nothing on trust but does not go to the absurdities of those sceptics who attempt to live as if nothing whatsoever could be taken for granted. Mitigated scepticism applied to questions of religion points in the direction of atheism, but stops short of it. The mitigated sceptic would not accept the Design Argument as proof of the Christian God's existence or attributes. But saying that there is insufficient evidence on which to base a belief in God's existence is not the same as asserting that God definitely does not exist. Hume might have considered atheism itself a dogmatic position, that is, one for which there is insufficient evidence. Perhaps, then, Hume really did believe, along with Philo, that the universe had some kind of intelligent creator. However, he certainly believed that human reason was insufficient to give us detailed knowledge of what that creator, if there was one, might be like. He died without holding out any hope of an afterlife.

DATES

See previous chapter.

GLOSSARY

analogy: a comparison between two things. Arguments from analogy rely on the supposition that if two things are alike in some respects, they are likely to be alike in others.

anthropomorphism: attributing human qualities to non-humans, in this case to God.

argument *a posteriori*: argument from experience. In the *Dialogues* Hume uses this phrase to refer to the Design Argument.

argument *a priori*: argument from reason rather than experience. In the *Dialogues* Hume uses this phrase to refer to the First Cause or Cosmological Argument.

atheism: the belief that no God or gods exist.

Cosmological Argument: an argument for God's existence based on the notion that if God didn't exist nothing would exist.

Design Argument: an argument for God's existence based on the evidence of design in the natural world.

fideism: the position of those who rely on faith in God's existence rather than on reason and argument.

First Cause Argument: an argument for God's existence based on the claim that there must have been a first uncaused cause of everything and that that is God.

monotheism: belief in the existence of one God.

natural religion: the belief that there is scientific evidence for God's existence; usually contrasted with revealed religion.

polytheism: belief in the existence of more than one god.

revealed religion: the belief that God's existence is demonstrated by the testimony of miracles, especially in the scriptures.

theism: belief in the existence of one God who is all-knowing, all-powerful and supremely benevolent.

FURTHER READING

J. C. A. Gaskin *Hume's Philosophy of Religion* (London: Macmillan, 2nd edn, 1988) provides a clear overview of this aspect of Hume's philosophy and contains extended discussion of the arguments used in the *Dialogues*.

J. L. Mackie *The Miracle of Theism* (Oxford: Oxford University Press, 1982) provides an excellent introduction to the philosophy of religion and includes a discussion of Hume's *Dialogues*.

Hume's 'Of a Particular Providence and of a Future State', which is chapter XI of *An Enquiry Concerning Human Understanding*, overlaps significantly with the discussion of the Design Argument in the *Dialogues*, in terms of both content and literary technique.

Michael Ignatieff gives a moving account of Hume's death in 'Metaphysics and the Marketplace', in his *The Needs of Strangers* (London: Vintage, 1994).

12

JEAN-JACQUES ROUSSEAU *THE SOCIAL CONTRACT*

'Man was born free, and everywhere he is in chains.' This, the opening line of *The Social Contract*, has stirred the heart of many a revolutionary over the past two hundred years. Yet it is balanced in the same book by the disconcerting thought that those who fail to act for the general good of the state should be 'forced to be free'. This sounds like a licence for oppression given the difficulty of ascertaining what is genuinely for the good of the state. Both these ideas convey the uncompromising nature of Rousseau's philosophy: he was never afraid to express controversial and even dangerous views. In an age when the convention was to publish such views anonymously, Rousseau wrote under his own name. As a result many of his works were banned and he lived in perpetual fear of persecution, several times having to flee his home for a safer retreat. In the circumstances it is not surprising that in later years he became paranoid, believing that he was the victim of an international conspiracy.

Rousseau's central aim in *The Social Contract* is to explain the sources and limits of legitimate authority. He believes that our duties towards the state stem from a social contract, or social pact, as he sometimes calls it, by means of which groups of individuals are transformed into a body politic: a whole which has its own general will which isn't necessarily simply a sum of the individual wills of the people of which it is composed.

SOCIAL CONTRACT

Like most writers in the social contract tradition, including Hobbes and Locke, Rousseau describes the social contract as if it were a historical event. However, he does not mean by this to unravel how actual states were created; rather it is simply a device to bring out the underlying structure of the state. He is not saying that there was a moment in history when people actually got together and made a deal with each other, but only that the relations between citizens and the state can best be understood by considering the hypothetical origins of the association.

The basic agreement made by members of a state is that they shall unite for their common good. There is a great deal to be gained by co-operating as part of a society rather than living alone. Society can provide protection of life and property. So individuals have a strong incentive to collaborate and form a state.

At first glance it might seem that Rousseau entertains two incompatible ideals since he both praises the freedom that all humans have, even outside society, and emphasises the great benefits of life within society. Our natural freedom is a necessary part of our humanity: if we give up our freedom entirely, or become slaves, then we cease to be fully human. If society were to take away our freedom entirely then there would be no point in joining it, since in the process we would lose our humanity. Rousseau sets himself the task of explaining how we can form a state without sacrificing freedom. This may seem impossible since the essence of life in society is that you give up most of your natural freedoms in order to reap the benefits of protection. However, Rousseau believes that his particular version of social contract theory does provide a formula that combines genuine freedom with the fruits of society. Central to his account is his doctrine of the general will.

THE GENERAL WILL

Once individuals have been transformed into a state by means of a social contract, they are united by common goals. The general will is the wish of the state as a whole: the general will pursues the common good.

The concept of the general will is probably easier to understand when it is compared with that of the will of all. It may be that all the individuals who together make up the state desire a certain outcome because they stand to gain individually by it: for instance, they might all desire a reduction in taxation. Thus the will of all the individuals is to lower taxes. However, if the whole state stands to gain by keeping taxes high, then that is the general will, even though the individuals with their personal interests do not wish to pursue this policy. For the common good, taxes should be kept high and anyone who resists this should be 'forced to be free'. Similarly, I might as an individual have a vested interest in a new road not being built through my back garden. However, if the new route turns out to be the best one for the common good, then as part of the state I must will this.

Rousseau's philosophy draws a sharp distinction between individuals with their personal interests and desires, which are largely self-serving, and those same individuals as parts of the state. In the latter public role, there is no scope for dissent from the general will: that would be like turning against your own better self. The self-interested desires that you have as an individual should always be subservient to the higher aims of the general will. The general will is for the common good, and the continued existence of the state depends upon its members setting aside their private interests where they conflict with the state's interests.

FREEDOM

This might seem to leave little room for freedom, at least as the term is generally understood. If you have to sacrifice your personal desires for the greater good of the state, then it seems that your freedom to act will often be limited. We have already seen that Rousseau is happy to advocate forcing people to be free when they refuse to acknowledge the force of the general will. However, Rousseau maintains that far from diminishing freedom, this organisation of the state provides it. Acting in accordance with the general will is the most important form of freedom. It is civil freedom, as opposed to the mere desire-satisfaction permissible outside society. For him there is nothing paradoxical about achieving such freedom by means of force.

THE LEGISLATOR

The success and longevity of a state depend on the nature of its constitution. Good and appropriate laws are needed for its continued survival. Rousseau suggests that these laws should be created by a legislator. The good legislator is a remarkable individual who brings about a transformation of the people by making a flourishing state possible. Rousseau argues that the legislator's only function should be to write the laws of the state. A legislator who was also a sovereign might be tempted to skew the laws in the direction of his interests, knowing that he would have the power to gain by this. Nor should the legislator draw up an ideal set of laws without taking into account the nature of the people and land for whom he is working. Laws have to be tailored to circumstances.

GOVERNMENT

Government should be clearly distinguished from the sovereign. Government's role is purely executive. This means that the government is the group of individuals who put into action the general policies that have been provided by the sovereign. The sovereign is the name Rousseau gives to the state when it is actively pursuing the general will. In less than perfect states the sovereign may take another form, but in Rousseau's ideal state it is composed of every citizen. His use of the word 'sovereign' can be quite confusing because for us it can simply mean 'monarch'. But Rousseau was thoroughly opposed to the idea that sovereign power should rest with a monarch. One reason why *The Social Contract* was considered to be subversive was its defence of rule by the people and its open attacks on the idea of a hereditary monarchy.

THREE TYPES OF GOVERNMENT

Rousseau considers three possible types of government, though he recognises that most actual states employ a mixture of types. The three basic types are democracy, aristocracy and monarchy. Unlike many political theorists, Rousseau does not prescribe one form of government for every state: a certain flexibility is appropriate, taking into account the circumstances, the size of the state, the nature and customs of the people, and so on. However, he does rank the types of government and clearly prefers an elective aristocracy above the rest.

Democracy

Although the governments of the United Kingdom and the United States are often described as 'democratic', for Rousseau they would more likely be counted as elective aristocracies. By 'democracy' he meant direct democracy, that is, the system by which every citizen is entitled to vote on every issue. Clearly such a system could only work in a very small state and with relatively simple business to decide, otherwise the logistics of getting the whole citizenship together and getting through the business of government would thwart all other activity. Rousseau recognises the attractiveness of such direct democracy when the practical difficulties can be overcome, but points out that 'so perfect a government' is better suited to gods than mortals.

Aristocracy

Rousseau recognises three types of aristocracy: natural, elective and hereditary. We usually only use the word to describe the last of these. He thinks hereditary aristocracy the worst kind of aristocracy, and elective the best. Elective aristocracy is government by a group of individuals who have been elected on grounds of their suitability for the job. Elections minimise the risk of those who put private interests before the common good exercising their power for long.

Monarchy

Monarchy puts the power of government into the hands of an individual. This system has many inherent dangers. For instance, Rousseau maintains that monarchs tend not to appoint competent officers, but select on the basis of their making a good impression at court rather than aptitude for the job. The result is bad government. He is particularly scathing about hereditary monarchies, which, he says, always run the risk of handing over supreme power to children, monsters or imbeciles, a view that would not have been sympathetically heard by those who believed in the divine right of kings, the idea that inherited monarchy was God's will.

CRITICISMS OF *THE SOCIAL CONTRACT*

Freedom

One common criticism of Rousseau's *The Social Contract* is that it seems to legitimise oppression of an extreme kind; that far from providing the conditions for freedom, it gives totalitarian governments a justification for removing them. This view is lent support not just by the sinister implications of the phrase 'forced to be free' but also by Rousseau's suggestion that the state should employ a censor whose responsibility it is to enforce morality. The civil freedom that Rousseau celebrates may turn out to be extreme oppression; it certainly needn't include the toleration that the word 'freedom' seems to hint at. Whether this is or is not so will depend on the nature of the general will.

This is not to say that Rousseau was deliberately providing a framework for oppression. His sincere aim was to describe a situation which would provide both freedom and the benefits of society. However, it is a weakness of his system that it could support oppression.

How do we discover the general will?

Even if we concede that we should sacrifice our individual interests for the sake of the general will, there still remains the problem of discovering what that general will is. Rousseau suggests that if the people voted on any issue without consulting each other, then the majority vote would be in the direction of the general will, minor differences of interest, as it were, cancelling each other out. However, this seems implausible: it would at the very least require a fully informed populace. Besides, to expect the people to vote without forming factions is unrealistic. So we are left with the practical problem of deciding what is for the common good. Without the possibility of discovering the common good, Rousseau's entire theory would crumble.

DATES

1712   born in Geneva, Switzerland.
1762   publishes *The Social Contract*.
1778   dies in Ermenonville, France.

GLOSSARY

aristocracy: an elite group of rulers who may owe their position to nature, election, or else heredity.

democracy: for Rousseau this usually means the direct participation of all citizens in any major decision.

executive: those responsible for putting state policies into action.

general will: whatever is in the common good. Not to be confused with the will of all.

legislator: the exceptional individual entrusted to write the state's constitution.

monarchy: a state which entrusts its fate to a monarch, usually selected on the basis of heredity. Rousseau strongly opposed monarchy.

social contract: the agreement of individuals to come together to form a state held together by their common interests.

sovereign: not to be confused with a monarch. For Rousseau the sovereign is, ideally, the state pursuing the general will.

will of all: the sum of what particular citizens happen to desire. This need not coincide with the general will: the will of all may not be in the general interest as individuals often choose selfishly.

FURTHER READING

Robert Wokler *Rousseau* (Oxford: Oxford University Press, Past Masters series, 1995) is a brief introduction to Rousseau's thought.

Timothy O'Hagan *Rousseau* (London: Routledge, Arguments of the Philosophers series, 2000) is a more substantial analysis of Rousseau's philosophy.

N. J. H. Dent *A Rousseau Dictionary* (Oxford: Blackwell, 1992) is a very useful reference book which gives clear explanations of all Rousseau's major philosophical concepts.

Rousseau's autobiography, *Confessions* (first published in 1782, several translations available), gives some remarkable insights into his life. Maurice Cranston's three-volume biography also provides a rich source of information about Rousseau the man.

IMMANUEL KANT
CRITIQUE OF PURE REASON

Immanuel Kant describes his approach as a 'Copernican Revolution' in philosophy. Copernicus put forward the theory that the earth moves round the sun rather than vice versa. Kant's revolutionary idea is that the world that we inhabit and perceive depends on qualities of the perceiver's mind, rather than simply existing independently of us.

If you look at the world through rose-tinted spectacles, then everything will appear pink. Before Kant, many philosophers assumed that we were, for the most part, passive recipients of information about the world. Kant, in contrast, argued that as perceivers of the world we impose certain features on all our experience. It is a condition of having any experience at all that we experience the world as including relations of cause and effect, being ordered in time, and that the objects we perceive are related spatially to each other. Cause and effect, and time and space, are contributed by the perceiving subject rather than being out there in the world, existing independently of us. The 'spectacles' that we wear colour all our experience. To carry the analogy further, we would not be able to experience anything at all if we removed the 'spectacles'.

The *Critique of Pure Reason* is, as its title suggests, an attack on the idea that by reason alone we can discover the nature of reality. Kant's conclusion is that knowledge requires both sensory experience and concepts contributed by the perceiver. Either without the other is useless. In particular, metaphysical speculation about what lies beyond the realm of appearances is worthless unless it is grounded in experience. Pure reason will not provide the key to the ultimate nature of a transcendent reality.

The book is complex and difficult to follow despite its carefully designed 'architectonic' or structure. Part of the difficulty stems from the intrinsic difficulty of the subject matter, the fact that Kant is investigating the limits of human knowledge; but much of it is a direct consequence of his use of technical language and his convoluted style. Another feature which makes it difficult to read is the interconnectedness of the parts; a full understanding of the work would involve knowing all its parts and how they interrelate. Here there is only space to sketch some of its major themes.

THE SYNTHETIC *A PRIORI*

Empiricist philosophers, such as David Hume, distinguished two sorts of knowledge: relations of ideas and matters of fact. Relations of ideas gave knowledge that was true by definition, such as that all kangaroos are animals. We can be sure of the truth of this independently of having any experience of kangaroos. It simply follows from the definition of 'kangaroo'. If someone claims to have discovered a kangaroo that isn't an animal, we know in advance of checking their story that they are confused about the meaning of 'kangaroo'. Kant calls statements like 'all kangaroos are animals' 'analytic'.

An example of the other sort of knowledge that Hume recognised is 'some bachelors have collections of etchings'. The way to determine whether or not such a statement is true is to make some sort of observation. You can't tell whether or not it is true independently of such observation. It is a statement about an aspect of the world. For Hume there are only these two possibilities: statements have to be either analytic or empirical. If they are neither, they make no contribution to human knowledge.

Kant, who describes himself as having been roused from his 'dogmatic slumbers' by reading Hume's work, recognises a third type of knowledge, knowledge of what he calls the synthetic *a priori*. 'Synthetic' is used in contrast with 'analytic'. If a statement is not true by definition, then it is synthetic. *A priori* is a Latin phrase which Kant uses to refer to any knowledge which is known to be true independently of experience; it is contrasted with the phrase *a posteriori*, which means acquired from experience. For an empiricist like Hume, the notion of the synthetic *a priori* would seem strange. He took it as obvious that if a statement was *a priori* it must be analytic. Kant thought otherwise.

It is perhaps easiest to understand what Kant means by looking at some more examples. Where Hume allowed for only two possibilities, Kant allowed for three: the analytic *a priori*, the synthetic *a posteriori* and the synthetic *a priori*. The analytic *a priori* includes judgements such as that all kangaroos are animals; it does not give us new knowledge about the world. The idea of being an animal is, as Kant puts it, 'contained' in the idea of a kangaroo. The synthetic *a posteriori*, in contrast, is the realm of empirical judgements such as that all philosophers wear glasses. This requires observation in order to verify or falsify it. The synthetic *a priori*, Kant's main interest in the *Critique of Pure Reason*, consists of judgements which are necessarily true, and can be known to be true independently of experience, yet which give us genuine knowledge of aspects of the world. Kant's examples of the synthetic *a priori* include most of mathematics (such as, for instance, the equation $7 + 5 = 12$) and 'every event must have a cause'. Kant claimed that we know 'every event must have a cause' and '$7 + 5 = 12$' are both necessarily true; yet they are informative about the world, so neither of them is analytic. The aim of the *Critique of Pure Reason* is to investigate how such synthetic *a priori* judgements are possible. The answer amounts to an explanation of what must be true if we, or any other conscious beings, are to have any experience at all.

APPEARANCES AND THE THING-IN-ITSELF

Kant distinguishes between the world we experience (the world of *phenomena*), and the underlying reality behind it. The underlying reality consists of *noumena*, about which we can say nothing at all because we have no access to them. We are restricted to knowledge of phenomena; noumena must for ever remain mysterious to us. Hence most metaphysical speculation about the ultimate nature of reality is misguided, since it purports to describe features of the noumenal world, and our lot is to dwell entirely in the phenomenal one.

However, we are not simply passive recipients of sensory information about the world. Perceiving involves more than receiving data. What is received has to be recognised and organised. In Kant's terminology, intuitions are brought under concepts. Without concepts experience would be meaningless; as he puts it, 'Thoughts without content are empty, intuitions without concepts are blind'. I couldn't have knowledge of the word-processor in front of me without the intuition (the sensory experience of it); but I also need to be able to recognise and re-recognise it for what it is, and that involves bringing it under a concept. The faculty of my mind which deals with intuitions is the sensibility; the one which deals with concepts is the understanding. It is through the collaboration of the sensibility and the understanding that knowledge is possible at all.

SPACE/TIME

Space and time are, in Kant's terminology, forms of intuition. They are necessary features of our experience rather than qualities found in the thing-in-itself. They are contributed by the perceiver. In other words, when I look out of the window at the street and see children playing, although it seems to me that the space in which the children are playing is simply a feature of reality, rather than something I contribute, Kant's point is that in order to have knowledge of what is going on I have to organise my perception in terms of space. I couldn't have a non-spatial perception. Similarly, the ordering of events in time is something that I bring to bear on intuitions rather than an intrinsic quality of what I perceive.

THE CATEGORIES

Kant identifies twelve categories, including those of substance and of cause and effect. These are what allow us to bring our intuitions under concepts. They are *a priori* concepts. They are the contribution of the perceiver to experience. It is not just a matter of fact that all our experience, for instance, can be understood in terms of causes and effects; this is a necessary condition of having experience at all, and something that we, as perceiving subjects, contribute rather than simply discover in the world. The categories together with the forms of intuition (space and time) are the rose-tinted spectacles that we all must wear if we are to have any experience at all; but they don't exist as a feature of the world independent of all subjects of experience. They are contributed by conscious subjects, not real features of the thing-in-itself or noumenal world.

THE TRANSCENDENTAL DEDUCTION

One of the most important sections of the *Critique of Pure Reason* is, unfortunately, also one of the most obscure and difficult to unravel. This is the transcendental deduction of the categories. If successful, this argument demonstrates that scepticism about the external world (the philosophical doubt about whether anything that we perceive exists objectively) is self-defeating. What Kant attempts is to prove that any experience whatsoever must conform to the categories and that the experience that is thus produced is of an objective world, not a merely personal subjective creation of each individual. Sceptics about the external world begin from their own experience and argue that they can't prove that it is really experience of an external world rather than a pure illusion. Kant argues that because they begin from experience, such sceptics undermine their own approach: the existence of an objective external world, always perceived in terms of the categories, is a condition of our having any experience at all.

The transcendental deduction of the categories is an example of the type of argument that Kant uses throughout the book, namely a transcendental argument. It is important not to confuse it with the word 'transcendent', which Kant uses to mean what lies beyond appearance. A transcendental argument is one which moves from some aspects of our experience to conclusions about what must necessarily be so if we are to have this sort of experience. In other words, it brings out what is presupposed by the very fact that we have the sorts of experiences that we do.

CRITICISM OF THE *CRITIQUE OF PURE REASON*

Transcendental deduction fails through incomprehensibility

Despite the attentions of numerous interpreters and reconstructors, Kant's transcendental deduction and its conclusion remain hopelessly obscure. This is unfortunate. If Kant had succeeded in refuting scepticism about our experience and its sources, and had done this in a way intelligible to mortals, then this would have been of immense significance.

Inconsistent about metaphysics

Much of Kant's *Critique of Pure Reason* is directed against rationalist metaphysics, that is, speculation about reality based on the assumption that you can glean knowledge about a transcendent reality by pure thought alone. Yet Kant is in places guilty of the very charge he lays against other metaphysicians. He postulates the existence of noumena; but that is, as Berkeley had shown, going beyond what can reasonably be concluded from our experience. In other words, by supposing that noumena exist behind the veil of appearance, Kant was unwittingly indulging in the sort of speculative metaphysics which he elsewhere makes clear that he abhors.

Although this inconsistency might seem a devastating criticism of Kant's interconnected system of thought, several recent commentators have suggested that a great many of Kant's philosophical insights are salvageable and can be reconstructed in a consistent and enlightening form.

DATES

1724	born in Königsberg, Prussia.
1781	publishes *Critique of Pure Reason*.
1785	publishes *Groundwork of the Metaphysic of Morals*.
1804	dies in Königsberg.

GLOSSARY

a posteriori: that which is discovered empirically.

a priori: whatever we know independently of experience.

analytic: true by definition.

the categories: very general concepts which (unlike many more ordinary concepts) have to be applied to experience. For Kant there are twelve such categories including cause and effect, and sub-stance.

concepts: classification-rules which allow us to recognise similar intuitions and to make sense of our experience.

the forms of intuition: space and time.

intuitions: the raw data of experience.

noumena: things-in-themselves. The inaccessible reality which lies behind appearances.

phenomena: the things which we can perceive. The phenomenal world is the world as it appears to us. It is contrasted with the noumenal world, the world as it really exists behind appearances.

synthetic: not true by definition.

transcendental argument: any argument from what actually exists to what therefore must exist.

transcendental deduction: Kant's argument which is supposed to demonstrate the existence of an objective reality independent of perceivers.

FURTHER READING

T. E. Wilkerson *Kant's Critique of Pure Reason: A Commentary for Students* (Oxford: Oxford University Press, 1976; 2nd, revised edn, London: Thoemmes, 1998) is a very useful introduction to this book. It is lucid and stimulating and relates Kant's ideas to recent debates.

Roger Scruton *Kant* (Oxford: Oxford University Press, Past Masters series, 1982) and S. Körner *Kant* (Harmondsworth: Penguin, 1955) are both good introductions to Kant's philosophy as a whole.

Sebastian Gardner *Kant and the Critique of Pure Reason* (London: Routledge, Philosophy Guidebook Series, 1999) is a more thorough introduction to *The Critique of Pure Reason*.

14

IMMANUEL KANT
GROUNDWORK OF THE
METAPHYSIC OF MORALS

Good intentions count. The morality of an action is not determined by its consequences, only by the intentions behind it. Morality is objective: it's not a matter of taste or culture, but applies equally to all rational beings. The point of Immanuel Kant's *Groundwork of the Metaphysic of Morals* is to make these claims plausible by establishing what he calls 'the supreme principle of morality', namely the categorical imperative. The book was written as a short prelude to his more complex and detailed work on moral philosophy. It has stood the test of time as a succinct statement of a duty-based or deontological moral theory.

THE GOOD WILL

The only thing in the world which is good without qualification is a good will. What Kant means by this is that good intentions are good unconditionally. Everything else which is good is only good under certain circumstances. So, for example, courage might be considered a good attribute to have, but on its own, it is not necessarily good: it requires good intentions, that is, a good will, to guarantee its goodness. Power, wealth and honour may be good; but equally without a good will, they can all serve evil ends.

A good will is good in itself, not because of anything else that it gives rise to. So, Kant tells us, provided that we have good intentions, it doesn't matter from a moral point of view if a 'niggardly endowment of step-motherly nature' prevents us achieving what we set out to do. Even when all our good intentions are thwarted by events outside our control the good will still shines like a jewel.

This view contrasts sharply with consequentialist moral theories, such as John Stuart Mill's utilitarianism (discussed in a later chapter). These judge the moral worth of an action by its actual or probable consequences. For Kant, however, this is a mistake. Consequences are irrelevant to assessments of moral worth, though they are, of course, relevant to most other aspects of life.

DUTY AND INCLINATION

The only appropriate motive for moral action is a sense of duty. Some people's actions conform outwardly with their duties, but inwardly they are acting only from self-interest. So, for example, a shrewd shopkeeper won't overcharge an inexperienced customer because he knows that ultimately this is bad for business. This is not acting from duty, but only from prudence: enlightened self-interest. Acting from a motive of duty is acting simply because you know that this is the right thing to do, not from any other motive.

Duty stands in contrast to mere inclination. Some people happen to have compassionate natures; if they see others in need, they are moved to help them. Kant says that actions done solely from compassionate inclinations have no *moral* worth whatsoever. The motive of duty is all-important. Someone who has no natural inclinations to sympathy or compassion, yet who helps others out of a sense of duty, is morally praiseworthy; those who act purely out of inclinations, no matter how admirable those inclinations happen to be, are not acting morally at all.

Kant's reason for these surprising statements is that morality is open to every rational being; yet our inclinations are outside our conscious control. Ultimately it is a matter of luck whether or not you happen to have a compassionate nature. He reinterprets the Christian 'love thy neighbour', arguing that here the relevant kind of love is what he calls a *practical* one, that is, acting out of a sense of duty, rather than *pathological* love, which is the emotional attitude which more usually goes by that name. In other words, Jesus Christ wasn't telling you how you should feel about your neighbour when he said 'love thy neighbour', but rather instructing you to act from your sense of duty.

MAXIMS

It is the underlying principles motivating an action which determine its moral worth, not the end result. Kant calls such principles maxims. The same behaviour could be the outcome of very different maxims. You might tell the truth on a particular occasion while acting on the maxim 'Always tell the truth'; but your behaviour would on this occasion be indistinguishable if you were acting on the maxim 'Always tell the truth unless you are sure you can get away with telling a lie.' Only the first maxim is a moral one. Kant provides a way of identifying moral from other maxims with his categorical imperative.

THE CATEGORICAL IMPERATIVE

Our moral duty arises from our respect for the moral law. The moral law is determined by what Kant calls the categorical imperative. A hypothetical imperative is a statement such as 'If you want to get other people's respect, then you should keep your promises': it is a conditional statement. A categorical imperative, in contrast, is a command such as 'Keep your promises': it applies unconditionally, irrespective of your goals. Kant thinks that there is one basic categorical imperative fuelling all our moral actions. He provides several formulations of this imperative.

Universal moral law

The first formulation of the categorical imperative is 'Only act on a maxim that you could will should become a universal law.' 'Will' here is very different from 'want': it means *rationally* intend. By 'law' he means a moral rather than a legal law (many actions which transgress moral laws are perfectly legal). The idea is that if a maxim is a genuinely moral one, then it ought to apply to everyone in relevantly similar circumstances: it should be universalisable. It should also be impersonal inasmuch as it shouldn't make a special exception for you. If an action is morally wrong, it is morally wrong for everyone, including you. If an action is morally right, it is morally right for anyone in relevantly similar circumstances.

In order to explain the implications of this formulation of the categorical imperative, Kant uses the example of making promises you don't intend to keep. You might find it convenient to make such promises sometimes, but, he says, you could not rationally will the maxim 'Break your promises when you are hard pressed' for everyone. If the maxim were taken up universally, then the whole institution of promising would be undermined. This would be self-defeating. You wouldn't be able to trust anyone to keep their promises. So the maxim can't be a moral one; you could not will it as a universal law. Thus the categorical imperative provides a way of distinguishing between moral and non-moral maxims. If you can't rationally universalise a maxim, it isn't a moral one.

Treat people as ends

The second formulation of the categorical imperative is 'Act so as to treat others and yourself always as ends, never simply means to ends.' Rational beings are persons, that is, they are ends in themselves; they have their own lives to lead, and we should not simply use them for what happens to suits us. We should recognise them as individuals capable of leading their own lives. To treat someone merely as a means to my own ends is tantamount to denying their essential humanity. Another way of putting this is that we should respect other people's autonomy. It would be treating someone as a means to an end if I promised to pay him back the money he leant me, even though I never really intended to do so. Recognising him as an end in himself would entail intending to and actually keeping my promise.

The kingdom of ends

A further formulation of the categorical imperative is expressed in terms of a kingdom of ends: 'Act as if through your maxims you were a law-making member of a kingdom of ends.' A kingdom of ends is an imaginary state whose laws protect individual autonomy, allowing everyone to be treated as an end rather than as a means to an end. Here Kant makes clear that morality is not just a matter of individual conduct, but also the foundation of societies. Kant's approach is designed to discriminate between principles which rational agents would adopt for their ideal state and those which they would reject. A principle which you could not will to be a law in this ideal state fails to pass this test, and so is not a moral principle.

KANT, ARISTOTLE AND MILL

Kant's approach to moral action contrasts sharply both with Aristotle's and Mill's. Kant treats emotions as either irrational or irrelevant to moral action; only the practical emotions, which aren't emotions in the ordinary sense of the word, have any direct part to play in morality. Aristotle, in contrast, argues that the cultivation of appropriate emotional responses is a central aim of moral education. Aristotle's philosophy is flexible, based on sensitivity to circumstances; Kant's is rigid in its adherence to general principles which admit of no exceptions.

Kant's approach to morality also contrasts with a utilitarian one such as Mill's. Kant dismisses the consequences of actions as irrelevant to our moral assessment of them; whereas for Mill the consequences of an action determine its moral worth. Mill's approach gives guidelines for discriminating between competing moral claims: assess the consequences and choose the option which will maximise aggregate happiness. Kant's moral philosophy gives no method of choosing between two actions both of which are moral; or for that matter between two actions both of which are immoral.

Aristotle, Kant and Mill provide three distinctively different approaches to morality. Like Aristotle's and Mill's, Kant's theory is open to a number of criticisms.

CRITICISMS OF *THE GROUNDWORK OF THE METAPHYSIC OF MORALS*

It is empty

A common criticism of Kant's moral theory is that it doesn't provide any content to ethics. It concentrates on the structure of moral judgements, their universalisability and impersonality, rather than helping us to discover precisely what we ought to do. Worse still, using Kant's own test for moral judgements, it seems that we could quite easily universalise some quite obviously immoral principles, such as 'Always use the most efficient means of farming regardless of animal welfare': there is nothing inconsistent about willing this principle. Because most animals would fail to meet the appropriate threshold of rationality for Kant, the version of the categorical imperative which enjoins us to treat others as ends and not means would not save them here. So Kant would have to say that this maxim was a moral one.

Even the example of promise-breaking that Kant uses seems open to criticism. If you have a maxim 'Break your promises whenever you can get away with it', then, provided that no one else knows that this is your policy, it might appear that there is nothing self-contradictory in willing it. If everyone acted on the same maxim, the institution of promising could still survive. However, Kant's response would be that breaking a promise is absolutely wrong and that you could not rationally will the maxim in question. This is because willing such a maxim would entail willing not only that I break promises when I can get away with it, but also that other people treat their promises to me in the same fashion. So I would, in willing the maxim, effectively be willing that I have promises broken to myself.

The role of emotion

Kant's moral philosophy treats the emotions and individual character traits as irrelevant to our moral assessments of individuals. It doesn't matter for Kant if you are hard-hearted, provided that you act out of a reverence for the moral law. Yet, for many of us, genuine compassion is the core of morality, not a potentially distracting quirk of individual psychology. We admire people who have a special capacity for sympathy and compassion, and this admiration seems to be an admiration of qualities relevant to them as moral beings. Kant's approach, which focuses on what any rational being should do, ignores the centrality of emotions to human moral interaction. The *practical* emotions which he wants to substitute for the pathological ones scarcely seem to merit the label 'emotion' at all.

A caricature of Kant's attitude to emotions suggests that he always considers them obstacles to genuine moral action. However, in fact what he argues is that emotions and inclinations can cloud the issue of whether or not you are acting morally. This is particularly relevant if you find yourself in a situation in which you happen to feel a strong emotional inclination to act in the way that the categorical imperative indicates anyway.

For example, you might, when walking around London, be approached by someone begging for money. The sight of this person stirs up feelings of compassion that have you reaching for your purse; but you also recognise a moral duty, following from the categorical imperative, enjoining you to give money to this person. In such a situation it may be difficult or even impossible to tell what your real motivation for giving money is: is it an inclination, or is it reverence for the moral law? However, if your immediate response to being asked for money was revulsion and irritation, yet you still acted according to the categorical imperative, then you would have no trouble in knowing that you had acted morally. Kant doesn't rule out the possibility that those who feel compassion also act from reverence for the moral law; what he does say is that acting from compassion alone will not make your action a moral one.

Nevertheless, Kant's dismissal of emotion dehumanises moral relations. The coldly rational responses which he points to as models of moral behaviour seem to be less human and less desirable than appropriately emotional ones.

DATES

See previous chapter.

GLOSSARY

autonomous: being able to choose and act for oneself.

categorical imperative: Kant's term for our basic moral duty, which is absolute.

consequentialism: any ethical theory which determines the rightness or wrongness of an action on the basis of the consequences which ensue from it rather than, say, the motivation with which it was carried out.

deontological ethical theory: a duty-based ethical theory. Duties rather than consequences determine the rightness or wrongness of an action.

hypothetical imperative: any statement of the form 'if you want x do y'.

kingdom of ends: an imaginary state whose laws protect individual autonomy.

maxim: the general principle underlying any action.

pathological love: love consisting simply of emotion.

practical love: a rational attitude based on respect for the moral law.

universalisability: if a principle is universalisable, this means that it could consistently be willed in any other relevantly similar situation. For Kant all moral judgements are universalisable.

FURTHER READING

H.J. Paton's translation of the *Groundwork of the Metaphysic of Morals*, which is published under the title *The Moral Law* (London: Routledge, 1991) contains a useful section-by-section summary of Kant's argument. H. B. Acton *Kant's Moral Philosophy* (London: Macmillan, 1976) is worth consulting if you can find a copy of it.

Roger Scruton *Kant* (Oxford: Oxford University Press, Past Masters series, 1982) and Stephan Körner *Kant* (Harmondsworth: Penguin, 1955) are both good introductions to Kant's philosophy as a whole. Both include discussions of his moral philosophy.

15

ARTHUR SCHOPENHAUER
THE WORLD AS WILL
AND IDEA

The World as Will and Idea has often been compared to a symphony in four movements. Each of its four sections has a distinctive mood and tempo, and Schopenhauer returns to and develops themes touched upon in earlier sections. The book opens with an abstract discussion of our relation to the world we experience, the world as we represent it to ourselves (the world as idea). In the second section this discussion broadens out, suggesting that there is a deeper reality than the world which science describes; this world, the thing-in-itself (the world as will), can be glimpsed when we observe our own willed bodily movements. The third section is an optimistic and detailed discussion of art. Here Schopenhauer develops his claim that art can provide an escape from the relentless willing that is the normal human condition, whilst revealing aspects of the deeper reality, the world as will. Finally, a darker pessimism takes over in the fourth section, in which he explains why we are doomed to suffering by our very nature. Yet there is a glimmer of hope if we are prepared to live a life of asceticism, relinquishing our desires.

THE WORLD AS IDEA

When Schopenhauer begins *The World as Will and Idea* with the line 'The world is my idea', he means that experience is always from the perspective of a perceiving consciousness. We represent the world to ourselves rather than have immediate access to the underlying nature of reality. But the world as idea doesn't yield knowledge of the true nature of things. If we rest satisfied with appearances we are like a man who goes round a castle trying to find its entrance, stopping every now and then to sketch the walls. According to Schopenhauer, this is all philosophers until now have done. His philosophy, however, purports to give us knowledge about what lies behind the walls.

The question of the ultimate nature of reality is the central question of metaphysics. Schopenhauer accepts Immanuel Kant's division between the world as we experience it, what Schopenhauer calls the world as idea, and the underlying reality of the thing-in-itself. Kant calls the reality behind experience the noumenal world; Schopenhauer calls it the world as will. We aren't simply passive recipients of sensory information; rather, we impose the categories of time, space and causation on all our experience. But at the level of the thing-in-itself, the world as will, these categories do not apply. The world as will is an indivisible whole. What Schopenhauer calls the *principium individuationis*, the division into particular things, only occurs in the phenomenal world. The world as will is the entirety of all that exists.

THE WORLD AS WILL

It might seem that the world as will is by definition inaccessible to human beings, since it would seem not to be accessible through experience. However, Schopenhauer declares that in our experience of willing, the power we have to move our bodies, the world as will shows itself. The will is not separate from bodily movement: it is an aspect of that movement. When we are conscious of our own willing, we go beyond the world as idea and can get a glimpse of the thing-in-itself. We experience our own body both as idea, another object encountered in the world, and as will.

For Schopenhauer it is not just human beings who are manifestations of will: ultimately everything is an expression of will. In other words, he uses the word 'will' in an extended sense. A lump of rock, for instance, is an expression of will. The will that he describes is not an intelligence; it is a blind, directionless striving which condemns most human beings to lives of suffering.

ART

Art has a pre-eminent position in Schopenhauer's philosophy. The contemplation of works of art allows us to escape momentarily from the relentless grind of willing that is otherwise inevitable. Art allows us a disinterested aesthetic experience. When we contemplate a work of art we can, and should, set aside any practical concerns and cares, any notion of the work of art serving a function for us. We lose ourselves in contemplation. The same is true of our experience of beauty in nature: we can achieve this state of peaceful contemplation looking at a waterfall or a mountain just as much as at a great painting.

Artistic geniuses can achieve this state of disinterested contemplation of objects and events, and have the intellectual ability to communicate their emotion to audiences of their work. Such geniuses have the capacity for pure knowing: they can experience the Platonic Forms of what they perceive. Plato famously believes that the chair I'm sitting on is an imperfect copy of an ideal chair, the Form of the chair. For Plato, an artist who paints the chair puts the view at several removes from the real chair, the Platonic Form. This is one of his reasons for banning artists from his ideal republic: they deal in distant copies of reality, and distance us from the Forms. Schopenhauer, in contrast, believes that artistic geniuses can, through their work, reveal the Forms or Platonic Ideas of the particular things which they depict or describe. Thus artistic geniuses allow us to escape from the power of will and achieve an impersonal knowledge of the Platonic Forms.

Beautiful objects and scenes are well suited to jolt us out of the endless stream of desiring. Some depicted objects, however, are better suited to this than others. We can contemplate the beauty of depicted fruit, for example, but our practical interest may make it very difficult to remain disinterested, particularly if we are hungry. Similarly, some paintings of nudes are easier to contemplate disinterestedly than others; some tend to arouse the viewer sexually, thereby reasserting a practical interest.

Sublime objects and scenes, in contrast to those which are simply beautiful, are ones which are in some way hostile to the human will. They threaten with their immensity or power. Black thunder-clouds, huge bare crags, a river rushing in torrent: all these can be sublime. The aesthetic experience of the sublime is achieved by consciously detaching yourself from the will, lingering pleasurably over what would otherwise be terrifying. This again reveals the Platonic Forms of the objects contemplated.

The Platonic Forms revealed in the aesthetic contemplation of art and nature are important to Schopenhauer because they allow us a kind of knowledge of the thing-in-itself, the world as will. We can't get direct knowledge of the thing-in-itself by this means; but the Platonic Forms give 'the most adequate objectification of the will'. This simply means that the world they reveal is not subjectively distorted, but is as close as is possible to the thing-in-itself.

MUSIC

Music differs from other arts in that it doesn't represent the world as idea. It doesn't usually represent anything at all. Yet it is undeniably a great art. Schopenhauer gives it a special place in his system. Music, he says, is a copy of the will itself. This explains its profundity: it can reveal to us the nature of reality.

Music which is sad doesn't express a particular person's sadness, or suggest sadness in a particular context: it expresses sadness in its essential nature, removed from particular circumstances. Ultimately, though, it is a copy of the will. A consequence of this view is that music is a kind of unconscious metaphysics. It gives us a picture of the thing-in-itself, just as the metaphysician attempts to explain to us what lies behind the veil of appearance. Schopenhauer is well aware that his views on music and its relation to the thing-in-itself are unverifiable: there is no way of comparing a Beethoven string quartet with the thing-in-itself to see if he is correct. However, he presents his account as a plausible explanation of music's power, and suggests that the reader should try listening to music bearing in mind the theory.

FREE WILL

All phenomena are bound by the principle of sufficient reason, the principle that for everything there is a reason why it is as it is. This applies as much to human beings as it does to rocks and plants. Our behaviour is, then, entirely determined by biology, past events, our character. We only have the illusion of acting freely.

However, the will, the thing-in-itself, is entirely free. So human beings are both determined and free. The suggestion that we are, even if only at the phenomenal level, determined is a pessimistic one. The stream of pessimism that runs through the whole book becomes a raging torrent when Schopenhauer focuses on the nature of human suffering.

SUFFERING AND SALVATION

Here he draws heavily on a tradition of Asian philosophy, including Buddhist and Hindu teachings. Sustained periods of happiness are an impossibility for human beings. We are so constructed that our lives involve constant willing, seeking satisfaction. When we achieve what we desire, we may enjoy momentary happiness, which is nothing more than the relief from wanting what we were seeking. But this is inevitably short-lived. We either sink into a state of *ennui* (an intense state of boredom), or else find that we still have unfulfilled desires which drive us on to seek their satisfaction. All human life is, then, tossed backwards and forwards between pain and boredom.

However, if we gain insight into the true nature of reality, if we see through the veil of Maya (i.e. gain knowledge of the world as will), then there is a chance of salvation and of a permanent escape from suffering, a state which is at least as blissful as the temporary states of aesthetic contemplation which art can afford.

A first step in this direction is the recognition that inflicting harm on others is a kind of self-injury, since at the level of will, the person who inflicts harm and the person who suffers it are one. It is only at the level of phenomena that we perceive them as different. If we see this, then we will recognise all suffering as in a sense our own, and be motivated to prevent such suffering. We will recognise that when one person harms another it is as if the will were a crazed beast which sinks its teeth into its own flesh, not realising that it was injuring itself.

The more extreme move which Schopenhauer outlines at the end of *The World as Will and Idea* is asceticism, a deliberate denial of the will to life. The ascetic lives a life of sexual chastity and poverty, not in order to help others, but rather to extinguish desire, and ultimately to mortify the will. By this extreme policy, the ascetic escapes the otherwise inevitable suffering of the human condition.

CRITICISMS OF THE WORLD AS WILL AND IDEA

Fragile metaphysical foundations

Schopenhauer's book sets out a system of thought which has fragile metaphysical foundations. The entire framework relies on our gaining knowledge of the thing-in-itself, or at least some access to it, via our awareness of our own willed bodily movements. But if Schopenhauer is mistaken about the possibility of such access to the world as will, then the entire work is undermined. It seems at times that Schopenhauer wants to have his cake and eat it: he wants to say both that the veil of Maya prevents us from knowing about the ultimate nature of reality *and* that we can see through this veil.

However, even if we reject the metaphysical foundations of Schopenhauer's thought, there are many insights about art, experience and suffering that can be gleaned from this book. The fact that the system as a whole may be flawed does not prevent Schopenhauer from providing us with a rich source of ideas and speculation. It is not surprising that practising artists have found Schopenhauer's work inspirational.

Hypocrisy

Schopenhauer preached asceticism as the route to salvation and an end to the suffering that would otherwise be an inevitable feature of the human condition. Yet he didn't practise what he preached: he didn't practise sexual chastity, and he enjoyed a good meal. So why should we take such a hypocrite seriously?

This attack doesn't seriously damage Schopenhauer's philosophy: it is entirely possible for someone to recognise the route to salvation without actually pursuing it himself. Whilst hypocrisy is an unattractive character trait, it does not affect the strength of his arguments. If Schopenhauer was right that asceticism provides a way of eliminating suffering, then this is completely independent of how he actually chose to live his life.

DATES

1788   born in Danzig (now Gdansk).
1819   published *The World as Will and Idea*.
1860   dies in Frankfurt.

GLOSSARY

asceticism: a way of living which involves extreme self-denial.

disinterestedness: the attitude of someone who has no practical motivation for looking at something.

ennui: boredom, listlessness.

idea: the world as we represent it to ourselves. Contrasted with the world as will.

Idea (Platonic): the perfect Form of anything. Plato believed that, for instance, the perfect Form of a chair exists. All the chairs we perceive are simply imperfect copies of this Form or Platonic Idea.

metaphysics: the study of the ultimate nature of reality.

phenomena: Kant's term for the world we experience, in contrast to noumena, which lie behind appearances.

principium individuationis: the division of reality into particular individual things: this does not occur at the noumenal level, the level of the world as will.

sublime: that which is threatening to humanity yet which, when made the object of aesthetic experience, reveals its Platonic Idea. A thunderstorm, for example, can be sublime rather than merely beautiful.

Veil of Maya: the barrier which prevents us perceiving the world as will, the world as it really is.

will: the thing-in-itself, the ultimate reality which lies behind phenomena, for the most part inaccessible to us, but which is glimpsed when we will bodily movements, and mirrored in music.

FURTHER READING

Christopher Janaway *Schopenhauer* (Oxford: Oxford University Press, Past Masters series, 1994) and Patrick Gardiner *Schopenhauer* (Harmondsworth: Penguin, 1963) are both good introductions to Schopenhauer's work. Both concentrate on *The World as Will and Idea*.

Bryan Magee *The Philosophy of Schopenhauer* (Oxford: Clarendon, rev. edn, 1997) is particularly good on Schopenhauer's influence on creative artists; it also provides a wide-ranging introduction to Schopenhauer's work.

16

JOHN STUART MILL
ON LIBERTY

My freedom to swing my fist ends where your face begins. That, in essence, is the message of Mill's *On Liberty*. The only ground for preventing me from doing what I want to do, or forcing me to do something against my will, is that someone else would be harmed by my actions. My private life is my business, and as long as I don't actually harm anyone else by what I do, then it is not for the state or society to interfere. Anyone who has reached adulthood and is capable of making informed decisions should be free to pursue their version of the good life without any interference. Even if I harm myself through my actions, this isn't sufficient grounds for state intervention. I can, for example, decide to neglect my physical health and degenerate into a couch potato, and should be free to do this. Paternalism, that is, controlling what people do on the grounds that you know better than they do what is good for them, is only justified towards children and those who, because of mental illness, are incapable of making responsible decisions for themselves. Mill also, more controversially, believes that paternalism is justified towards 'uncivilised' peoples who are incapable of judging what is best for them. The rest of us, however, should be given a free rein because that's the best way of increasing the overall level of happiness in the world.

AUTHORSHIP

Although *On Liberty* is always referred to as by John Stuart Mill, in his introduction to the book and in his autobiography he emphasises that it was in fact co-written with his wife, Harriet Taylor, who died before it was finished. Historians of philosophy dispute the degree of influence she had on the content of the finished book, but it is clear that Mill himself saw her role as co-author (though he didn't go so far as to include her name on the title page).

THE HARM PRINCIPLE

In his autobiography Mill describes *On Liberty* as 'a kind of philosophic textbook of a single truth'. The single truth is usually known as the Harm Principle or the Liberty Principle. This is the idea outlined above that potential harm to other people is the only acceptable ground for preventing me from doing whatever I want to do. This is very different from arguing for unlimited freedom. Mill thought that life in society would be impossible without imposing *some* restrictions on freedom: the question he addressed was where to draw the line between what should and should not be tolerated.

The Harm Principle is underpinned by Mill's commitment to utilitarianism, the view that the right action in any circumstances can be calculated by assessing its consequences: whatever is likely to give rise to the greatest happiness just is the morally right thing to do (though not all types of happiness are given equal weight in Mill's calculation). Mill argues that if individuals are allowed space to pursue what interests them, the whole society benefits. I know better than other people the sort of life that is best for me. Even if I'm mistaken about this, choosing for myself is probably preferable to being forced to accept someone else's conception of the good life 'off the peg'. Mill believes that a situation in which individuals are allowed to pursue a wide range of incompatible lifestyles is far preferable to one in which they are coerced into a pattern of social conformity. He is an empiricist, and as such believes that the way to discover the truth on most matters is by experiment. Only by trying out different solutions to the human predicament will a society flourish; this was the route to social improvement. He approved of what he called 'experiments of living'. In contrast, unthinking conformity leads to stagnation and a cramping of choice, the net result of which is misery and a stunting of human potential. It is important to realise that Mill is not arguing that we all have a natural right to liberty: he does not believe that the idea of natural rights makes sense at all. For convenience we might talk about a 'right' to freedom, but, for Mill, this must always be translatable into a generalisation about what is most likely to promote happiness. Utilitarianism rather than a natural rights theory underpins the policies of *On Liberty*.

On Liberty is partly directed at those who want to impose laws to restrict what consenting adults do in private (and consequently it has in recent years provided intellectual support for law reform on such issues as film censorship and homosexuality). But it is also directed at what Mill called 'the tyranny of the majority', the way that social pressures imposed by majority views can prevent some people from carrying out experiments of living even though there is no law which prohibits them from doing so. If my neighbours are affronted by the eccentric way I choose to live, even if nothing I do directly harms them, they may well make my life intolerable and thereby effectively prevent me from exercising the freedom I have within the law. The social pressure to conform can, Mill believed, undermine freedom and level everyone down to an unthinking mediocrity that is in the end worse for all.

This brings out clearly a point that some people who want to use Mill's Harm Principle find convenient to ignore, namely that merely causing offence to other people doesn't count as harming them. If you are offended by the knowledge that I choose to live in an unconventional way, with several homosexual partners, or as a nudist, perhaps, or maybe as a transvestite, then that doesn't provide sufficient grounds for coercing me by law or by social pressure to behave otherwise. Mill's principle would have been completely implausible if it had allowed offence to count as harm since almost every style of life is found offensive by someone or other. What exactly Mill *does* mean by 'harm' is not always clear and has been the focus of much discussion; but he is explicit in rejecting the idea that causing offence to others counts as harm. The sort of toleration that Mill advocates does not mean that you have to approve of other people's eccentric life choices. You are entitled to be disgusted by how others live. You can try to educate them into making better choices; and the state is justified in imposing an education system on children that will make them less likely to pursue self-destructive lives as adults. But your disgust at the way other adults have chosen to live is never on its own enough to justify any intervention forcing them to behave differently. A mark of a civilised society is that it can tolerate diversity.

Mill's principle is not meant to be an abstract philosophical ideal with no relevance to real life. He wants to change the world for the better. To that end he focuses on applications of the principle. The most important of these is his discussion of freedom of thought and discussion, usually known as freedom of speech.

FREEDOM OF SPEECH

Mill is a passionate defender of free speech. He argues that thought, speech and writing should only ever be censored when there is a clear risk of incitement to violence. The context in which words are uttered or written can affect their dangerousness. As Mill pointed out, it would be acceptable to print in a newspaper the view that corn-dealers starve the poor. However, if the same words were spoken to an angry mob outside a corn-dealer's house then we would have good grounds for silencing the speaker. The high risk of inciting a riot would justify the intervention. Today's debates about freedom of speech often focus on pornography or on racism; for Mill, writing in the nineteenth century, the central concern was with writing or speech which criticised orthodox views in religion, morality or politics. He thinks that greater damage is caused by suppressing a view, even if that view is false, than by allowing it to be freely expressed. In *On Liberty* he gives a detailed justification of this stance.

If someone expresses a controversial opinion, there are two basic possibilities: that the view is true, or that it is false. There is also a less obvious third possibility: that, though false, it contains an element of truth. Mill considered each of these possibilities. If the view is true, then suppressing it involves denying us the opportunity of ridding ourselves of error. His assumption is that truth is better than falsehood. If the view is false, then to silence it without giving it a hearing undermines the possibility of providing a public refutation of the view in which, he believes, truth would be seen to be victor in its collision with error. So, for example, Mill would tolerate the expression of racist opinions, provided that they did not incite violence, because they can then receive a public refutation and be demonstrated to be false (assuming that the views were indeed false).

If the view expressed contains an element of truth, silencing it can prevent the true part becoming known. For example, a racist might point to the fact that members of a particular ethnic group on average left school with fewer qualifications than the norm. The racist might take this as evidence that members of that ethnic group were innately inferior. However, even though this view is very probably false, the evidence might contain some truth: the truth here might be that members of this ethnic group *do* actually leave school with fewer qualifications. The true explanation of the evidence might be that they are discriminated against by the education system, not that they are innately inferior. Mill thinks that by silencing opinions that you are convinced are false you run the risk of overlooking the fact that even false opinions can contain elements of truth.

In order to silence a view you must be confident of your own infallibility (inability to make mistakes). But none of us can have complete confidence in this respect. No human being is immune from mistakes about what is true. History is brimming with examples of truth being suppressed by people who genuinely believed the suppressed view to be misguided nonsense. Think of the suppression by the Church of the view that the earth goes round the sun rather than vice versa. Galileo and his followers were persecuted for their beliefs; their persecutors were convinced that their own views were correct.

But surely censors are justified in making judgements on the basis of probability? They may not be infallible, but in some cases surely they can be almost certain that they are right? There are very few issues on which we can achieve absolute certainty: won't a demand for certainty paralyse us into inaction? Mill's response to this is that allowing others the freedom to contradict us is one of the principal ways in which we gain confidence in our judgements. We can be more confident about a view which survives scrutiny and criticism than one which has never been challenged. Besides, even if a view is obviously true, the act of defending it against false views keeps the true view alive and prevents it from becoming a dead dogma incapable of stirring anyone to action.

If a view is neither entirely true nor entirely false, by silencing it we will run the risk of jettisoning the element that is true along with the false part. The true element may never enter the public debate, thus setting back the cause of truth in the name of suppressing falsehoods.

CRITICISMS OF ON LIBERTY

Religious objections

Despite the fact that Mill was very keen to promote religious toleration, his views on liberty are sometimes attacked on religious grounds. Some religions teach that part of the state's role is to enforce the God-given moral code. For members of such religions it may be inconceivable that they could be misled about their religious duty. If, for example, you are a member of a religion which dictates that all homosexual activity is a sin, and your religion is the official state religion, then you may believe that the state should prohibit all homosexual activity despite the fact that it does no direct harm to anyone. Whether or not this prohibition would be conducive to happiness is irrelevant, you might think. In contrast, Mill would argue that *because* this prohibition would tend to decrease happiness and restrict human potential it should not be imposed. The two views are in such direct contradiction that there is no obvious compromise between them.

Vague notion of harm

The Harm Principle provides the core of *On Liberty*, but Mill is vague about what he means by harm. He rules out being offended as not counting as being harmed. However, at one point in the book he allows that some acts which are permissible and harmless in private (presumably he is thinking of sexual acts) should be prevented from taking place in public. This seems inconsistent with what he says elsewhere in the book, since he argues there that only if an action causes harm is there any justification for intervention. And in the example mentioned the only possible harm that can occur would be that members of the public find it offensive. Furthermore, it is not clear, even with physical harms, what threshold of harm needs to be reached before intervention becomes justified.

In Mill's defence, his *On Liberty* was not intended as the last word on the subject.

Private immorality harms society

One alleged justification for state intervention to prevent some activities which are carried out in private and harm no one or else only consenting adult participants is that a society only exists in virtue of a common underlying set of moral principles. If these principles are undermined, whether in public or private, then the society's continued existence may be threatened. So intervention may be necessary, for the preservation of society, which is the basis of the possibility of individual happiness.

The assumption that this last sort of criticism is based on is controversial. There is a great deal of evidence that societies can tolerate moral diversity without disintegrating.

Not utilitarian

Mill is explicit about the theoretical justification of the doctrines of *On Liberty*: utilitarianism provides the ultimate justification for the Harm Principle. However, a number of critics have pointed out that, at times, Mill seems to be arguing for freedom as something having *intrinsic* value whether or not it contributes to overall happiness. *Intrinsic* value is usually contrasted with *instrumental* value. Intrinsic value is the value that something has in itself; instrumental value is the value that it has because it can be used to get something else (money, for example, has instrumental value because its value to us lies in its use rather than in the coins or notes themselves). A utilitarian believes that the only thing that has intrinsic value is human happiness: everything else which is of value is of instrumental value in bringing about human happiness. So, we would expect a utilitarian to say that the only value in freedom is that it is conducive to happiness. But such a view does not obviously lead to Mill's conclusion that we should always preserve individual freedom except in cases where harm to others is likely. Indeed, a strict utilitarian might claim that, for example, regarding freedom of speech, in certain specific cases there might be good grounds for silencing some true views because happiness would thereby be increased. If I have reliable information that the whole of humanity will be destroyed by a comet which will collide with our planet in the next few weeks, you might have good utilitarian grounds for suppressing my freedom of speech. If it were generally known that our species was about to be wiped out it is fairly obvious that the overall level of human unhappiness would increase significantly as compared with a situation of ignorant bliss.

Mill suggests that freedom of speech is always for the best except in the situation where there is a serious risk of direct harm as a result. It is not obvious that utilitarianism provides a theoretical justification for such a strong position. This sort of objection doesn't necessarily undermine Mill's conclusions, but just points to the fact that he has not provided a convincing *utilitarian* justification for them.

Over-optimistic

Many of Mill's views about freedom and its consequences are optimistic, some, perhaps, over-optimistic. For example, he assumes that adults are generally in the best position to know what is likely to promote their own happiness. But is this obviously so? Many of us are experts at self-deception and easily seduced into short-term gratification at the expense of the chance of long-term happiness. We tell ourselves stories about what will make our lives go well which, on sober reflection, often turn out to be convenient fictions. If this is so, it's possible that someone else, who is not so involved in the matter, might be better suited to assessing how I should live. However, any benefits which might ensue from letting other people choose how I live will have to be offset against the accompanying loss of my own self-direction.

Another area in which Mill is perhaps over-optimistic is that of freedom of speech. He assumes that in the collision between truth and error, truth will triumph. But this may not be the case. He underestimates the power of irrationality in human life. Many of us are strongly motivated to believe things which aren't true. Allowing false views to be circulated freely may actually allow them to take root amongst the gullible in a way that they would not have done had they been silenced. Also, changes in technology have resulted in a much wider dissemination of views. There is no evidence whatsoever that amongst the diverse and widely disseminated views there has been a strong tendency for truth to triumph over error. In the circumstances, some people might think that there are good grounds for censorship. However, any would-be censor will have to face up to Mill's point that if you suppress someone else's opinion this involves an assumption that you are infallible and that the beneficial effects of silencing the view outweigh the detrimental ones.

Positive freedom

A further criticism of Mill's account of freedom is that, by concentrating on freedom from interference and by making the case for tolerance, he missed a more important sense of the term 'freedom'. Mill provided an account of what is usually known as *negative* freedom, or freedom *from*; what is needed, some of his critics believe, is an account of *positive* freedom or freedom *to*. Those who defend positive freedom argue that since society is imperfect, simply allowing people space to get on with their lives isn't sufficient to guarantee them freedom. There are numerous obstacles to achieving freedom, ranging from lack of material and educational resources to psychological obstacles to success. Those who argue for the positive sense of freedom believe that in order to fulfil your potential as a human being and thereby be genuinely free, all kinds of state intervention may be necessary, and at times this may result in individuals having their range of activity curtailed, even though it does not directly harm anyone else. Some of the more extreme defenders of positive freedom even believe that it is acceptable to force people to be free, and that there is no contradiction involved in this notion. In contrast, in Mill's terminology, if you are forced to do something then you cannot, by definition, have done it freely.

DATES

1806   born in London.
1859   publishes *On Liberty*.
1863   publishes *Utilitarianism*.
1873   dies in Avignon, France.

GLOSSARY

coercion: use of force to make someone do something.

fallibility: the fact that we are prone to make mistakes.

the Harm Principle: the only justification for coercing another's actions is that they are otherwise likely to harm someone else. Sometimes known as the Liberty Principle.

negative freedom: freedom from constraints. The principal kind of freedom advocated by Mill.

paternalism: forcing someone to do or refrain from something for their own good.

positive freedom: freedom actually to do what you really want to do. Obstacles to positive freedom can be internal as well as external: for instance, weakness of will can prevent you from being free in this sense.

toleration: allowing people to conduct their lives as they wish, even though you disapprove of the choices they have made for themselves.

utilitarianism: the moral theory which declares that the morally right action in any circumstances is the one which is most likely to maximise happiness.

utility: for Mill 'utility' is a technical term meaning happiness rather than usefulness. If an action increases utility, this simply means that it increases happiness.

FURTHER READING

Isaiah Berlin 'John Stuart Mill and the Ends of Life' and 'Two Concepts of Freedom', both in Isaiah Berlin *Four Essays on Freedom* (Oxford: Oxford University Press, 1969) are two important essays which address the central issues raised in *On Liberty*.

Alan Ryan ed. *Mill* (New York: Norton, 1997) includes the texts of *On Liberty* and *The Subjection of Women*, together with a selection of commentaries. It also includes an annotated bibliography.

John Skorupski *John Stuart Mill* (London: Routledge, Arguments of the Philosophers series, 1989) provides a detailed account of Mill's philosophy as a whole and includes a discussion of *On Liberty*.

Nigel Warburton *Freedom: An Introduction with Readings* (London: Routledge and the Open University, 2001). This book, originally written as part of an Open University philosophy course, includes an examination of Mill's arguments in *On Liberty*.

For details of Mill's life, see Michael St John Packe *The Life of John Stuart Mill* (London: Secker & Warburg, 1954), Nicholas Capaldi *John Stuart Mill: A Biography* (Cambridge: Cambridge University Press, 2004), or Mill's own very readable *An Autobiography* (first published in 1873, London: Penguin, 1989).

17

JOHN STUART MILL
UTILITARIANISM

Maximise happiness. That is a caricature of utilitarianism, but it captures something true and central to the theory. John Stuart Mill is the most famous utilitarian philosopher; in his book *Utilitarianism* he develops and refines the cruder version of the theory which had been put forward by his mentor Jeremy Bentham. In order to understand Mill's approach it is important to see how it differs from Bentham's.

BENTHAM'S UTILITARIANISM

For Bentham, the morally right action in any circumstances is the one that will tend to maximise total happiness. He conceives of happiness as a blissful mental state: pleasure and the absence of pain. The more of this that occurs in the world, the better. It doesn't matter how the pleasure is produced: Bentham famously declared that pushpin (a pub game) was as worthwhile as poetry provided that they produced equal amounts of pleasure. Each individual counts equally in the calculation of how much pleasure is produced by an action, and the total of pleasurable states is summed to determine how we should act. This is utilitarianism in its most straightforward form.

So, for instance, if a utilitarian wanted to decide whether to leave her money to one poor relative or divide it between twenty reasonably well-off friends, she would calculate how much total pleasure would be produced by each. Although the inheritance might make the poor relative very happy, the total amount of happiness may still be less than making twenty reasonably well-off friends moderately happy. If this were true, the woman should leave the money to the friends rather than the relative.

Mill shared many of Bentham's beliefs. Mill's Greatest Happiness Principle, for example, is simply 'actions are right in proportion as they tend to promote happiness, wrong as they tend to produce the reverse of happiness'. Both Bentham and Mill were hedonists in the sense that their approach to ethics was founded upon the pursuit of pleasure (not, however, merely the pursuit of individuals' own pleasure, but rather the pursuit of the greatest overall pleasure). Actions for both philosophers were to be judged according to their probable consequences, not according to any religious code or set of binding principles to be followed whatever consequences ensued.

The phrase 'the greatest happiness of the greatest number' is sometimes used to describe the utilitarian approach to ethics, but this can be misleading. What both Bentham and Mill were interested in was achieving the greatest *aggregate* happiness (that is, the largest total sum of happiness) irrespective of how that happiness was distributed. It would be consistent with this approach to think that it would be better to make a few people extremely happy than to make a much larger number slightly happier, provided that the sum of happiness in the first case was larger than the sum in the second.

Mill's utilitarianism differs from Bentham's in that he gives a more sophisticated account of happiness. For Mill, there are qualitatively different sorts of pleasure: higher and lower pleasures. Higher pleasures are to be preferred to lower ones. Bentham, in contrast, treats all pleasures as on a par.

MILL ON HIGHER AND LOWER PLEASURES

One common criticism of simple versions of utilitarianism, such as Bentham's, is that they reduce the subtleties of human life to a stark calculation of animal-like pleasures, with no concern for how these pleasures are produced. Utilitarianism of this kind was ridiculed as a doctrine only worthy of swine.

Mill meets such criticisms with his distinction between higher and lower pleasures. As he puts it, it is better to be a dissatisfied human being than a satisfied pig; and better to be a dissatisfied Socrates than a satisfied fool. Human beings are capable of intellectual pleasures as well as the brute physical ones; pigs cannot have intellectual pleasures. Mill argues that the intellectual pleasures, those he calls higher pleasures, are intrinsically more valuable than the physical lower ones. His argument in support of this is that those who have felt both kinds of pleasure will certainly prefer the intellectual kind. This leaves him with the awkward fact that some people who are capable of experiencing sublime intellectual pleasures throw themselves into lives of debauchery and sensual gratification. His response to this sort of case is that they are led astray by the temptation of immediate sensual gratification; they know full well that the higher pleasures are more worthwhile.

THE 'PROOF' OF UTILITARIANISM

The obvious question to ask is 'Why maximise happiness?' Mill's answer is controversial, though it is important to realise that he never claims that it provides a conclusive justification for his theory: he does not believe that a theory such as utilitarianism can be proved to be true.

Happiness, he says, is pursued as an end in itself. The ultimate end of all human activity is happiness and the avoidance of pain. Everything else which is desirable is desirable because it contributes to such a life. If you spend your life collecting beautiful works of art, this activity is a way of getting pleasure. If someone, for example, argues against Mill by claiming that they pursue virtue as an end in itself independently of any happiness that might arise from it, Mill answers that virtue is then an ingredient in their happy life; it becomes part of that person's happiness.

The Greatest Happiness Principle claims that the end or purpose of all human life is happiness and the avoidance of pain. These are the only things that are desirable as ends; everything else desirable is desirable as a means to these ends. So the question 'Why maximise happiness?' is really just a question about what makes happiness desirable. Mill suggests an analogy to answer this question. The only way that we can prove that an object is visible is by demonstrating that people actually can see it. Analogously, he claims, the only evidence we can give that happiness is desirable is that people actually do desire it. Each person finds his or her own happiness desirable, so general happiness is the sum of the individual happiness, and itself desirable.

CRITICISMS OF *UTILITARIANISM*

'Proof' is based on bad arguments

Mill's attempt to justify the belief that we ought to maximise happiness contains some allegedly bad arguments. Most of these were pointed out by Henry Sidgwick. First, the move from what is visible to what is desirable is misleading. Mill suggests that because we can tell what is visible by identifying what is seen, it follows that we can tell what is desirable by identifying what people actually do desire. But on closer inspection the analogy between 'visible' and 'desirable' does not hold. 'Visible' means 'can be seen', but 'desirable' doesn't usually mean 'can be desired'; what it usually means is 'should be desired' or 'is worthy of being desired', and that is certainly the sense in which Mill employs it in his argument. Once the weakness of the analogy between the two words has been pointed out, it is difficult to see how describing what people actually do desire is likely to reveal anything about what people *should* desire.

But even if Mill had established that happiness is desirable in the appropriate sense, this would lead logically to a form of egoism, each person pursuing his or her own happiness, rather than the more benevolent approach of utilitarianism which makes the greatest happiness possible its aim. Mill thinks that because each individual wants his or her own happiness, the total of all the individual happinesses can simply be added up to give an aggregate which would then itself be desirable. But this does not follow at all. He needs a far stronger argument to prove that the general happiness, rather than just our own individual happiness, is something that we all ought to pursue.

Difficulties of calculation

Even if Mill had established that there were good grounds for adopting a utilitarian approach to ethics, there are still some objections to the theory and its application which he would need to meet. One practical difficulty is that of calculating which of the many possible actions is most likely to produce the most happiness overall. This might be a particularly vexing issue when you had to make a moral decision quickly – for instance, if you were faced with a dilemma about whom to save from a burning building, given that you could only save one person and there were three people trapped inside. In such a situation you just would not have time to sit down and calculate probable consequences.

Mill's response to this sort of objection was that throughout human history people have been learning from their experience about the probable courses of different sorts of action. The solution is to come up with some general principles about which sorts of actions tend to maximise happiness, rather than to go back to the Greatest Happiness Principle whenever you are faced with a moral decision. Mill, then, suggests that the rational approach to life involves adopting such general principles rather than forever calculating possible consequences. Thus his utilitarianism has two stages: the derivation of general principles on utilitarian grounds, and then the application of those principles to particular cases.

Higher/lower pleasures

Mill's division of pleasures into two categories creates problems of several sorts. Because these pleasures are different in kind rather than just degree it makes the calculation and comparison of consequences of actions far more complex. Higher and lower pleasures are incommensurable: that is, there is no common currency in which both can be measured and compared. So it is not at all clear how we are to apply Mill's version of utilitarianism in circumstances where both higher and lower pleasures enter into the calculation.

Furthermore, the higher/lower pleasure distinction looks like a self-serving one. It is no surprise to find an intellectual defending the idea that intellectual activity produces pleasures of a more satisfying kind than merely physical ones. This in itself doesn't prove the theory is false; it just reveals the fact that Mill might have had a vested interest in the intellectual pleasures being intrinsically more valuable than others.

Unpalatable consequences

The strict application of utilitarian principles in some cases has consequences which many people would find unacceptable. For example, if there had been a gruesome murder, and the police had found a suspect who they knew hadn't committed the murder, there might be utilitarian grounds for framing him and punishing him accordingly. Presumably most members of the public would be very happy that the culprit had been caught and punished; they would remain happy just as long as no one found out that he was in fact innocent. The innocent man's suffering would be great for him, but in the calculation of consequences would be far outweighed by the sum of pleasure that many millions of people would feel at seeing what they believe to be justice to have been done. Yet, this consequence of utilitarian morality would be unpalatable for most of us: our intuitions are that punishing the innocent is unjust and should not be permitted whatever the beneficial consequences of this practice.

One response to this sort of criticism is to modify utilitarianism into what is known as rule utilitarianism. Here general principles of conduct are worked out on utilitarian grounds, such as that in general punishing innocent people produces more unhappiness than happiness. These general principles are then adhered to even in the few particular cases in which, for example, punishing an innocent person would in fact produce the greatest sum of happiness possible from available options. Some have claimed that Mill is himself a rule utilitarian. However, it is more plausible that what Mill says about working out general guidelines of behaviour before you are faced with a situation in which you must act quickly (rather than having to do a calculation on the spot) is only intended to produce rules of thumb, generalisations which can be broken in particular cases and are not binding principles of conduct.

DATES

See previous chapter.

GLOSSARY

altruism: being helpful to others for their own sake rather than any more selfish motivation.

egoism: acting solely from one's own interests.

Greatest Happiness Principle: the basic tenet of utilitarianism, namely that the morally right action in any circumstances is the one which is most likely to maximise happiness.

hedonism: pursuit of pleasure.

higher pleasures: the more intellectual pleasures of thought and artistic appreciation. Mill assigns these much higher value than the lower physical pleasures.

lower pleasures: the physical pleasures which animals as well as humans can experience, such as those which come from eating, or from sex.

rule utilitarianism: a variety of utilitarianism which, instead of focusing on particular actions, looks at the kinds of action which tend to maximise happiness.

utilitarianism: the moral theory which declares that the morally right action in any circumstances is the one which is most likely to maximise happiness.

utility: for Mill 'utility' is a technical term meaning happiness rather than usefulness. If an action increases utility, this simply means that it increases happiness.

FURTHER READING

Roger Crisp *Mill on Utilitarianism* (London: Routledge, 1997) is a clear critical study of Mill's moral philosophy.

Jonathan Glover (ed.) *Utilitarianism and its Critics* (New York: Macmillan, 1990) is an excellent selection of readings on the topic of utilitarianism. It contains relevant extracts from a variety of utilitarian writers, including Mill, and provides brief and lucid introductions to each reading.

For further reading on Mill, see the recommendations at the end of the previous chapter.

18

SØREN KIERKEGAARD
EITHER/OR

Either/Or is more like a novel than a philosophical treatise. And like most novels it is resistant to paraphrase. Nevertheless, its central concern is clear: it is the question asked by Aristotle, 'How should we live?' Kierkegaard's answer to this question is oblique enough to leave a trail of contradictory and sometimes confusing interpretations in its wake. On the surface, at least, it explores two fundamentally different ways of life, the aesthetic and the ethical. But it does this from within: the views are not summarised, but rather expressed by two characters who are the fictional authors of the work.

PSEUDONYMOUS AUTHORSHIP

Kierkegaard's writing has a playful quality. One aspect of this is his use of pseudonymous authorship: it is not just that Kierkegaard writes under a series of pseudonyms; rather he creates fictional characters, different from his own, in whose voices he writes.

The tone of *Either/Or* is set in the preface. The narrator, who is called Victor Eremita, tells the story of how he came by the manuscripts which are published as *Either/Or*. He had bought a secondhand writing desk, an escritoire, which he had long admired in a shop window. One day, just as he was leaving for a holiday, a drawer of the desk jammed. In despair he kicked the desk, and a secret panel sprang open revealing a hoard of papers. These, which appeared to be written by two people whom he labelled 'A' and 'B', he put into order and published. It emerges that B is a judge called Wilhelm; we never learn the identity of A. This story is, of course, a fiction; and A and B are fictional characters. The story of the escritoire provides a metaphor for a central theme of the book: the discrepancy between appearances and reality, or as Kierkegaard usually puts it, 'the inner is not the outer'.

The technique of using pseudonymous authors allows Kierkegaard to distance himself from the views explored and expressed in the book and to hide his own position behind that of his characters. But it also allows him to get inside the various positions he evokes; to investigate them from the point of view of the inner life of imagined individuals rather than by means of the cool abstractions which philosophers typically employ. This is an aspect of Kierkegaard's method of indirect communication: a self-conscious attempt to convey truths about living human beings by showing aspects of their lives rather than describing abstract and impersonal concepts.

EITHER

The first part of the book, called *Either*, is the part that is usually read. Most readers find that A's writing is more interesting and diverse than the solid, somewhat laborious section written by B. Very few of those who enjoy *Either* bother to slog through every page of *Or*, even in the abridged versions in which it usually appears. Nevertheless, parts of *Or* provide a detailed if biased commentary on A's approach to life, the aesthetic approach, while defending B's own ethical approach. A's writing does not provide a direct description of his approach to life; rather it exemplifies it through its concerns and style of writing.

THE AESTHETIC APPROACH TO LIFE

In simple terms the aesthetic approach to life has at its heart the hedonistic pursuit of sensual pleasure. But this does not adequately characterise Kierkegaard's use of the term, since it suggests a brutish craving after physical satisfaction; whereas for Kierkegaard the aesthetic approach includes the more refined pleasure-seeking of the intellectual aesthete. The aesthete's pleasures may come from the contemplation of beauty, and the refined appreciation of works of art; or they may include delight in the sadistic exercise of power, an attitude revealed in the section of *Either* called 'The Seducer's Diary'. All these pleasures are sought by A.

For Kierkegaard the aesthetic approach to life involves a restless seeking after new pleasures, since the worst that can happen to someone who adopts this way of life is that they become bored. Boredom for the aesthete is the root of all evil. So A suggests a half-serious strategy for avoiding boredom, which he jokingly labels 'Crop Rotation'.

CROP ROTATION

Crop Rotation involves arbitrarily changing your attitude to life, or to whatever you happen to be involved in. Like the method by which farmers replenish the soil's nutrients, the arbitrary shifting of viewpoint should replenish the individual and help stave off boredom. A's example is of having to listen to a bore: as soon as A started concentrating on the drops of sweat running down the bore's nose the bore ceased to be boring. At this point Kierkegaard seems to sow the seeds of surrealism in his celebration of arbitrary and perverse approaches to life: he suggests just going to the middle of a play, or reading only the third part of a book, thereby getting a new and potentially stimulating angle on what could otherwise be tedious.

The restless shifting of topics and styles in the essays that make up *Either* reflects the constant search for new stimulation characteristic of the aesthetic approach to life. This is most apparent in the opening section, called *Diapsalmata* (Greek for 'refrains'), which is a series of fragmentary comments and aphorisms. Other parts of *Either* are presented as quasi-academic papers, or else, most notably, in one case as a diary.

'THE SEDUCER'S DIARY'

'The Seducer's Diary' is a novella within *Either*. It is a brilliantly written account of the cynical seduction of a young woman, Cordelia, incorporating, as the title suggests, a diary, but also letters from the woman to her seducer. It stands as a work of literature in its own right; but within *Either/Or* it provides a case study of one way of living within the aesthetic approach, an attempt to live life poetically rather than ethically.

In the preface to *Either/Or*, Victor Eremita, the fictional editor of the whole work, introduces the diary, which he claims to have found amongst the papers in the escritoire; but there is a further level of concealment of authorship in that the diary itself has a preface, allegedly written by someone who knew the protagonists. Eremita draws attention to what he calls this Chinese box, suggesting that the diary's editor might well be a fiction used by the seducer to distance himself from what it describes. Of course as readers of *Either/Or* we are immediately at a further level of remove from the events than was Eremita, well aware that Eremita is simply another mask worn by Kierkegaard, and that the events that the diary describes are almost certainly creations of the philosopher's imagination rather than a description of something that actually happened. We might also take his account of this distancing technique to apply equally to Kierkegaard's own use of pseudonyms and puzzles of authorship throughout *Either/Or*: Eremita describes A's attitude to 'The Seducer's Diary' as possibly being like someone who scares himself as he recounts a frightening dream, suggesting that this might be why he has to hide behind the mask of an imagined editor.

The seducer's aim is to get a particular young woman to fall in love with him. He succeeds in this, and then withdraws all affection. His pleasure is not a simple physical gratification but a kind of psychological sadism.

Seduction is the quintessential pastime of those who adopt the aesthetic approach to life, and it is significant that an earlier essay in *Either*, 'The Immediate Stages of the Erotic', is devoted to an examination of Mozart's *Don Giovanni*, an opera which follows the fortunes of a serial seducer. For A, *Don Giovanni* is the supreme achievement of a great composer. The underlying suggestion is that A is drawn to this opera because in important ways the central character's lifestyle mirrors his own.

THE ETHICAL APPROACH TO LIFE

Whereas in *Either* the reader has to work hard to extract a sense of the view that the writing illustrates and exemplifies, in *Or* views are stated explicitly and mostly directed against aspects of A's lifestyle. The pseudonymous author of *Or*, B, or Judge Wilhelm, not only sets out his own approach to life, but also criticises A's own: thus, a far clearer picture of *Either*'s meaning emerges when you read *Or*.

In contrast to A's life spent in pursuit of pleasure, B advocates a life in which the individual chooses his or her actions. As B describes it, the life of the aesthete puts the individual at the whim of outside events and circumstances, since we cannot simply choose the sources of our pleasure, but must rely on aspects of the world to stimulate us. The ethical approach, in contrast, is always motivated from within: it is not a matter of learning a set of rules and obeying them, but rather of transforming yourself into someone whose choices coincide with duty. From this point of view, the aesthete A is merely hiding behind a set of masks, shirking responsibility for his freedom. B believes that such an approach requires a kind of self-deception. The ethical approach requires self-knowledge. The point of adopting it is to transform yourself into what B calls 'the universal individual', that is, somehow to choose to become a model of humanity. This, B claims, reveals the true beauty of humanity, in a way that the aesthete's purported pursuit of beauty never can.

READINGS OF *EITHER/OR*

An existentialist interpretation

According to the existentialist interpretation of *Either/Or*, the reader is faced with a radical choice between the two approaches to life. There are no guidelines which indicate how to choose: we must choose one or the other, and thereby create ourselves through that choice. However, contrary to the views which dominated the Enlightenment period, there is no such thing as a 'right' answer to the question 'How should I live?' The reasons for choosing the ethical above the aesthetic only make sense if you are already committed to the ethical approach to life; to suggest that the aesthetic approach is evil is to imply that you have already accepted that there is a good/evil distinction to be drawn.

Similarly, the justifications for the aesthetic approach only appeal to the aesthete, and would be ruled out as inconsequential by one committed to the ethical way of life: the pleasures of seduction, for example, would count for nothing in Judge Wilhelm's reckoning. On this reading *Either/Or* reflects the anguished position of all humanity. We find ourselves forced to choose, and through our choices we create what we are. That is the human condition. Existentialists have thus seen *Either/Or* as a key text in the history of the existentialist movement. On this view Kierkegaard was one of the first philosophers to recognise the importance of radical choice in the face of a world in which no pre-ordained value can be discerned, thereby anticipating many of the themes which would occupy Jean-Paul Sartre a century later. It is certainly true that most twentieth-century existentialists have been influenced by Kierkegaard's writing.

The case for the ethical

Whilst there is much in Kierkegaard's text which supports the existentialist reading, some interpreters have seen the book as a thinly veiled advocacy of the ethical above the aesthetic. B sees through A's aestheticism and presents him with a solid, if staid, alternative. Only through seizing control of your life and putting it beyond contingent events can you fulfil your nature. The aesthete is more or less at the whim of what happens; the ethical approach ensures that the self remains intact, even if chance events thwart your goals and desires.

One point against this interpretation of *Either/Or* is that it contradicts his claim that there is no didacticism in the book. A further objection is that so skilful a writer as Kierkegaard would not have presented his favoured approach to life in so dry and unpalatable a form. It is far from obvious why he would have given the aesthete A all the best lines, and invented the staid and pontificating Judge Wilhelm as the defender of his favoured view.

Thinly veiled autobiography

Kierkegaard met Regine Olsen when she was only 14; he was 21. Not unlike the seducer in 'The Seducer's Diary' he befriended her family, and even her suitor. When Regine reached 17, Kierkegaard asked her to marry him and she accepted. However, Kierkegaard could not go through with the marriage and broke off the engagement in 1841, just two years before *Either/Or* was published, leaving Regine humiliated and in great distress. Some commentators have seen parts of *Either/Or* as a response to his situation: of more psychological than philosophical interest.

On this reading, *Either* presents the life of sensual pleasures that Kierkegaard had led in his youth and would have to relinquish if he married; *Or*, on the other hand, presents the case for marriage and the acceptance of social responsibilities that that entails. The book *Either/Or* can thus be seen as a literary expression of the torment that led to the broken engagement; the philosophical surface is simply another screen scarcely concealing the agonised soul in turmoil at the most significant choice he had to make in his life.

This interpretation of *Either/Or* may well be accurate, but is entirely compatible with either of the two interpretations sketched above. It is interesting and informative to learn these biographical facts about the man Kierkegaard. But ultimately his writing stands or falls independently of its relation to his life and the psychological motivations which gave him the energy to write.

CRITICISMS OF *EITHER/OR*

False dichotomy?

It is not obvious that the two ways of life exemplified by A and B cover all the options. There may be C, D, E, F and G to take into account. In other words, Kierkegaard seems to suggest that if you reject the aesthetic the only option is the ethical, and vice versa. However, this is a simplistic reading of Kierkegaard's position. Kierkegaard, or at least the character Victor Eremita, considers the possibility that one person has written the texts of both *Either* and *Or*, suggesting that perhaps the two positions need not be as incompatible as they initially seem. And Kierkegaard need not be read as suggesting that these are the only two options available: indeed, in subsequent writings he explicitly outlines a third approach, the religious attitude to life.

Indeterminacy

It should be clear by now that *Either/Or* is open to a wide range of interpretations and that his original intentions are by no means easy to discern. It is a book which seems to have a profound message; yet

critics are not agreed upon what that message is. Some sa
is because Kierkegaard is unacceptably indeterminate about v
means. This is a consequence of the style of writing he has cho:
with fictional characters exploring lived philosophical positions. Since
characters exemplify rather than state their positions, there is some
latitude for interpretation. Those who want simple views clearly
stated in unambiguous prose will be disappointed by Kierkegaard's
more poetic approach to philosophy.

DATES

1813   born in Copenhagen, Denmark.
1843   publishes *Either/Or*.
1855   dies in Copenhagen.

GLOSSARY

aesthetic approach: a way of life built on the pursuit of sensual pleasure, including sensual pleasure of more intellectual kinds.

Crop Rotation: A's technique for staving off boredom, involving arbitrarily changing your attitude to life.

ethical approach: the way of life advocated by Judge Wilhelm. A life
of responsible choices.

hedonism: the pursuit of pleasure.

pseudonymous authorship: Kierkegaard's technique of attributing
the various parts of his texts to fictional authors.

FURTHER READING

Patrick Gardiner *Kierkegaard* (Oxford: Oxford University Press, Past
Masters series, 1988) gives a concise account of Kierkegaard's work,
including *Either/Or*, setting it in its philosophical background.

Donald Palmer *Kierkegaard for Beginners* (London: Writers and
Readers, 1996) provides a light-hearted, accessible and informative
overview of the central themes of Kierkegaard's philosophy.

Joakim Garff *Søren Kierkegaard: A Biography* trans. Bruce H.
Kirmmse (Princeton and Oxford: Princeton University Press, 2005) is
a superb account of Kierkegaard's difficult life and bizarre character.

19

KARL MARX AND FRIEDRICH ENGELS *THE GERMAN IDEOLOGY*, PART ONE

We are what we are as a result of our position in the economic situation of our time; in particular, our relation to the means of material production shapes our lives and thoughts. There is no timeless, unchanging human nature. We are products of the historical period in which we find ourselves. This is the message at the heart of the first part of Karl Marx and Friedrich Engels' *The German Ideology*, a book which sets out the theory of historical materialism. Most of the book is negative, attacking almost line by line the work of some German reinterpreters of Hegel's philosophy, the so-called Young Hegelians. Much of it is devoted to a discussion of Ludwig Feuerbach, a writer who, together with Georg Hegel, exercised a powerful influence on Marx's intellectual development.

Most present-day readers of *The German Ideology* concentrate on the positive theories set out in the first part of the book, before the authors get immersed in the minutiae of their opponents' work. Isaiah Berlin's assessment of the book as a whole acknowledges its more tedious aspects while justifying its status as a classic: 'This verbose, ill-organised and ponderous work, which deals with authors and views long dead and justly forgotten, contains in its lengthy introduction the most sustained, imaginative and impressive exposition of Marx's theory of history.'

When reading *The German Ideology* it is important to recognise the radical approach that Marx and Engels advocated, an approach encapsulated in the last of Marx's 'Theses on Feuerbach', which he wrote around the time that he was working on *The German Ideology*: 'The philosophers have only *interpreted* the world in various ways; the point is to *change* it.' It is not good enough simply to recognise that capitalism traps many people in a life of meaningless work and impoverished home life. What is needed is a revolution: a complete overturning of the status quo. No one can deny that Marx and Engels succeeded in their aim of changing the world. Unlike many of the writers discussed so far, these two managed to have a profound effect not just on academics, but on the world at large. Almost miraculously, their writings inspired successful revolutions, the after-effects of which are still being felt today.

HISTORICAL MATERIALISM

Marx and Engels' theory of historical materialism, or 'the materialist conception of history', as they prefer to call it, is the theory that your material circumstances shape what you are. 'Materialism' has several uses in philosophy. In the philosophy of mind, for instance, it is the view that the mind can be explained in purely physical terms. This is not how Marx and Engels use it. Rather for them 'materialism' refers to our relationship with materials of production: at its most basic, this amounts to the labour that we have to do in order to feed and clothe ourselves and our dependants. In more complex societies it takes in the property that we may or may not own and our relationship to the means of producing wealth.

Materialism in this sense is directly opposed to the kind of philosophy that forgets the nature of real human life and hovers in a world of abstract generalisations. It concentrates on the harsh realities of most human life, which perhaps explains its wide appeal. This materialism is *historical* in the sense that it recognises that material circumstances change over time, and that, for example, the impact of a new technology can completely transform a society, and thus the individuals who compose it. For instance, the abolition of slavery was made possible by the invention of the steam engine, a machine which could work harder and longer than a hundred slaves.

DIVISION OF LABOUR

As soon as human beings begin to produce what they need to survive, they set themselves apart from animals. The particular demands of what they produce and how they produce it shape their lives. As societies grow, so the social relations necessary for successful production become more complex; the more developed a society, the greater division of labour that occurs.

Division of labour is simply the allocation of different jobs to different people. For example, in a very simple society each individual might farm, hunt and build for him or herself. In a more developed one each of these roles would be likely to be carried out by different people.

Marx and Engels saw the extreme division of labour characteristic of capitalist economies as a powerful negative influence on what human life can be. It gives rise to alienation, the distancing of an individual's labour from his or her life. The division of labour renders individuals powerless victims of a system that enslaves and dehumanises them. This is particularly damaging when the division of physical and intellectual labour occurs, since it reduces the chances of those who only do harsh and tedious physical work of achieving a fulfilled existence. More importantly, for Marx and Engels, it goes against the common interest. The vision that Marx and Engels put in its place is of a world in which private property has been abolished and each individual is free to take on a number of roles in the course of a working day. As they put it, in such a society it would be possible for me 'to do one thing today and another tomorrow, to hunt in the morning, fish in the afternoon, rear cattle in the evening, criticise after dinner, just as I have a mind, without ever becoming hunter, fisherman, herdsman or critic'. This is a vision of work as a freely chosen and fulfilling activity rather than as an enforced treadmill the only alternative to which is starvation. Marx and Engels' sympathies always lie with the working-class labourer trapped in a job which is unsatisfying; a victim of a faceless economic system.

IDEOLOGY

All religious, moral and metaphysical beliefs are as much a product of our material relations as are any other aspects of our lives. The dominant ideas of an age, which have traditionally been treated as independent of class interest, are in fact nothing more than the interests of the ruling classes writ large and rationalised. 'Ideology' is the word Marx and Engels use to refer to these ideas which are the by-product of a particular economic and social system. Those who are in the grip of ideology typically see their conclusions as being the outcome of pure thought. In this they are simply mistaken: their ideas are the outcome of their historical and social circumstances.

REVOLUTION

When the proletariat, that is, the class of workers who own no property but their own labour, become sufficiently disgruntled with their condition and with the ideologies used to suppress them, revolution is possible. Marx and Engels were fervent advocates of revolution: they saw it as inevitable and praiseworthy. When the conditions of the proletariat become sufficiently impoverished and precarious, this is the time for them to rise up and rebel against the system that enslaves them. After the revolution, private property would be banned, leaving the way open for communal ownership. This vision of the future was, according to Marx and Engels, a prediction based on hard empirical evidence about the patterns of history and the effects of alienation. It follows directly from their historical materialism: the way to change people's ideas is to change the system of material production that gives rise to them.

CRITICISMS OF *THE GERMAN IDEOLOGY*

Deterministic

One criticism often levelled at Marx and Engels' historical materialism is that it is deterministic. It does not leave any room for free will since what we do is entirely shaped by our roles in a complex web of causes and effects. The causes are to do with the individual's socioeconomic position. Who and what you are is outside your control. You are a product of the situation in which you find yourself.

This sort of criticism only makes sense if you hold that human beings do genuinely have free will of some kind, and not just the illusion that they have it. Marx and Engels might have been happy to have had their theory labelled 'determinist', provided that it is recognised that determinism can be a matter of degree, rather than an 'all or nothing' concept. Marx and Engels clearly believed that you could choose to revolt against an oppressive system, and that human choices could accelerate the turning of the wheels of history. To this extent, then, they were not complete determinists about human behaviour.

Unrealistic vision of work

A further criticism of *The German Ideology* is that it paints too rosy a picture of work in the future and fails to recognise the importance of division of labour to the state. The idea that you could pick and choose jobs as you felt like it in a true communist society is absurd. Division of labour is often based on a division of skills: some people just are better at woodwork than others, so it makes sense to let those who are good become carpenters, and to steer the botchers into some other task.

If I were to try to make a dining table, this could well take me five or six times as long as it would take a carpenter to do the same job; and anyone employing me or relying on me to produce a table would run the risk of getting a badly made piece of furniture. The carpenter works with wood every day and has acquired the skills needed to make tables. I only occasionally work with wood, and never produce anything of worth. So of course it makes sense to divide jobs up amongst those who are best suited to them. It would be absurd to suggest that you could be a surgeon in the morning, a train driver in the afternoon and a professional footballer in the evening.

It is ideological itself

Marx and Engels' theory cannot escape being ideological. If the theory is correct, then the theory itself must be a product of the system of material production in which it arose. It might seem as if the theory is purely the outcome of rational thought about the nature of history and of work, but this is an illusion. It is the consequence of an industrial economy in which large numbers of people were employed on low wages doing jobs which gave them little control over their lives.

Marx and Engels would no doubt happily accept that their own theories were ideological, so drawing attention to their ideological nature doesn't necessarily undermine their approach. Presumably what distinguishes their work from the bourgeois ideologies they were so keen to expose is that theirs is an expression of a proletariat ideology. Their views serve the interests of the working class and so redress the balance.

Nevertheless, if we accept that the views expressed in *The German Ideology* are themselves ideological, this does have the consequence that it would be a mistake to expect them to hold for all human beings in all material circumstances. As societies, and in particular the modes of material production, change, so must philosophical theories about human nature and society.

Incites revolution

The German Ideology, like many works by Marx and Engels, did not stop short of advocating revolution. It was intended to change the world, not simply describe it. Some critics see this as a step too far. You can recognise the deficiencies of the current system without suggesting that it needs to be overthrown by force. Revolution causes bloodshed. The cost of revolution in human terms can outweigh any benefits that would ensue from its having taken place. Add to this the very high risk of failure, and the revolutionary aspects of Marx and Engels' thought can seem irresponsible.

This criticism does not undermine their arguments so much as question the morality of advocating revolution. Only if the communist ideal could genuinely be achieved would the human cost of a revolution be worth paying. The historical evidence of recent decades is that the ideal is not so easy to achieve, let alone maintain, as many of its admirers believe.

DATES

Marx

1818   born in Trier, Prussia.
1845–6 with Engels, publishes *The German Ideology*.
1883   dies in London.

Engels

1820   born in Barmen, Prussia.
1895   dies in London.

GLOSSARY

alienation: the distancing of labour from other aspects of an individual's life with a debilitating effect.

division of labour: the assigning of different jobs to different people.

historical materialism: the theory that your relation to the means of production determines your life and thought.

ideology: ideas which are the by-product of a particular economic system. Those in the grip of ideology often see their thought as the outcome of pure thought when in fact it is a product of class interests.

proletariat: the working class who have nothing to sell but their own labour.

FURTHER READING

Jonathan Wolff *Why Read Marx Today?* (Oxford: Oxford University Press, 2002) is a clear and pertinent assessment of the current relevance of Marx's ideas.

David McLellan *Karl Marx* (London: Fontana, Modern Masters series, 1975) is a brief and accessible introduction to Marx's thought.

Ernst Fischer *Marx in his Own Words* (Harmondsworth: Penguin, 1970) provides an introduction to the key concepts in Marx's thought largely through a selection of quotations.

Isaiah Berlin *Karl Marx* (London: Fontana, 4th edn, 1995) is an interesting biography which also serves as a lucid critical introduction to all of Marx's major works.

Francis Wheen *Karl Marx* (London: Fourth Estate, 1999) is a highly entertaining recent biography.

20

FRIEDRICH NIETZSCHE
BEYOND GOOD AND EVIL

According to Sigmund Freud, Friedrich Nietzsche had a more pene-trating knowledge of himself than any other man who ever lived or was ever likely to live. This deep self-knowledge is revealed in a string of books which have stood the test of time both as literature and as philosophy. They are idiosyncratic, fragmentary, infuriating, and at times exhilarating. They defy simple analysis, and summaries cannot do justice to the richness and diversity of their contents. Most contain passages which, it must be said, are little more than the ranting of a madman and which anticipate his eventual mental break-down. A shadow is cast over all of them by the fact that anti-semites and fascists have, by selective quotation, found support for their views in them; however, the ideas that some Nazis found so attrac-tive are, for the most part, caricatures of Nietzsche's philosophy.

Beyond Good and Evil pulsates with ideas, not all of them fully formed and some of them quite unpleasant. It is a flawed master-piece by an eccentric genius. Within it there are many deep phil-osophical insights; but these sit alongside a range of misogynist jibes, and bizarre generalisations about national character traits and religion. Nietzsche was undoubtedly one of the most influential phil-osophers of the nineteenth century. His ideas influenced a wide range of twentieth-century thinkers, including Sigmund Freud, Jean-Paul Sartre and Michel Foucault, but also, amongst others, the novelists

Thomas Mann and Milan Kundera. Despite his later reputation, however, in his own lifetime very few of his contemporaries recognised the importance and significance of his work.

From summaries of this book you might imagine it a coherent and well argued series of related theses in which Nietzsche lays out his positions on truth, morality and psychology. This is very far from the case. It is fragmentary and in large part difficult to paraphrase – more a collage of thoughts than a developed argument. One whole section consists entirely of aphorisms – short, pithy statements. Another is a poem. The most overtly philosophical sections consist of loosely connected mini-essays. But these are not always easy to follow, and some are scarcely more than tirades; others could be pages torn from a notebook, printed without editing. Yet throughout this book any sensitive reader is likely to be struck by Nietzsche's brilliance.

Despite the wide-ranging nature of Nietzsche's thinking, major themes do emerge, most of them signalled by the section titles. Some of these complement the ideas expressed in the book discussed in the next chapter, *On the Genealogy of Morality*. Broadly, in *Beyond Good and Evil* Nietzsche begins by diagnosing the shortcomings of modernity, and moves on to outline the kind of thinking that will allow humanity to progress. His aim is to clear the way for what he calls 'free spirits': the philosophers of the future. In the great tradition of philosophy he is concerned with truth and appearance. But he believes that to date philosophers have failed to see things as they are. They have been seduced by Plato's view that there is an objective reality beyond appearance, a world of absolute values. In contrast with this he asserts that truth is necessarily truth from a perspective. In place of absolute good or evil, he reveals the dark psychological origins of everything those around him believe to have intrinsic value and worth. His method is a diagnosis of the ills of his society. His stance is for the most part that of an anthropologist examining the values of the culture in which he finds himself, but not a scientific anthropologist – more of a poet-prophet.

THE TITLE

The title of the book describes Nietzsche's intended position: whoever is interested in truth will stand beyond the simple black/white moral categories of good and evil, and will recognise morality for what it is. Morality is an expression of the fundamental life force he calls the Will to Power. The cherished values of his contemporaries, far from originating in compassion and universal love, have their deepest origins in cruelty and the desire to surpass others. The philosophers of the future will come to recognise this. As a result they will revalue all values.

THE WILL TO POWER

The Will to Power is the basic life force that drives us all. Nietzsche believes that most people deny the truth about existence: for many that is the only way they can cope with living at all. They fail to recognise that exploitation and oppression can't be eliminated since these are a fundamental part of nature. It is for Nietzsche an essential feature of life that the strong oppress the weak. This Will to Power is the source of everything that we are. All that is valued as good or benevolent has its beginnings in this life force. We hide from this difficult truth, but the free spirits of the future embrace it.

ON THE PREJUDICES OF PHILOSOPHERS

Nietzsche opens *Beyond Good and Evil* by turning his gaze on philosophers themselves, attacking their misplaced confidence in the power of reason which they allege leads them to the conclusions they hold. In a series of acid critiques, Nietzsche argues that, without realising it, philosophers simply rationalise their prejudices: they provide reasons for what they happen to believe already. What passes for the product of impartial thought is really unconscious confession: accidental autobiography. Kant's moral philosophy, for example, is simply his heart's desire made abstract; Spinoza's quasi-geometrical 'proofs' for his ethical philosophy mask his highly personal moral commitments that he presents as if they were the conclusions of neutral logic. This attack on his predecessors indirectly justifies Nietzsche's own more openly personal approach to writing philosophy. Nietzsche's voice is rarely neutral and transparent to what is being said. It would be difficult to read his philosophy as the product of a disinterested, supremely rational intellect. It also justifies the ambition of his preface to the book, in which he sees philosophy as it has been as something to be surpassed, a phase in history like astrology in the progress of science.

TRUTH

One prejudice of traditional philosophers is that truth is more important than appearance. In place of this absolute antithesis, *truth or appearance*, Nietzsche substitutes the hypothesis that there can be a spectrum of darker or lighter shades, not an absolute black/white dichotomy, just as in a painting there are different tonal 'values'. At times Nietzsche seems to toy with a radical subjectivism about truth in which 'true' just means 'true for me'; but most commentators interpret his position as perspectivism. On this account there are different perspectives on any matter, no absolute neutral point from which to observe; yet some perspectives are superior to others – they are not all of equal value (the position usually taken by relativists).

A further prejudice of the philosophers is that they assume that knowledge of the truth will produce a better outcome than a life based on falsehoods. Nietzsche again questions this, recognising that there can be such a thing as *dangerous knowledge*, knowledge that far from being life-enhancing can be unbearable. There are many aspects of truth from which we shy away. He includes in this category the insight that unconscious processes can be the source of our most revered values. Superficial falsehood may be a pre-requisite for survival. Religion, which he takes to rest on a falsification of reality, plays an important part for many in maintaining optimism in the face of a world that Nietzsche believes to be ultimately explained by the force of the Will to Power. In this thought Nietzsche echoes Karl Marx's famous comment about how religion acts as an opiate for the people.

UNCONSCIOUS DRIVES

Nietzsche's uncovering of unconscious drives influenced Freud. Nietzsche suggests that humanity has moved beyond a *pre-moral* stage (when all that matters are consequences) and through a *moral* phase (where emphasis is on intentions – most obviously exemplified in Kant's ethics). In order to progress to the *extra-moral* –

humanity's next important stage – we need to move beyond good and evil and recognise that the value of our actions lies in unconscious rather than conscious motivation.

RELIGION

Like Freud after him, Nietzsche believed that religion was a kind of neurosis. In *Beyond Good and Evil* he attacks what he calls the religious disposition, diagnosing in it a range of psychological problems and hypocrisies. The values he embraces of nobility, superiority and natural hierarchies, and of the triumph of the few elevated geniuses who can go beyond herd morality, are completely at odds with Christian values. Religion, then, like all other existing value systems, is for Nietzsche something to anatomise and ultimately to explain away. The philosophers of the future will be as beyond religion as they are beyond the conventional moral categories which often flow from religion.

CRITICISMS OF *BEYOND GOOD AND EVIL*

Anti-egalitarianism

The ideal, for Nietzsche, seems to be a strong, heroic individual opposed to what he disparagingly describes as herd morality. He advocates strength and free spirit. For him freedom is the prerogative of the strong, not a right of the weak. He has no concern for the general welfare of the majority. More than that, he seems to despise ordinary people: in *Beyond Good and Evil* he comments that books for common people are always bad-smelling, with the odour of little people clinging to them. The only value of the herd's existence for Nietzsche is that it may inadvertently provide the conditions of adversity in which genius seems to flourish. This is one aspect of Nietzsche's thinking that is particularly attractive to fascists, and anyone who is inclined to believe themselves far superior to the people around them, and so not bound by the ethical rules of the majority. Critics of Nietzsche see him as fuelling anti-egalitarian prejudices. His admirers, on the other hand, are inclined to praise him for being bold enough to dismiss what they see as the myth that everyone is of equal value.

Anti-feminist

Nietzsche's anti-egalitarianism is perhaps most obvious in his misogynistic comments and attacks on the idea that the sexes should be treated equally. For Nietzsche the attempt to give women equality with men is a sign of shallowness. In contrast with, for example, his predecessor John Stuart Mill, who in his *The Subjection of Women* made a passionate case for equality of treatment between men and women, Nietzsche simply asserts some rather unpleasant prejudices and suggests that it would be good if women stopped asserting their rights to equality. Comments like these reveal what is so often smoothed over: Nietzsche's work is uneven and lurches between comments of great philosophical insight and vituperative generalisations that can fuel the thought of the worst deniers of human equality and freedom.

Vagueness

Nietzsche's styles of writing in this book and elsewhere leave the reader with substantial interpretive work to do. It is rarely clear what Nietzsche is arguing for, whether he is being ironic or earnest, for example. Nietzsche scholars dispute at length about the interpretation of his work often generating new philosophical positions in the process. Even Nietzsche's basic position on truth is unclear: is he a consistent perspectivist, or does his position collapse into subjectivism?

The grand sweep of Nietzsche's ideas can be exhilarating, and inspiring. Yet the collage of thoughts that he presents is so open to different interpretations and emphases that it is likely to frustrate anyone looking for a simple straightforward understanding of his major theses.

It is true that Nietzsche rarely writes with the precision or clarity of David Hume or John Stuart Mill. But this same point can, however, be taken as a positive one rather than a criticism. Nietzsche's work has a similar merit to imaginative literature, and as such gains force from the multiplicity of possible interpretations. His is a poetic philosophy, similar in many ways to Kierkegaard's. Like a work of art, Nietzsche's books are open rather than closed: they have the power to stimulate the reader to thoughts of his or her own – either in support of or in reaction against the ideas they entertain.

DATES

1844   Friedrich Nietzsche born in Röcken, Saxony.
1886   publishes *Beyond Good and Evil*.
1887   publishes *On the Genealogy of Morality*.
1900   Nietzsche dies, eleven years after a severe mental breakdown.

GLOSSARY

Perspectivism: the view that truth is always truth from a particular perspective.

Subjectivism: the idea that truth is always truth for a particular individual and that there is no objectivity whatsoever.

Will to Power: the life force that drives everything that we are and ultimately motivates all our actions whether we realise this or not.

FURTHER READING

Michael Tanner *A Very Short Introduction to Nietzsche* (Oxford: Oxford University Press, 2000) provides an overview of Nietzsche's main works.

Alexander Nehamas *Nietzsche: Life as Literature* (Cambridge, Mass.: Harvard University Press, 1985) is a fascinating attempt to make sense of Nietzsche's output as part of a single project. Although the ideas it discusses are complex, it is written in lucid prose.

Ronald Hayman *Nietzsche: A Critical Life* (London: Weidenfeld & Nicolson, 1980) analyses the philosopher's development and subsequent mental decline.

Lesley Chamberlain *Nietzsche in Turin* (London: Quartet, 1996) is a study of Nietzsche's last year of sanity.

21

FRIEDRICH NIETZSCHE
ON THE GENEALOGY
OF MORALITY

On the Genealogy of Morality, which is one of the most important of Nietzsche's works, is the closest in style to a conventional philosophical treatise, at least at first glance. In other books, such as *Thus Spake Zarathustra*, Nietzsche resorted to aphorisms: short, pithy remarks which force the reader to pause and reflect, and which demand a special kind of reading. *On the Genealogy of Morality*, in contrast, consists of three essays, each on a related theme. The central theme is the origins of morality: the literal translation of the book's title is *On the Genealogy of Morality*, though it has sometimes been translated as *On the Genealogy of Morals*. The implicit argument is that the moral concepts we have inherited from a Christian tradition are now obsolete and inferior to their pagan predecessors. Nietzsche had declared the death of God in his earlier book, *The Gay Science*: 'God is dead; but given the way of men, there may still be caves for thousands of years in which his shadow will be shown' (*Gay Science*, section 108). *On the Genealogy of Morality* is in part a working out of the implications of the absence of any God and the consequences for morality. We have inherited outmoded moral concepts based on Christianity's false beliefs. Laying bare the origins of these concepts in bitter resentful emotions, Nietzsche seems to believe, will allow us to see them for the soul-cramping injunctions that they are, and free us to replace them with a more life-enhancing approach. This, it must be stressed, is implicit rather than explicit in the text: most of the book is devoted to an analysis of the origins, both psychological and historical, of several key moral concepts.

But Nietzsche's aim is not simply to replace one morality with another; he wants to call into question the value of morality itself. If moral goodness is little more than the product of envious and resentful emotions, and the response of particular groups to their circumstances rather than some unchanging part of the natural world, what ultimate value does it have? It is not clear that Nietzsche provides an answer to this question, but this is his aim. His basic methodology is genealogical. But what does this mean?

GENEALOGY

Genealogy is literally the activity of tracing your ancestors, establishing your pedigree. Nietzsche means by it tracing the origins of particular concepts, largely by examining the history of the changing meanings of words. His training in philology (the study of languages and the origins of words) equipped him to trace the changing meanings of the words he investigates. His application of the genealogical method in *On the Genealogy of Morality* is intended to show that received opinion about the source of morality is misleading, and that, historically, concepts such as moral goodness, guilt, pity and self-sacrifice originated in bitter emotions turned against others, or against oneself.

Genealogy, however, is meant to provide not just a history of these concepts, but also a critique of them. By uncovering their true origins, Nietzsche intends to reveal their dubious pedigrees and thereby question their exalted place in the morality of his day. The fact that moral concepts have a history undermines the view that they are absolute and apply to all people at all times. This approach to moral philosophy is, like most of Nietzsche's thought, highly controversial, both as a methodology and in terms of its alleged findings.

FIRST ESSAY: 'GOOD AND EVIL' AND 'GOOD AND BAD'

In the first of the three essays that constitute the book, Nietzsche puts forward his theory about the origins of our basic moral terminology of approval and disapproval: the words 'good' and 'evil' when used in a moral context. He develops his ideas by criticising the views of English psychologists who claimed that 'good' was originally applied to unselfish actions not so much because the actions themselves were good, but because they were useful to those who benefited from them, those to whom goodness was shown. Gradually people forgot the term's origins and came to think of unselfish actions as good in themselves rather than because of their effects.

Nietzsche attacks this account, which, like his own, provides a genealogy of a moral concept. He maintains that the term 'good' was first used by the nobility, who applied it to themselves in order to set themselves apart from the common people. They had a sense of their own self-worth; anyone who could not live up to their noble ideals was obviously inferior and so 'bad'. In this essay, Nietzsche's use of the good/bad distinction (as opposed to the good/evil one) is always from the point of view of the nobility: the actions of nobles are good; those of the common people, in contrast, bad.

His account of how the word 'good' came to stand for what is unselfish is in terms of *ressentiment*. Nietzsche uses the French word for resentment to refer to the psychological origins of modern uses of the terms 'good' and 'evil'. Notice that when Nietzsche refers to the contrast between good and evil (as opposed to good and bad), he is seeing things from the perspective of the common people rather than the nobility: he is referring to the modern use of 'good' as unselfish and 'bad' as selfish action.

RESSENTIMENT

Ressentiment is the emotion felt by the oppressed. *Ressentiment* as Nietzsche uses it is not synonymous with 'resentment'; rather it is a specific kind of resentment. It is the imaginary revenge wreaked by those who are powerless to react to oppression with direct action. From hatred and a desire for vengeance felt by those who were kept in check by the nobility came the loftiest values of compassion and altruism, according to Nietzsche. This is intended both as a historical description of what actually happened and as an insight into the psychology of those who brought it about. The common people, who could not aspire to the lifestyle of the nobility, in their frustration overturned the good/bad value-system. In place of the nobility's perspective on morality, the common people put their own, which subverted the status quo. The morality of the common people declared the nobility's approach to life, based on power and the ethos of warriors, to be evil; the wretched, the poor and the lowly were the good.

Nietzsche attributes this 'radical revaluation of their enemies' values' to the Jews and the subsequent Christian tradition, and calls it the first slave revolt in morality. We have, without realising it, inherited the consequences of this revolt, a revolt that served the interests of the oppressed. For Nietzsche morality is not something fixed for all time to be discovered in the world; rather it is a human creation, and as a consequence moral terms have a history, a history which is influenced by human psychology as well as by the interests of particular groups. In Nietzsche's metaphor, the lambs decided that birds of prey were evil, and so they thought to themselves that the opposite of a bird of prey, a lamb, must be good. His comment on this is that it is absurd to deny those who are powerful the natural expression of their power. His choice of language throughout the book makes it clear that his sympathies lie with the birds of prey rather than with the lambs.

SECOND ESSAY: CONSCIENCE

The main theme of the second essay is the evolution of conscience, and specifically of bad conscience. Bad conscience is the sense of guilt with which modern humanity is burdened yet which is necessary for life in society.

The essence of Nietzsche's argument is that the psychological source of the sense of guilt is frustrated instinct. Human beings instinctively get pleasure from their powerful actions, and particularly from inflicting suffering. But when, through socialisation, a block is put on acting on our desires to inflict cruelty on others, the expression of the desire is thwarted and turned inwards. We torture ourselves inwardly with guilty feelings because society would punish us if we tried to torture other people. This is a particular instance of Nietzsche's general principle that all instincts not discharged outwards turn inwards, a principle which Sigmund Freud would later elaborate.

In the course of his discussion of the origin of conscience, Nietzsche points out that punishment was originally independent of any notion of responsibility for one's actions: you would be punished simply for breaking an agreement whether or not it was your fault. The original meaning of the German word for guilt was 'debt'. The guilty were those who had failed to repay their debts. Yet 'guilt' has become a moral concept. The hidden history of the concept which Nietzsche unveils is supposed to reveal the contingency of the modern use: it could have been otherwise and is not a natural 'given'. The unstated implication of this and the earlier discussion of the origins of 'good' seems to be that the meanings of key moral concepts are not fixed for all time but can be transformed by an immense creative act of will.

THIRD ESSAY: ASCETICISM

The third essay is less focused than the first two and meanders from topic to topic. Nevertheless, the central theme is reasonably clear. Nietzsche addresses the question of how asceticism, the philosophy of life which encourages abstinence and self-denial, could have arisen. Ascetics typically advocate chastity, poverty, self-flagellation (either literal or metaphorical) and so on; they deliberately turn away from the pleasures and fulfilments that life offers. Nietzsche identifies ascetic impulses in artists, philosophers and priests. Indeed, he suggests that viewed from a distant star, earth would be seen to be teeming with creatures riddled with self-loathing and disgust, their only pleasure being to inflict as much harm on themselves as they possibly can: not on each other, but on themselves. How could such a widespread trend have evolved? How could life have so turned against itself?

Nietzsche's answer is, once more, in terms of genealogy. Self-denial was the last resort of the almost powerless. Frustrated in their attempts to exert influence on the world, rather than ceasing to will anything at all, they directed their power against themselves. One of Nietzsche's characteristic psychological insights is the joy that human beings take in inflicting cruelty. This cruelty is not just directed at others: we even take delight in inflicting it upon ourselves. The ascetic impulse, which for Nietzsche is an apparently absurd drive to self-destruction, is a kind of self-torture which was the last resort of those who cannot exert their will in the world, yet it has become an ideal to be celebrated.

CRITICISMS OF *ON THE GENEALOGY OF MORALITY*

The genetic fallacy

A fundamental criticism of Nietzsche's methodology in *On the Genealogy of Morality* is that it commits the genetic fallacy. The genetic fallacy is the unreliable method of reasoning from what something at one stage was to what it now is. For instance, from the fact that the word 'nice' originally meant 'fine', in the sense of fine distinctions, it in no way follows that this will reveal anything important about present uses of the term. Or, to take another example, from the fact that oak trees come from acorns we cannot conclude that oak trees are small greenish brown nuts, or that they have much in common with them at all. Some of Nietzsche's critics have argued that the genealogical method always commits this fallacy, and so sheds little or no light on current uses of moral terms.

However, in *On the Genealogy of Morality*, although in places Nietzsche does seem to be suggesting that because certain moral concepts originated in bitter emotions their ultimate value is undermined (and so here might be accused of committing the genetic fallacy), for the most part his method is intended to reveal that moral concepts are not absolute and that revaluations of value have taken place in the past, and so might do so again. The genealogical method is particularly good at revealing that concepts which we have taken to be fixed for all time can be changed. This use of the method does not involve the genetic fallacy. In order to cast doubt on the absolute nature of moral uses of the word 'good', for instance, it is sufficient simply to show that it has been applied very differently in the past. There is no need to suggest that because it was used differently in the past this past meaning of the word must somehow affect present uses.

Lack of evidence

A more serious criticism of Nietzsche's approach in *On the Genealogy of Morality* is that in each of the three essays he provides scant evidence for his hypotheses. Even if we accept that 'good' might have been used differently in the past, or that conscience and asceticism evolved from thwarted desires, Nietzsche's evidence for the specific accounts of these genealogies is extremely thin. Although psychologically astute, his discussions are, as historical accounts, virtually unsupported. Without the historical evidence to back up his assertions about the origins of moral concepts, we have no reason to believe that his accounts reflect what actually happened. The best that could be said in Nietzsche's defence on this point is that if he has provided reasonably plausible accounts of what might have happened, then he has succeeded in raising doubts about the allegedly fixed and unchanging moral concepts that we have inherited. Perhaps the important point is to understand that moral concepts can change their meaning, that they are human creations, rather than part of the natural world waiting to be discovered.

Evil uses of his ideas

Perhaps the most frequent criticism of Nietzsche's philosophy as a whole is that it has been cited approvingly by anti-semites and fascists. For instance, some Nazis felt that his ideas were in tune with theirs. Some comments in *On the Genealogy of Morality* if taken in isolation could be thought anti-semitic: though he shows a grudging admiration of the Jews' transvaluation of values, he stresses that it was the last resort of the weak. He cannot disguise his own sympathy for the noble morality of the powerful. Throughout his philosophy, he repeatedly celebrates power even at the expense of the weak.

However, there are two important points to consider in relation to the criticism that his ideas have been used for evil ends. First, many of those who have used Nietzsche's philosophy in this way have had to distort it to achieve this. For instance, although isolated sentences of Nietzsche's writing might be taken to be anti-semitic, these have to be balanced by other passages which are explicitly opposed to anti-semitism. The second point is that the fact that his ideas appear to glorify power does not thereby prove them wrong. One of the reasons why reading Nietzsche's work can be so challenging is that he is constantly gnawing at our most cherished beliefs. Even if he hasn't succeeded in undermining these beliefs, his writings force us to reflect on the foundations and assumptions on which all our lives are built.

DATES

See previous chapter.

GLOSSARY

altruism: being helpful to other people for their own sakes.

asceticism: self-denial as a way of living.

bad conscience: a sense of guilt that arises from frustrated instinct; inward self-torture.

genealogy: the method of explaining a concept through an analysis of its ancestry.

ressentiment: a specific kind of resentment felt by the oppressed. The imaginary revenge wreaked by those who are powerless to act against their oppression.

FURTHER READING

Richard Schacht (ed.) *Nietzsche, Genealogy, Morality* (Berkeley: University of California Press, 1994) is a wide-ranging collection of articles about *On the Genealogy of Morality*. Some of the articles are quite difficult.

Brian Leiter *Nietzsche on Morality* (London: Routledge GuideBook series, Routledge, 2001) gives a useful critical analysis of the major themes of *On the Genealogy of Morality*, setting it in its intellectual context.

Aaron Ridley *Nietzsche's Conscience: Six Character Sketches from the 'Genealogy'* (Ithaca: Cornell University Press, 1998) is an original interpretation of the book.

See also the suggestions for further reading at the end of the previous chapter.

22

BERTRAND RUSSELL
THE PROBLEMS OF PHILOSOPHY

Bertrand Russell described this little book as his 'shilling shocker' –
a cheap, short book, written quickly for a general readership, yet it
has remained in print for almost a century. Although by no means
his major philosophical work, this, along with his opinionated
survey, *A History of Western Philosophy*, is one of his most read
books. Indeed, until the early 1980s, *The Problems of Philosophy*
was the book most likely to be recommended reading for students
considering studying the subject at university, despite having been
written in 1911 and first published in January 1912.

The most plausible reason for its continued use, apart from its
brevity, is the vision of what philosophy is that Russell presents
within it. Much of the book consists of brief summaries of the work
of Descartes, Berkeley, Hume, Kant and other major philosophers.
There are also some original contributions within this. But it is when
he expounds his own view of the limits and value of philosophy that
Russell's sincerity and enthusiasm for the subject emerges. This is
where the book moves on to a higher plane and can be inspiring. In
contrast, some other parts of the book are like a dusty and rather
abstract lecture that has already been given many times to under-
graduates. In places, too, the book fails to serve its purpose as an
introduction: only someone with a firm grasp of the basics of philosophy would be in a position to follow every sentence of Russell's
at times condensed argument.

THE TITLE

Despite its title, this book covers quite a narrow range of philosophical problems. Its main focus is the limits of what we can know: the area of philosophy known as epistemology. Ethics, aesthetics, political philosophy, philosophy of religion, and many other important areas are only mentioned in passing, if at all.

The choice of the word 'problems' in the title suggests the equivalent of mathematical problems: equations and the like that need to be solved. But Russell points out that philosophy differs from those subjects where there can be straightforward right answers. This is an aspect of the vision of philosophy that he presents throughout the book, but particularly in its two concluding chapters.

WHAT IS PHILOSOPHY?

Many people, including some great philosophers of the past, have come to the subject hoping it will solve major metaphysical questions about the ultimate nature of reality, right and wrong, beauty and so forth, but, Russell says, this is a vain hope. Philosophy doesn't give simple answers. Philosophers ask questions; often they cannot answer those questions. Indeed, Russell acknowledges that philosophy has not been particularly successful in answering with any certainty most of the questions that philosophers ask. But that does not mean that philosophy is a waste of time. By asking deep questions we make life more interesting and reveal that a little below the surface of our comfortable assumptions lies a much stranger world.

So anyone coming to philosophy expecting it to provide knowledge of reality is likely to be disappointed. What philosophy can provide, however, is the possibility of ordering our less than certain beliefs and getting some insights into the ways in which we acquire them. Even if it can't provide us with certainties, philosophy can make us less likely to be wrong about our basic beliefs than if we had left them unexamined.

There is a clear distinction between philosophy and science, though historically many of the problems of philosophy have later become scientific questions. Science can be extremely useful to us even if we never study it: all of us have the potential to benefit from medical science, science-based technology and so on, whether or not we understand the science underpinning the inventions. Philosophy differs from this. Studying philosophy can have a profound effect on the student who thinks through the issues; but those who don't study the subject are only likely to benefit from the effects on the student of philosophy. There are no direct benefits from philosophy for those who don't actually study it themselves.

The real value of philosophy, however, Russell declares, lies in its uncertainty. If you never question your beliefs, then you can cling to prejudices that need never be subjected to critical assessment. If, however, you begin to question beliefs that have previously seemed uncontroversial, with the help of a philosophical approach you will free yourself from the 'tyranny of custom' and awaken a less dogmatic sense of wonder at the strangeness of the world and our position in it. This opening up of possibilities enriches our imaginations. Philosophical contemplation takes us away from the purely individual concerns of our lives, moving us towards becoming 'citizens of the universe'. Our minds become great by contemplating greatness in this impartial spirit. In the combination of these factors lies philosophy's value to humanity.

One traditional approach to philosophy (usually known as rationalism) has been to attempt to prove truths about the nature of reality *a priori*, that is independently of any experience, by pure reason alone. In place of this Russell offers something much closer to John Locke's account of the philosopher as 'underlabourer' to science (though Russell does not identify the source of this idea). For Russell, philosophy is the activity of investigating the principles that we use both in science and in everyday life, and subjecting them to a critical scrutiny that reveals any inconsistencies. This, Russell believed, shouldn't result in a destructive scepticism that leaves everything in doubt. Indeed, one theme of *The Problems of Philosophy* is that there are beliefs, such as that our perceptual experiences exist, that are beyond doubt. In contrast, the belief that physical objects are really as they appear to us, is open to philosophical doubt. Much of the book focuses on questions about our knowledge of the world as it is acquired through the senses and by reason.

APPEARANCE AND REALITY

Is there any knowledge so certain that no reasonable person could doubt it? This is Russell's opening question. If we look at a table it seems a particular shape, colour and texture to us. But do we really know that it is as it seems? If we analyse our experience more closely we very soon discover that, for example, the 'real' shape of the table is something inferred from what we see. A rectangular table does not appear to have right-angled corners from almost any angle it is viewed. When I say I see a table over there I am in some senses begging the question about what I see. Russell uses the more neutral term 'sense data' (the singular is 'sense datum') to refer to what we see – the patches of colour and shape. Sensations are mental; sense data are the things that we see, and are, he presumes, not entirely mental. What I see, what appears to be in front of me are sense data. I have data that I take to be of a real table. I see something of a particular colour and particular shape: the sense data are our means of access to the real table. But the sense data don't seem to correspond perfectly with what we take to be the real table. The table doesn't seem to be the sense data: we take the table to have an oblong top and a brownish red colour, perhaps, but as I experience it now, the sense data are of a parallelogram of yellowish brown.

Bishop Berkeley's solution to this problem was to declare that there is no real table independent of sense data: matter doesn't exist. To be is to be perceived. Russell rejects such idealism. He recognises that there is no *logical* absurdity in supposing that there is nothing more than my mind and its experiences. Nor is there any logical absurdity in thinking the whole of life a dream. But the commonsense hypothesis that objects exist independently of us and differ from their appearances, an example of what he calls an *instinctive* belief, is a simpler explanation and so we should prefer it. (In passing he comments that beliefs about moral values are also instinctive, but he later changed his mind about this.) Russell believed that all our knowledge ultimately rests on and is built up from such instinctive beliefs.

KNOWLEDGE BY ACQUAINTANCE AND BY DESCRIPTION

The distinction between knowledge by acquaintance and knowledge by description is an important one for Russell. For him it is clear that we have knowledge of truths and knowledge of things. Our knowledge of things comes by either acquaintance or description.

Knowledge by acquaintance is the foundation of all our knowledge. Knowledge by acquaintance involves a direct awareness of the thing that we know. So, for example, I have direct knowledge – knowledge by acquaintance – of my sense data. I am acquainted with what I see. But we also have knowledge by acquaintance of our own memories, and, when we introspect, we have knowledge by acquaintance of our sensations.

In contrast, knowledge by description is the kind of knowledge that takes us beyond our direct acquaintance. Knowledge by description would include the knowledge that someone who had never visited Australia might have that Canberra is the capital city of Australia. So, for Russell, as we have seen, we don't have direct knowledge of physical objects, only of sense data, so our knowledge of real physical objects, as opposed to sense data, is knowledge by description too. Knowledge by description is how we move beyond our own personal direct experience and get to know things that we haven't experienced ourselves. In *The Problems of Philosophy* Russell declares that every proposition that we understand must ultimately be dependent on some things that we know by acquaintance.

THE *A PRIORI*

Immanuel Kant famously argued that we can learn by pure thought about principles that must apply to all our experience – these are the very conditions of thought at all. So-called *a priori* knowledge, what we know independently of experience, was traditionally restricted to the category known as analytic truths: those that are true by definition, such as 'All bachelors are unmarried.' Against this Kant announced that there could be synthetic *a priori* knowledge: *a priori* knowledge of matters that weren't true by definition. He put our knowledge of time, space and cause and effect in this category: he believed that it was a feature of our understanding rather than of the world that all our experiences and all possible experiences included these elements. Russell, however, rejects Kant's conclusions, arguing that *a priori* knowledge is only ever of relations and qualities, never of facts directly about the world.

INDUCTION

Russell's outline of the so-called Problem of Induction in Chapter 6 of his book follows David Hume's quite closely. Why are we all convinced that the sun will rise tomorrow? Simply because it has always risen in the past. Have we got good reason to believe that the future will be like the past? We assume a uniformity of nature in this respect. But consider the chicken fed by the farmer every day. As Russell points out, on the day that the farmer wrings its neck 'more refined views as to the uniformity of nature would have been useful to the chicken'.

We are left recognising that experience of past uniformity of nature is not a completely reliable guide to the future. Just because we have never had an exception to an apparent uniformity of nature, it does not follow that there never could be one. It just makes it improbable that this will occur. As Russell points out, this cuts two ways. We can't prove the reliability of the principle of induction using experience, since that would be begging the question: using induction to justify the principle of induction. But equally we can't prove that the future *won't* be like the past

CRITICISMS OF *THE PROBLEMS OF PHILOSOPHY*

Wrong about the point of philosophy?

Russell characterised philosophy as a way of stepping back from our individual concerns, revealing our uncertainties to ourselves, and as an antidote to dogmatism. This view of the subject can be challenged. Ludwig Wittgenstein, Russell's sometime pupil, hated *The Problems of Philosophy*. This may well have been in part because Wittgenstein had a very different vision of what philosophy was. For Wittgenstein, at least in his later years, philosophy was something that required a kind of intellectual therapy: philosophical problems often arose from a strange forcing of language to do things that it couldn't do. Philosophy should be a process of taking away mystery, not creating a sense of mystery.

From a different direction, Friedrich Nietzsche's claim in *Beyond Good and Evil* that philosophy is a kind of involuntary autobiography wrapped up to make it seem impersonal, if true, would undermine

Russell's suggestion that philosophy takes us away from the merely personal to a more general level. If Nietzsche is right, all philosophy is riddled with philosophers' own personal prejudices and heartfelt desires.

Over-optimistic bibliographical note

At the very end of his book, Russell claims that students who want to learn more about philosophy will find it 'both easier and more profitable' to read some original works of the great philosophers than to turn to handbooks of philosophy. He lists works by Plato, Descartes, Leibniz, Berkeley, Hume and Kant. Russell's assertion may reflect the kind of introductory books available in 1911. Some of the texts he recommends, notably Spinoza's *Ethics*, are far from an easy read for beginning students, or anyone else.

Whilst it is certainly still true that most students would benefit from reading some primary texts early on in their study of philosophy, it is no longer true, if it ever was, that it is either 'easier' or 'more profitable' to do this than to read the best available introductory works, such as those that I recommend in the 'Further Reading' sections of each chapter here. This is an example of a widespread phenomenon that still persists: professional philosophers are notoriously bad at appreciating how difficult philosophy can be for a beginning student. For many students it would be just as profitable to recommend battering your head against a brick wall as to attempt to read Spinoza's *Ethics* without any commentary or introduction to its main themes.

DATES

1872   Bertrand Russell born.
1911   Writes *The Problems of Philosophy*.
1912   *The Problems of Philosophy* published.
1970   Russell dies.

GLOSSARY

a priori: knowledge which is independent of experience.

epistemology: the theory of knowledge.

knowledge by aquaintance: what we know from direct experience.

knowledge by description: what we learn about indirectly.

metaphysics: branch of philosophy that studies the nature of reality.

rationalism: the attempt to discover truths about reality by thought alone.

scepticism: questioning of fundamental beliefs.

sensations: the mental representations of what we experience.

sense data: the things we see and otherwise sense.

FURTHER READING

Ray Monk, *Bertrand Russell* (2 vols, London: Vintage, 1997 and 2001) is a controversial biography. Some critics disliked Monk's lack of personal sympathy with Russell's character and private life; others appreciated Monk's thoroughness, literary style and combination of philosophical understanding and clarity. For Russell's own account of his life, see his *Autobiography* (London: Routledge, 2000).

23

A. J. AYER *LANGUAGE, TRUTH AND LOGIC*

Most people talk and write nonsense some of the time; and some people talk and write nonsense all of the time. But it can be difficult to detect precisely who is talking and writing nonsense when. In *Language, Truth and Logic* Ayer presents what he believes to be an infallible nonsense detector, a two-pronged test for meaningfulness which he calls the Verification Principle. With this test he demonstrates that a huge swathe of philosophical writing doesn't deserve to be called philosophy at all, since it is simply nonsensical. He suggests that we set it aside and get on with the real business of philosophy, which is to clarify the meaning of concepts. The subject that is left after he has wielded his Verification Principle is very much slimmer than philosophy as traditionally conceived: there is no place for metaphysics, for example.

Language, Truth and Logic, which Ayer published before his 26th birthday, is, then, an iconoclastic book, one which attempts to transform the nature of philosophy and of philosophising. The book is not itself wholly original, since most of its ideas are to be found either in the work of David Hume, or else in that of the so-called Vienna Circle, a group of intellectuals who met regularly in the late 1920s to discuss philosophy and who founded the school of thought known as logical positivism. Nevertheless, Ayer's was the first, and best-known, synthesis of these ideas to appear in English.

THE VERIFICATION PRINCIPLE

It is tempting to think that all statements are either true or false. However, there is a third important class of statements, namely those which are neither true nor false, but literally meaningless. Ayer's Verification Principle is designed to pick out this third class of statements. So, for example, it is true that I am typing this on a word processor; false that I am writing it by hand; and meaningless to say 'colourless green ideas sleep furiously'. This last statement is the equivalent of saying 'blah': although it uses words, it can be neither true nor false since it is impossible to come up with any criterion for determining whether it is true or false.

The Verification Principle asks two questions of any statement. First, 'Is it true by definition?' And second, if not, 'Is it in principle verifiable?' Any statement which passes the test, that is, is either true by definition or else in principle verifiable, is meaningful. Any statement which fails the test is meaningless, and so should not be taken seriously.

Actually, Ayer usually does not talk of statements, but rather of propositions. Propositions are the underlying logical structures of statements: the point is that 'The cat sat on the mat' expresses a proposition which could equally well be expressed in another language. It doesn't affect the truth of the statement if it is in French or Swahili. So statements made in different languages can express the same proposition. Also, Ayer usually talks of 'putative' propositions: here the word 'putative' is used so as to leave open the possibility that they might not be propositions at all (i.e. that they might be nonsensical): 'putative' just means 'supposed'.

Let's consider the first prong of the Verification Principle, the question 'Is it true by definition?' An example of a proposition that is true by definition is 'All bachelors are unmarried men.' There is no need to conduct a survey to establish that this statement is true: anyone who purports to be a bachelor and yet is married has simply misunderstood the meaning of the word 'bachelor'. The statement is a tautologous one, that is, one that is logically true. Another example of a statement that is true by definition is 'All cats are animals.' Again, there would be no need to conduct any research in order to assess whether or not this statement is true: it is true simply by virtue of the meanings of the words. This kind of statement is sometimes also called an analytic truth ('analytic' is used here in a technical sense).

In contrast, statements such as 'Most bachelors are untidy' or 'No cat has ever lived longer than thirty years' are empirical statements. Some kind of observation is needed in order to assess whether or not they are true. You can't tell conclusively whether or not they are true unless you do some research into the matter. These statements purport to be factual ones. They are not just about the meaning of words, but report on features of the world referred to by the words. They are the sort of statement covered by the second prong of the Verification Principle.

Ayer asks of empirical statements such as those given in the previous paragraph 'Are they in principle verifiable?' Here 'verifiable' simply means capable of being shown to be true or false. The word 'verifiable' is slightly confusing since in ordinary language to verify something is to show that it is true; however, Ayer allows that showing something to be false is also a case of verifying it. He includes the words 'in principle' in the question because there are very many meaningful statements that cannot practically be tested. For instance, prior to space travel, a scientist could have claimed that the moon was made of limestone. This might have been practically difficult to refute; nevertheless, in principle it is easy to see how it could be refuted: get a specimen of moon rock and see if it is limestone. So it is a meaningful statement, despite the fact that at the time of being uttered it was not possible to test it. Similarly, even so absurd a statement as 'The moon is made of cream cheese' is meaningful since it is obvious how it can be shown to be false. Again it is important to recognise that Ayer is using the word 'meaningful' in a specialised sense, since in ordinary language we rarely call statements which we know to be false 'meaningful'. Statements about what happened in the past can be particularly difficult to verify in practice; specifying that these need only be verifiable in principle gets around the problems that would otherwise arise in assessing the status of such statements.

What emerges from this is that, when considering any putative proposition, for Ayer there are just three possibilities: that it is meaningful and true; that it is meaningful yet false; and that it is completely meaningless. The last category, that of completely meaningless utterances, is his main target in *Language, Truth and Logic*.

According to Ayer many philosophers have been duped into believing that they were making meaningful statements when in fact, as application of his Verification Principle reveals, they have been writing nonsense. His favourite word for such nonsense in the realm of philosophy is 'metaphysics'. A metaphysical sentence is one which purports to say something genuine (i.e. meaningful) but, because it is neither true by definition nor empirically verifiable, is actually meaningless.

STRONG AND WEAK SENSES OF 'VERIFIABILITY'

One problem that would arise for Ayer if he demanded that meaningful statements that weren't true by definition had to be conclusively verified is that general empirical claims are not subject to conclusive proof. For instance, take the general statement 'All women are mortal.' However many cases of mortal women you observe, you will never prove once and for all that this statement is true, only that it is very probably true. This is good enough for practical purposes. But if Ayer had adopted what he calls the strong sense of verifiability, that is demanded conclusive empirical proof for any empirical generalisation to be meaningful, he would have set too high a standard.

Instead he adopts a weak sense of 'verifiability'. For an empirical statement to be meaningful there need only be some observations which would be relevant to determining whether it was true or false. These observations need not make it certain that it is true or that it is false.

Some critics of Ayer's work have pointed out that the distinction between strong and weak senses of verification is itself a meaningless one since no empirical statement could ever in practice or in principle meet the rigorous demands of the strong principle. Ayer, however, in the introduction to the second edition of the book, suggests that there are what he calls 'basic propositions' which can be conclusively verified. These are the kind of proposition expressed by statements such as 'I am in pain now' or 'this lemon tastes bitter to me'. These are incorrigible, meaning that you cannot be mistaken about them.

METAPHYSICS AND POETRY

One line of defence for metaphysics is to claim that although literally meaningless it can have the same sort of effect as poetry and thus be a worthwhile activity in its own right. Ayer is scathing about this attempt at a justification of metaphysics. First, he points out, this attempted justification is based on a misapprehension about poetry. Poetry is rarely meaningless, though it sometimes expresses false propositions. And even when it is meaningless, the words have been chosen because of their rhythm or sound. Metaphysics is intended to be meaningful and true. Metaphysicians don't attempt to write nonsense. It is just an unfortunate fact that this is what they do. No defence in terms of its poetic qualities will mask this fact.

Ayer's main aim throughout *Language, Truth and Logic* is to eliminate metaphysics. He focuses on language, because he believes that language frequently misleads us into believing that we are making sense when we are not. This concentration on language is a distinctive feature of a great deal of philosophy which was written in Britain and the United States in the first half of this century, and is sometimes referred to as the *linguistic turn* in philosophy.

Here we'll examine the consequences of Ayer's radical approach to meaning. But first, what does Ayer understand by 'philosophy'?

PHILOSOPHY

For Ayer philosophy has a very narrow role. Philosophy is not an empirical subject: this is what distinguishes it from the sciences. Whereas the sciences involve statements about the nature of the world, and thus contribute factual knowledge, philosophy's role is one of clarification of the implications of definitions of concepts, and particularly of the concepts used by scientists. Philosophy is focused on language rather than on the world described by language. It is essentially a branch of logic. In fact the activities that Ayer is engaged in within *Language, Truth and Logic*, namely the clarification of our concept of 'meaningfulness' and following through its implications, are paradigm instances of philosophical activity.

THE PROBLEM OF INDUCTION

Ayer's treatment of the problem of induction provides a good example of his approach to traditional philosophical disputes. The problem of induction as it is usually understood is the difficulty of coming up with a satisfactory justification for our belief that empirical generalisations based on past observations will hold good for the future. How can we be sure that the future will be like the past? The sun rose yesterday, and every day that anyone ever observed before that, but this does not prove conclusively that it will rise tomorrow. Yet we all of us confidently rely on inductive generalisations of this kind, and they are the basis of all science.

Since David Hume first formulated the problem in the eighteenth century, philosophers have been attempting to justify the use of inductive reasoning. Ayer's approach is very different. He attempts simply to dissolve the problem. He dismisses it as a pseudo-problem, not a genuine problem. He does so on the grounds that there could not possibly be a meaningful answer to the question. Since every genuine question can in principle be answered meaningfully, and this one cannot, we should set it aside.

His reasoning is as follows. There are only two possible types of meaningful justification of induction, and both are non-starters. The first would be to give a justification based on truth by definition, perhaps on the definition of 'induction', or of 'true'. However, this is a non-starter because to attempt such a justification would be to make the fundamental mistake of assuming that any factual conclusions can be derived from statements about definition. Statements about definition simply inform us about the use of words or other symbols.

The second type of justification would be an empirically verifiable one. For instance, someone might argue that induction is a reliable method of reasoning since it has worked well for us in the past. But this, as Hume saw, would be to use induction to justify induction. Clearly this cannot be acceptable either, since it begs the question; it assumes that induction is reliable when this is the very point at issue. So, Ayer concludes, no meaningful solution is possible. The problem of induction so-called is not, then, a genuine problem.

MATHEMATICS

It is clear that the propositions expressed in mathematics must, on the whole, be meaningful ones. If they did not come out as meaningful on Ayer's analysis we would have very good grounds for dismissing his theory. How, then, can he show that they are meaningful? He has only two choices: they must be either true by definition or else empirically verifiable (or perhaps a mixture of the two).

Very few philosophers have claimed that $7 + 5 = 12$ is simply a generalisation based on adding together seven things and five things and getting twelve each time. This is a highly implausible view to hold. So Ayer is left with the consequence that $7 + 5 = 12$ is true by definition, simply a question of how we use the symbols '7', '+', '5', '=', and '12'. But if $7 + 5 = 12$ is true by definition in the same way that 'All bachelors are unmarried men' is true by definition, Ayer needs to explain how we can be surprised by mathematical 'discoveries' since, according to this theory, the solution must be implicit in the phrasing of the problem. Ultimately all equations will be the equivalent of the obviously tautologous $A = A$. So how can we have a sense of making a discovery in mathematics?

Ayer's answer is that although mathematical statements are true by definition, some mathematical truths are not obviously true at first sight. For instance, take the equation $91 \times 79 = 7,189$. This is far less obvious than $7 + 5 = 12$. Yet it is still true by definition. We need to use calculation to check that it is true; this calculation is ultimately nothing more than a tautological transformation. But because we cannot immediately see that the answer is correct, we find it interesting, although ultimately it does not give us any new factual information.

ETHICS

Ayer's treatment of ethics is one of the most controversial aspects of *Language, Truth and Logic*. His basic belief is that judgements about right and wrong are for the most part simply expressions of emotion and as literally meaningless as the expressions 'Boo!' and 'Hooray!' He arrives at this extreme conclusion by application of his Verification Principle.

Examining ethical philosophy he finds four types of statement. First, there are definitions of ethical terms; for instance, we might find in a book of ethics a detailed definition of 'responsibility'. Second, there are descriptions of moral phenomena and their causes; for instance, a description of pangs of conscience and how they might originate in early moral or religious training. Third, there are what Ayer calls 'exhortations to moral virtue'. A simple example of this would be a plea for readers to keep their promises. And last, there are 'actual ethical judgements'. These are statements such as 'Torture is a moral evil.'

Ayer examines each of these four types of statement. The first class, of definitions, is the only one which he considers acceptable as ethical philosophy. This class (the definitions of ethical terms) consists of statements which are true by definition and so pass his test for meaningfulness. The second class of statement, descriptions of moral phenomena, although passing the second prong of the test, and so meaningful, are not the province of philosophy. They are empirically verifiable, and so their treatment belongs to a branch of science, in this case either psychology or sociology. The third class of statement, exhortations to moral virtue, can be neither true nor false and are thus literally meaningless. They cannot belong to either science or philosophy.

The last class, the ethical judgements, Ayer treats at greater length. These are the statements that are usually thought to constitute ethical philosophy, and have traditionally been assumed to be meaningful. Ayer agues that they are neither true by definition nor empirically verifiable, and so are literally meaningless. If I say 'You acted wrongly in breaking into my house', then I am saying the equivalent of 'You broke into my house' in a particular tone of voice. The claim that you acted wrongly adds nothing meaningful to the statement. If I make the generalisation 'House-breaking is wrong', provided that 'wrong' is being used in an ethical rather than a legal sense, then I make a completely meaningless statement, one which is neither true nor false. It is simply an expression of an emotional attitude towards house-breaking, an expression which may also be calculated to arouse a similar emotional attitude in the listener. If you turn back to me and disagree, saying 'There is nothing wrong with house-breaking', there is no fact of the matter which will decide between us. You would simply be expressing an alternative emotional attitude towards house-breaking.

This account of ethical judgements, known as emotivism, has the consequence that it is impossible to have a genuine dispute about whether an action is wrong. What seems like a dispute will always turn out to be a series of expressions of emotion; and there is no point of view from which we can judge the truth or falsity of the ethical positions since the positions are not capable of being either true or false. They do not express genuine propositions at all.

RELIGION

Ayer's treatment of the statement 'God exists' is at least as challenging as his dismissal of most of ethical philosophy. He claims that the statement is neither true by definition nor empirically verifiable even in principle. It can't be true by definition, since definitions only indicate word use, and so cannot show the existence of anything. Ayer rejects out of hand the idea that there could be an empirical proof of God's existence. Consequently, he declares, 'God exists' is literally meaningless and can be neither true nor false.

This view does not have a name, but it differs significantly from the traditional approaches to the question of God's existence. Traditionally individuals either believe in God's existence, are atheists (i.e. believe that God doesn't exist), or else are agnostics (i.e. claim there is insufficient evidence to decide the issue either way). However, Ayer's position differs from all three of these since they all take the statement 'God exists' to be meaningful and, respectively, true, false or unproven. 'God exists' is, then, a metaphysical statement, one which Ayer concludes is completely nonsensical and so should not be addressed by philosophy. Thus, at a stroke, the problem of whether or not God exists, one which has occupied the greatest philosophers for thousands of years, has been dismissed as unanswerable, and so not worth exerting any philosophical energy upon.

CRITICISMS OF *LANGUAGE, TRUTH AND LOGIC*

Practical difficulties

Even if we were to accept Ayer's Verification Principle as a way of discriminating between meaningful and meaningless statements, there are some quite serious practical difficulties which would have to be met. How, for example, are we to determine whether or not a proposition is verifiable *in principle*? In other words, what does 'in principle' mean in this context? With a bit of imagination someone might claim that the statement 'Reality is one', an example Ayer uses of a metaphysical statement, is *in principle* verifiable. Imagine that the veil of appearances dropped for a split-second, and that we got a glimpse of the true nature of reality; then we would be able to make an observation relevant to the assessment of whether or not 'Reality is one' is true or false. Does this mean that 'Reality is one' is verifiable in principle? Ayer does not give us enough information about what 'verifiable in principle' means in practice to determine in particular cases whether or not a statement is metaphysical.

A further practical difficulty about applying the Verification Principle is that of identifying non-obvious tautologies. In his discussion of mathematics Ayer allows that some statements can be true by definition even though we cannot immediately appreciate that this is so. A consequence of this sort of view is that we might easily overlook the tautologous nature of many seemingly metaphysical statements.

Treats propositions in isolation from each other

A different sort of objection which can be levelled at Ayer's general approach is that it treats propositions as if they could be separated out from the complex web of meanings in which they are in fact embedded. This point has been made by the philosopher W. V. O. Quine (1908–2000).

For example, Ayer seems to suggest that I could determine the truth or falsehood of the statement 'Gravity caused the spaceshuttle to fall back towards earth' in isolation from other statements. However, in order to determine whether or not this was a metaphysical statement I would need to draw on scientific theory and a range of other assumptions, many of them built into the way we use language.

Self-refuting

The most serious criticism of Ayer's book is that the Verification Principle does not seem to pass its own test for meaningfulness. Is the principle itself true by definition? Not obviously so. Is it empirically verifiable? It is hard to see how it could be. So, according to its own dictates it is itself nonsensical. If this criticism holds, then the whole of Ayer's project collapses since it all depends on the truth of the claim that any meaningful proposition will pass the test.

Ayer's response to this criticism is that the Verification Principle is true by definition. Like the mathematical equation $91 \times 79 = 7{,}189$, it is not obviously true by definition: that is why it can be found interesting and is a discovery. However, Ayer does not demonstrate from what he derived this Verification Principle, nor does he provide any equivalent of mathematical calculation by which we can check to see if he came up with the correct answer.

Or perhaps the Verfication Principle is simply a proposal, a recommendation that we ought to use 'meaningful' in the way that the principle indicates. But if this were so, it would by its own standards be a metaphysical statement equivalent to the expression of an emotion: exactly the sort of statement that Ayer is so keen to eliminate from philosophy.

So, on either account, the criticism that his Verification Principle is self-refuting has a devastating force.

DATES

1910   born in London.
1936   publishes *Language, Truth and Logic*.
1989   dies in London.

GLOSSARY

emotivism: the theory that moral judgements are meaningless expressions of emotion which can be neither true nor false.

empirical: derived from experience.

logical positivism: the school of philosophy that advocates rigorous use of the Verification Principle.

meaningful: either true by definition or else verifiable in principle.

metaphysics: for Ayer this is always a term of abuse. It is for him synonymous with 'nonsense'.

problem of induction: the problem of justifying our widespread reliance on inductive reasoning. Logically we have no guarantee that the future will be like the past, yet we act as if we had such a guarantee.

proposition: the thought expressed by a sentence. The same proposition can be expressed in different languages.

pseudo-problem: not a genuine problem; something that has traditionally been thought to be a problem, but isn't.

tautology: a statement which is necessarily true, such as 'Whatever is, is' or 'All bachelors are unmarried men.'

Verification Principle: the two-pronged test for meaningfulness that dismisses as meaningless nonsense any statement which is neither true by definition nor, in principle, empirically verifiable or falsifiable.

FURTHER READING

Stephen Priest *The British Empiricists* (Harmondsworth: Penguin, 1990) includes a chapter on Ayer's work.

Bryan Magee *Men of Ideas* (Oxford: Oxford University Press, 1988) includes an interview with A. J. Ayer.

Oswald Hanfling *Ayer* (London: Phoenix, 1997) gives a brief overview of Ayer's philosophy and its importance.

Ben Rogers *A. J. Ayer: A Life* (London: Vintage, 2000). This biography provides an introduction to Ayer's philosophy in the course of giving a sensitive portrait of the man.

JEAN-PAUL SARTRE
BEING AND NOTHINGNESS

Being and Nothingness is the bible of existentialism. Yet despite its centrality in the movement which swept through Europe and North America in the postwar years, it is surprisingly obscure. Few of the café existentialists could have read and understood much of this book. In particular, the introduction is fiendishly difficult to make sense of, especially if you don't have a background in continental philosophy. Yet despite the initial feelings of hopelessness that most of those who attempt to read the book from cover to cover experience, it is worth persevering. *Being and Nothingness* is one of very few philosophical books written this century which genuinely grapple with fundamental questions about the human predicament. In its more lucid passages it can be both enlightening and exhilarating. Sartre's experience as a novelist and playwright is apparent in the memorable descriptions of particular situations which form a substantial part of the book.

The central theme of *Being and Nothingness* is encapsulated in the enigmatic line 'the nature of consciousness simultaneously is to be what it is not and not to be what it is'. Whilst this might on first reading sound like pseudoprofundity, it is in fact a summary of Sartre's account of what it is to be human. The full meaning of the line should become apparent in the course of this chapter.

PHENOMENOLOGICAL APPROACH

A distinctive feature of Sartre's writing in *Being and Nothingness* is its focus on real or imagined situations described at some length. This is not just a stylistic quirk but rather a feature of Sartre's phenomenological approach. Sartre is influenced by the philosopher Edmund Husserl (1859–1938). Husserl believes that by describing the contents of consciousness, setting on one side the question of whether or not what appears to consciousness actually exists, insight into the essence of things can be achieved. For Husserl an important part of philosophy is descriptive: we should describe our experiences, not simply reflect at an abstract level.

Sartre accepts this last aspect of Husserl's thought, but rejects the assumption that scrutiny of the contents of our consciousness reveals the essential nature of what is being thought about. What phenomenological method means in practice for Sartre is that he concentrates on life as it is lived and felt, rather than on human beings as described by science or empirical psychology. The result is a strange mixture of highly abstract discussion interspersed with vivid and memorable novelistic scenarios and descriptions.

BEING

The whole of *Being and Nothingness* rests on a fundamental distinction between different forms of existence. Sartre draws attention to the difference between conscious and non-conscious being. The former he calls 'being for-itself'; the latter, 'being in-itself'. Being for-itself is the kind of existence characteristically experienced by human beings, and most of *Being and Nothingness* is devoted to explaining its main features. Unfortunately Sartre provides no answer to the question of whether or not non-human animals can reasonably be categorised as examples of being for-itself. Being in-itself, in contrast, is the being of non-conscious things, such as of a stone on a beach.

NOTHINGNESS

Nothingness, as the title of the book suggests, plays a key role in Sartre's work. He characterises human consciousness as a gap at the heart of our being, a nothing. Consciousness is always consciousness of something. It is never simply itself. It is what allows us to project ourselves into the future and to reassess our past.

Concrete nothingness is experienced when we recognise that something is absent. You arrange to meet your friend Pierre in a café at four. You arrive a quarter of an hour late and he is not there. You are aware of him as a lack, an absence because you expected to see him. This is very different from the absence of, say, Muhammad Ali from the café, since you had not arranged to see him there: you could play an intellectual game listing all the people who weren't in the café, but only Pierre's absence in this case would be felt as a genuine lack, since only Pierre was expected. This phenomenon, the ability of human consciousness to see things as missing, is part of what Sartre calls the transcendence of consciousness. It is linked up with his idea of freedom, since it is our ability to see things as unrealised, or as to be done, that reveals to us a world brimming with possibilities. Or rather in some cases it reveals to us such a world; in others the peculiar kind of self-deception that Sartre labels 'bad faith' gets a grip, and we don't let ourselves recognise the true extent of our freedom.

FREEDOM

Sartre believes that human beings have free will. Consciousness is empty; it does not determine what we choose. We are not constrained by the choices we have made in the past, though we may feel that we are. We are free to choose whatever we wish. It is true that the world won't always allow us to fulfil our wishes. But that, like the facts of when we were born and who our parents were, is an aspect of what Sartre terms our 'facticity', those aspects of our lives which are given. Yet even though we can't change these things, we can choose to change our attitude to them.

Sartre takes an extreme position on the question of individual freedom, disregarding any theory which suggests that human beings are entirely shaped by their genetic endowment and their upbringing. For Sartre human beings are characterised by their ability to choose what they become. However, Sartre does point out that things aren't quite so simple: human consciousness is constantly flirting with what he calls bad faith, which is at bottom the denial of our freedom.

BAD FAITH

Sartre's discussion of bad faith is justly celebrated as one of the classic passages in twentieth-century philosophy. Here his skills as philosopher, psychologist and novelist are combined most successfully; here his phenomenological method yields fruit in a way that so many barren and abstract philosophical discussions of self-deception have failed to do.

It is important to realise that Sartre is not interested in self-deception as a general philosophical topic: bad faith is a particular kind of self-deception which only makes sense within a theory which postulates free will. Bad faith is a lie to oneself which is chosen as a flight from freedom. It is a condition to which human consciousness is particularly prone.

Consider Sartre's description of a woman on a first date with a man who has sexual intentions towards her. She is aware of the nature of his interest, yet denies it to herself, lies to herself about the significance of such comments as 'I find you so attractive!', turning them into innocuous non-sexual compliments. She manages to sustain her self-deception throughout the conversation. But then he takes her hand. To leave her hand in his would be to flirt with him; to take it away would 'break the troubled and unstable harmony which gives the hour its charm'. What does she do? She leaves her hand there, but inert, a thing, neither consenting nor resisting, while she talks loftily of her life, emphasising herself as personality rather than as body. She is in bad faith because she deceives herself about the nature of the man's intentions. She pretends to herself that he is really interested in her mind in order to avoid admitting the possibility that she might reciprocate his desire. But she is also in bad faith because she denies that she is her body and in doing so denies her freedom to act, and the responsibility she has for her actions. She attempts to make of her hand an in-itself rather than accept that it is her hand in his.

Sartre's most famous example of bad faith is of a café waiter. This waiter seems determined by his role as a waiter. It is as if he is acting a role. His movements are exaggerated: the way he bends forward to the customer, or balances his tray. It is all a kind of ceremony, an elaborate dance. Sartre points out that the waiter, however hard he tries to become his role, cannot be a waiter as an inkwell is an inkwell. A for-itself cannot by an act of will power metamorphose into an in-itself (except, perhaps, by committing suicide). Sartre diagnoses the waiter as someone trying to deny his freedom, as if he didn't have the choice of staying in bed rather than getting up at 5 o'clock, even though that would mean getting the sack. His mechanical movements betray a desire to be what he cannot be, an in-itself. Thus the waiter is in bad faith because he is deceiving himself about the limits of his freedom.

In a different example, Sartre describes a homosexual man who will not admit to his friend or indeed to himself that he is a homosexual. True, his pattern of conduct has been that of a homosexual. But he plays on two senses of the word 'is' when he claims he *is* not a homosexual. In his own eyes he cannot be a homosexual because no human individual is strictly determined by his or her past in the way that a red-haired man is red-haired. As a being for-itself he cannot simply make of his character an in-itself. Yet, in another sense, given his past behaviour, he clearly *is* a homosexual: his past sexual liaisons have been with men. The honest answer to the question 'Are you a homosexual?' would be 'In one sense no, and another yes.'

His friend demands that the homosexual be sincere and come out as homosexual. Yet the friend is as much in bad faith as the homosexual since the demand for sincerity is a demand to make of yourself an in-itself, to deny your freedom to act differently in the future from the way you have done in the past. So sincerity is itself a kind of bad faith.

The term 'bad faith' suggests that there is something bad about being in this condition, that it is, perhaps, a moral fault. It also suggests that authenticity, the opposite of bad faith, might be a virtue. However, in *Being and Nothingness* Sartre's approach is to describe rather than to judge: this is not an instruction manual on how to live but an account of what it is like to live. Sartre promised to write a sequel to *Being and Nothingness* in which he would present an existentialist ethics; however, he never published such a book. Nevertheless, it is difficult to read Sartre's account of bad faith without concluding that Sartre thought that, on the whole, bad faith was culpable and a denial of what we truly are, namely free individuals.

Bad faith is possible because human beings are both transcendence and facticity. Transcendence refers to our ability to think beyond the facts of what is happening now and project ourselves into future possibilities; facticity refers to the facts of our past, of what is now happening, the givens of our existence which we can't change at will. We maintain ourselves in bad faith by keeping our transcendence and facticity separate from each other, by thinking of ourselves either as wholly different from our bodies (denying an aspect of our facticity, as, for example, does the woman on her date) or else as wholly different from our possibilities (pretending to be an in-itself, as, for example, does the café waiter).

This discussion of transcendence and facticity goes some way to explaining the meaning of the quotation about consciousness given earlier in the chapter: 'the nature of consciousness simultaneously is to be what it is not and not to be what it is'. We are in one sense our possibilities, our transcendence: not what we are now but what we may become (i.e. consciousness 'is what it is not'). And yet we aren't simply our facticity, a product of where we were born, how we were brought up, what colour hair we have, how tall we are, how intelligent, and so on.

CRITIQUE OF FREUD

Freud's theory of the unconscious could have provided Sartre with a convenient account of how it is that an individual can lie to himor herself. According to Freud the psyche is divided into a conscious and an unconscious part. Unconscious motives and thoughts are censored and transformed before they can enter consciousness. The censor represses some thoughts altogether, allowing others to emerge into consciousness in disguised form, particularly in dreams or in so-called 'Freudian slips'. Psychoanalysts frequently talk of the patients' resistances to certain interpretations which get near to the truth; these resistances are the work of the censor. If Sartre had accepted this Freudian account, he could have explained bad faith as arising from unconscious beliefs and their conscious denial. On this model the human mind is fundamentally divided, almost the equivalent of two people, so it is relatively easy to understand how someone could lie to himor herself and yet believe the lie: it would simply be the unconscious lying to the conscious.

Sartre criticises the Freudian picture of the mind. He argues that if there were a censor between the unconscious and conscious aspects of our minds, then this censor would have to be conscious of both sides of the divide. In order to censor effectively, the censor would have to know what is in the unconscious mind in order to repress or transform it. If the censor is part of the unconscious, then there is a consciousness within the unconscious. The Freudian is left with the absurd situation of the conscious censor as part of the mind being aware of what is in the unconscious in order to appear unaware of what is in the unconscious (i.e. in order to repress all knowledge of it). In other words, the censor would find itself in bad faith. So the problem of how bad faith is possible would still remain for a Freudian; the notion of the unconscious solves nothing since the problem is simply moved on to the censor.

SHAME

Shame is an emotion which particularly interests Sartre because of what it reveals of our relations with other people, or 'the Other', as he usually expresses this. I see a man walking by some benches in the park. My awareness of him as another for-itself causes me to reorganise my experience of the park; I am suddenly aware of the fact that he sees the grass and the benches from his own conscious point of view, one which is not directly accessible to me. It is as if the Other steals the world from me. My confident position at the centre of my world is destabilised.

The impact of other people on our consciousness is most apparent when we are aware of being watched. Being seen by the Other forces me to be aware of myself as an object viewed by someone else, as the following example from *Being and Nothingness* illustrates. Moved by jealousy, I peer through a keyhole to see what is going on on the other side of the door. I am completely immersed in what I see. In this mode of consciousness, which Sartre labels non-thetic, or prereflective, I am not aware of my self as a self, but only of what I see or am thinking about. My mind is as it were entirely in the room behind the door.

Suddenly, I hear footsteps in the hall behind me. I am aware that someone is there looking at me. I am thrown into shame, judged by this other person. I am jolted into an awareness of myself as an object viewed by another consciousness: my own freedom escapes me as I become objectified by the look of this other person.

LOVE

In love too there is the danger that our freedom will escape us. For Sartre love is a kind of conflict: a struggle to enslave another without becoming enslaved yourself. Yet the lover does not simply want to possess but wants to be desired, and so needs the beloved to be free. The complex play of wills can lead to masochism, the desire to be an object for your lover. Yet even in masochism, the impossibility of transforming yourself into an in-itself is apparent. Alternatively, sadism, which flirts with the idea of turning the other person into pure flesh, is equally futile in its goals. A glimpse into the eyes of the other person reveals that he or she exists as a free individual, and that total enslavement of that freedom is not possible.

MY DEATH

It can be tempting to think of death as part of life, as, perhaps, the final chord of a melody giving meaning to what has gone before. Sartre rejects this view. He thinks death is absurd: it has no meaning at all. It is in almost every case impossible to be absolutely sure when you will die. Sudden death is always a possibility; but it is not *my* possibility. It is rather the removal of all my possibilities in the sense that it takes away what makes me human: my ability to project myself towards the future. It takes away all meaning for me since the only meaning my life can have is that which I choose to give it. At death we become 'prey to the living'. What this means is that, though while living we choose the meaning of our actions, at death our actions are interpreted and given meaning by other people: we cease to have any responsibility for them, and other people can make of them what they will.

EXISTENTIAL PSYCHOANALYSIS

As we have seen, Sartre rejects out of hand the idea that there is a split between the unconscious and the conscious mind. He wants to replace Freudian psychoanalysis with his own freedom-based approach to the mind, which he calls 'existential psychoanalysis'. Central to this is his notion of a fundamental choice of being or original project. This is the core around which each of us organises his or her personality, a choice about what fundamentally we are. It is the aim of existential psychoanalysis to lay bare this original project, a choice which informs the individual's every subsequent choice. Existential psychoanalysis differs from most other approaches to human psychology in that it makes the individual entirely responsible for his or her choice of being. We are not simply the products of society or our genes, according to Sartre, but rather of our own choices. That is what makes us human.

CRITICISMS OF *BEING AND NOTHINGNESS*

Overestimates human freedom

A major criticism of Sartre's existentialism is that it presupposes a degree of freedom that human beings don't in fact have. He sometimes writes as if we could choose to be anything; as if we could think beyond the limitations imposed on us by our social situation and upbringing. We make the choices that we do because of what we are, and we are what we are because of what has happened to us. Sartre's focus is almost entirely on the individual and the choices he or she makes, rather than on the social context in which groups of people live. For many people, social, political and economic pressures are far more constraining than Sartre seems to acknowledge.

This sort of deterministic criticism would not have discouraged Sartre: he would simply deny that it is true, and probably suggest that you reflect on your experience and see whether or not it really was true of your life, or whether the adoption of the belief that it is is a kind of bad faith in the face of extreme freedom. A reply to this might be that feeling free is not necessarily the same as being free. We might simply have the illusion of free will rather than the genuine item. Perhaps all our actions are completely determined by what has happened to us, and yet we have misleading feelings that they are freely chosen.

Too pessimistic?

Whilst Sartre's treatment of human freedom is perhaps over-optimistic, his account of human relations is extremely pessimistic. We are constantly on the brink either of turning the other person into an object, an in-itself, or of attempting to turn ourselves into objects for him or her. He even goes so far as to describe humanity as 'a useless passion'. Perhaps this is an overly bleak description of what it is to be human. Sartre simply disagrees. In his defence it must be said that for many readers his account of freedom and bad faith has a liberating effect and a direct influence on their lives. They take responsibility for what they are rather than trying to find excuses for failing to achieve what they want from their lives.

DATES

1905   born in Paris.
1943   publishes *Being and Nothingness*.
1980   dies in Paris.

GLOSSARY

bad faith: a particular kind of self-deception that involves denying your own freedom.

being for-itself: Sartre's term for any being capable of self-consciousness.

being in-itself: Sartre's term for inanimate objects, and anything which lacks self-consciousness.

existentialism: a philosophical movement based on the belief that for conscious beings existence precedes essence. For further explanation see the next chapter.

facticity: those things which are givens, which cannot be changed, such as where you were born, or who your parents were.

non-thetic consiousness: being aware of something without being aware that you are aware.

original project: the basic choice you make about the direction of your life which colours most of your other choices.

phenomenological approach: a philosophical approach which was based on the idea that if you gave an accurate description of your experience, this would somehow reveal the essence of the things you were experiencing.

transcendence: the capacity of the for-itself to project itself into the future.

FURTHER READING

Donald Palmer *Sartre for Beginners* (London: Writers and Readers, 1995) is a readable introduction to Sartre's work in comic-book form. Arthur C. Danto *Sartre* (London: Fontana Modern Masters series, 1975) provides an introductory overview of Sartre's main themes.

Joseph P. Catalano *A Commentary on Jean-Paul Sartre's Being and Nothingness* (Chicago: University of Chicago Press, 1980) is useful. It explains the book section by section. Though quite difficult in places, it is never as difficult as *Being and Nothingness* itself.

Gregory McCulloch *Using Sartre: An Analytical Introduction to Early Sartrean Themes* (London: Routledge, 1994) provides a dynamic introduction to some of the main lines of Sartre's thought in *Being and Nothingness*.

Eric Matthews *Twentieth Century French Philosophy* (Oxford: Oxford University Press, 1996) sets Sartre in the context of a French tradition. It provides a clear and interesting account of a number of notoriously difficult philosophers.

Annie Cohen-Solal *Sartre: A Life* (London: Heinemann, 1987) and Ronald Hayman *Writing Against: A Biography of Sartre* (London: Weidenfeld & Nicolson, 1986) are two absorbing accounts of Sartre's very full life. His own much briefer autobiography is *Words* (Harmondsworth: Penguin, 1967).

25

JEAN-PAUL SARTRE
EXISTENTIALISM AND HUMANISM

Abandonment, anguish, despair: these are the key concepts in Jean-Paul Sartre's public lecture 'L'Existentialisme est un humanisme' (literally 'Existentialism is a humanism'). The lecture, first delivered in Paris in October 1945, and later translated and published as the short book *Existentialism and Humanism*, is probably his most read philosophical work. He later regretted its publication. Yet despite its flaws, it can still fire the imagination and offer genuine insight into aspects of human choice and responsibility. It also serves as a bridge to his more complex work *Being and Nothingness*.

Sartre delivered his lecture on existentialism in the wake of the Nazi occupation of Paris. This was a time when people who might otherwise have led relatively uneventful lives had just emerged from a situation in which they could not avoid issues of integrity, betrayal and commitment, in relation to the occupation, the resistance movements and the Vichy government. Sartre had himself been a prisoner of war before returning to occupied Paris where he spent most of the war. Yet many of Sartre's thoughts are still directly relevant to anyone deciding what they want to do and be today.

WHAT IS EXISTENTIALISM?

Existentialism is a philosophical movement that exercised an influence on many of the arts as well as on philosophy and psychology.

Gabriel Marcel first coined the word 'existentialist' when talking of Sartre. It took several years before Sartre was prepared to accept this label.

Existentialists are diverse in their beliefs. In *Existentialism and Humanism* Sartre suggests that what all existentialists have in common is a belief that for human beings 'existence precedes essence'. By this he means that there is no pre-existing blueprint for humanity; no human nature to which we must conform. We choose what we become. In Sartre's version of existentialism there is no God in whose mind our essence lies. We exist first and, through our actions, make of ourselves what we will. In our choices we determine what sort of a being each of us is. We are completely free to determine what we want to become, but at the same time, as we shall see, for Sartre this freedom carries with it an inescapable burden.

An artefact, such as a penknife, in contrast, is determined by its function: if it won't cut and hasn't got a folding blade, then it isn't a penknife. The essence of a penknife – what makes it a penknife and not something else – was in the mind of its maker before the knife was made. A human being is different in that we have no predetermined function and no Divine Artisan as maker, in whose mind our essence could have been determined. Unlike Aristotle, for example, Sartre did not believe in a common human nature which could be the basis of morality.

The emphasis on human freedom to choose what we are and what we become is characteristic of all existentialist thinkers. Although Sartre was an atheist, other existentialists, such as Gabriel Marcel, have been Christians.

WHAT IS HUMANISM?

The main drive of Sartre's lecture was to demonstrate that his own brand of existentialism was a form of humanism. 'Humanism' is a term that has many related meanings, so it is important to be clear about how Sartre uses the word. In one sense it simply applies to any theory that puts human beings at the centre of things. So, for instance, the humanism of the Renaissance was characterised by a movement away from speculation about the nature of God to a concern with the works of humanity, especially in art and literature. Humanism has the positive connotation of being humane. It is also a term for secular movements – those who reject the idea that there is a God who is the source of morality.

When Sartre declares that existentialism is a humanism, part of what he is doing is emphasising the dignity of humanity, the centrality of human choice to the creation of all values. It is another way of saying that human beings create what they are and indeed create morality. In an important sense we are responsible for what and who we are and what we value. But he also wanted to identify existentialism as a humanism in order to answer his critics who caricatured his approach as a dark and dangerous pessimism about the human psyche and human potential.

ANSWERING HIS CRITICS

Some of Sartre's critics thought that existentialism was a philosophy that could only lead to 'a quietism of despair'. In other words they thought it a philosophy of inaction, a merely contemplative philosophy that would discourage people from committing themselves to any course of action. Others chided the existentialists for being overly pessimistic and for concentrating on all that is ignominious in the human condition – Sartre quotes a Catholic critic, Mlle Mercier, who accused him of forgetting how an infant smiles.

From other directions came the criticism that because existentialism concentrates so much on the choices of the individual it ignores the solidarity of humankind. It treats the individual as an island, rather than as an integrated part of a wider society. Marxists and Christians alike made this point. A further attack came from those who saw existentialism as licensing the most heinous crimes in the name of free existential choice. Since existentialists rejected the notion of God-given moral laws, it seemed to follow that everyone could do whatever they liked.

Sartre's response to these criticisms focussed on his analysis of the concepts of abandonment, anguish and despair. For Sartre these words have specific meanings – they are technical terms and their connotations are significantly different from those they have in ordinary usage, though they do still draw on those connotations. All three terms in everyday usage (in their English forms at least) typically connote helplessness and suffering of various kinds. For Sartre, though, they also contain an optimistic aspect, one which a superficial reading of the text might miss.

ABANDONMENT

For Sartre 'abandonment' means specifically abandonment by God. This doesn't imply that God as a metaphysical entity actually existed at some point, and went away. Sartre is echoing the famous pronouncement made in Nietzsche's *Thus Spake Zarathustra*: 'God is dead'. Nietzsche's point was that in the late nineteenth century belief in God was no longer tenable. By using the word 'abandonment' in a metaphorical way Sartre emphasises the sense of loss caused by the realisation that there is no God to underwrite our moral choices; no divinity to give us principles that will ensure our salvation. The choice of the word reminds us that we are alone in the universe when seeking guidance about how we should act.

The main consequence of abandonment is the absence of any objective source of morality. Our moral choices must be made from a subjective position, though this did not mean for Sartre that any arbitrary choice was as acceptable as any other, as we shall see.

Sartre objected strongly to the kind of atheistic moralist who recognised that God didn't exist, yet clung to a secular version of Christian morality without the reassurance of a God to back it up. This kind of humanist did not follow through the logical implications of abandonment but took refuge in a kind of wishful thinking. In contrast, the Sartrean existentialist recognises the full impact of the non-existence of a creator. The position of someone making choices about his or her life is one of anguish.

ANGUISH

Sartre believes wholeheartedly in the freedom of the will. He is strongly anti-determinist about human choice. Believing that you are forced to be one way or another is almost always a kind of self-deception which he labels 'bad faith' – the denial to yourself of your true freedom. Although he rejects the idea that humanity has any essence, he declares that human beings are fundamentally free. That is the core of what we are. Yet in Sartre's almost paradoxical phrase we are not just free, but 'condemned to be free'. Instead of liberation, the knowledge and experience of our own freedom to choose our action and our attitude to the world brings with it a weight of responsibility.

Anguish, then, is in part the recognition that we are alone without excuses. There is no one else on whom we can blame our plight. We are responsible for everything that we are. Obviously we can't choose who our parents were, where we were born, whether or not we will die, and so on. But Sartre does go so far as to claim that we are fully responsible for how we feel about every aspect of our situation. We choose our emotions, and to deny this is bad faith.

Sartre goes beyond even this. Not only am I responsible for everything that I am, but, when choosing any particular action I inevitably act 'as a legislator deciding for the whole of humanity'. In Sartre's example, if I choose to marry and to have children I thereby commit not only myself but the whole of humanity to the practice of this form of monogamous reproduction. This echoes Immanuel Kant's notion of the universalizability of moral judgements: the view that if something is morally right for one person to do, it must also be morally right for anyone else in relevantly similar circumstances. For Sartre the full sense of the term 'anguish' becomes apparent when we realise the implications of any of our choices. Whatever we choose, we are painting a picture of what it is to be human. When we realise this we will feel the tremendous responsibility of someone whose actions have far-reaching implications for others. Like the Biblical Abraham whom God instructed to sacrifice his only son, we are in a state of anguish because, like him we are 'condemned' to choose our actions in situations where we cannot possibly know what will happen until it is too late to make any difference. And yet, it is as if the whole of humanity is watching us to see what we will make of this human life.

DESPAIR

Despair, like abandonment and anguish, is an emotive term. For Sartre despair is simply a reaction to the obstinate character of the world. I can desire anything, but I can't necessarily get what I desire. I might, for example, want to be a concert violinist, but through no fault of my own break several fingers on my left hand, and as a result never be able to achieve the coordination and speed needed by a professional musician. Other people, events, circumstances can prevent the realisation of my goals. But just because things may not turn out the way we had hoped, Sartre does not believe that we should abandon ourselves to inaction. Rather he urges action and commitment, since we are simply the totality of what we actually do, not what we might have done had circumstances been different. And we still choose how we react to unfortunate obstacles to the achievement of our desires.

SARTRE'S PUPIL

The central example Sartre uses in *Existentialism and Humanism* is a real one. During the occupation of France one of Sartre's pupils was faced with a genuine moral dilemma. He had two options, as he saw it: to stay in France to look after his mother who doted on him; or to set off to join the Free French in England to fight for the liberation of France. He knew that the consequences of his leaving would be very bad for his mother; yet at the same time his attempt to join the Free French might end in total failure and his attempt to do something worthwhile with his life might 'vanish like water into sand'. The stark choice was between a son's loyalty and the attempt to fight for the liberation of his homeland.

Sartre begins by demonstrating that neither Christian nor Kantian moral doctrines could guide the pupil. Christian teaching would tell the youth to act with charity, love his neighbour and be prepared to sacrifice himself for the sake of others. This, however, doesn't solve the problem, since he would still be left choosing between love of his mother and love of his country. The Kantian ethic teaches never to treat others as means to an end. But this doesn't help much either, since staying with his mother would be treating her as an end, but at the same time treating those fighting on his behalf as a means to an end. But if he joins the fighters, he would be treating them as ends, but at risk of treating his mother as a means to an end.

Here the pupil experiences the meaning of abandonment: he is forced to make significant choices in a world without fixed pre-ordained values. There are no simple solutions. Ultimately he is forced to choose for himself. Even if he goes to someone for advice, he can choose to reject that advice. And his choice of advisor would probably to some extent be a result of his expectation of the kind of advice he would get from them. Sartre's advice to his pupil was straightforward, but perhaps not particularly helpful. He left the student bearing the full weight of the anguish of the human predicament with the words: 'You are free, therefore choose.'

CRITICISMS OF *EXISTENTIALISM AND HUMANISM*

Overestimates human freedom

In *Existentialism and Humanism*, just as in his earlier book *Being and Nothingness*, Sartre asserts that human beings are free and that our free choices determine what we are. Yet, many philosophers are sceptical of his assumption of the extent of free will (see the similar criticism of *Being and Nothingness* in the previous chapter). You needn't be a complete determinist to believe that we have less freedom about our emotions, for example, than Sartre suggests.

Too individualistic

Sartre's existentialism emphasises the individual alone, responsible for everything he or she does, not bound by any human nature or social conventions that fix what a human being should do. Yet this approach is atomistic. Sartre writes as if we weren't integrated into particular societies with resulting obligations and responsibilities. Society shapes us, and, many believe, conditions what it is possible for us to think and do. Sartre's approach is unashamedly subjective: he begins from the individual. In his later book, *The Critique of Dialectical Reason*, he attempted to reconcile the individual existentialist position with Marxism, acknowledging the social, political and historical aspects of the human predicament which he had underplayed in his earlier writing. Unfortunately most of that book is almost unintelligible, perhaps because he wrote large parts of it under the influence of amphetamines.

Why should my choices hold for all humanity?

In order to rebut his critics, Sartre needs to demonstrate that his existentialism does not support the worst form of subjectivism, whereby moral choices are really a matter of individual taste, and any choice of action is as morally good as any other. If his existentialism collapses into this position, then it would be a fair criticism of it to point out that it has the consequence that the most horrific examples of torture, murder and sadism are according to this theory morally acceptable if people genuinely desire to perform them.

His argument for his version of universalisability, however, on which the whole edifice of his argument stands, is rather weak. He begins with the claim that when we choose to do something what we choose is always what we believe to be the better course of action. But then, controversially, he goes on to claim that nothing can be better for us unless it is better for everyone. So, for Sartre, because I choose what is in my view best for me, this somehow implies that it must be best for everyone – presumably meaning everyone in a similar situation. The image of humanity that I create when making my choices must hold for anyone in an entire epoch. Thus our responsibility is supposed to extend far beyond the individual. Yet the swift moves in this argument from individual choice to responsibility for the whole of humanity in an epoch, do not seem justified or, indeed, justifiable.

The case of the sincere yet evil person

Even if Sartre's position had been well supported, it might have some extremely unpalatable consequences which he does not consider. For example, take the case of a sincere yet evil person, such as Adolf Hitler. From an existential viewpoint Hitler's choices – his repulsive anti-semitism, the Holocaust, his eugenics programmes – were all delivered in good faith. Hitler's fashioning of an image of himself did indeed fashion an image of what humanity could be like in an epoch. An existentialist Hitler could claim that his choices had been made in a world without pre-existing values and that they were not just binding on him but on the whole of humanity.

Existentialism and Humanism does provide the material for a response to this criticism. There Sartre asserts that someone who genuinely chooses to be free cannot not wish freedom for other people too. Quite clearly Hitler did not respect the freedom of those who did not agree with him. He murdered millions of Jews, homosexuals, political opponents, Gypsies, those with severe psychiatric problems. If Sartre's principle is accepted then this provides a retort to the objection that his philosophy would not provide a position from which to judge Hitler as immoral. Yet the principle that anyone who chooses to be free must want other people to be free only makes sense if you assume that logically whatever you want for yourself you must also want for other people. Sartre, however, as we have already seen, does not provide adequate argument to move from the individual to the whole of humanity.

DATES

See previous chapter.

GLOSSARY

abandonment: a metaphorical way of referring to the absence of God.

anguish: the experience of free choice with the weight of responsibility of choosing for humanity.

despair: the realisation that the world may be resistant to our will in various ways so that our projects may not be realised through events outside our control.

essence: the feature that makes something what it is, without which it would be something else.

existentialism: the philosophical and literary movement particularly identified with Sartre that emphasises that for human beings existence precedes essence.

humanism: the secular movement that makes human beings the source of value in the world.

quietism: a philosophy of inaction and withdrawal from the world.

FURTHER READING

Stephen Priest (ed.) *Jean-Paul Sartre: Basic Writings* (London: Routledge, 2001) includes the complete text of *Existentialism and Humanism* together with extracts from other key texts by Sartre. Priest's clear and succinct introductions are extremely useful in coming to terms with a quite difficult writer. His short biographical summary of Sartre's philosophical career is also very helpful.

For further reading about Sartre, see suggestions at the end of the previous chapter.

26

LUDWIG WITTGENSTEIN
PHILOSOPHICAL INVESTIGATIONS

Ludwig Wittgenstein did not want to spare other people the trouble of thinking for themselves. *Philosophical Investigations* was intended to stimulate his readers to have their own thoughts rather than to present them with pre-packaged ideas for convenient consumption. This is reflected in the style of writing, which is fragmentary and oblique, flitting from one topic to the next and back again. The answers to philosophical questions are not given in a straightforward way, but rather suggested through particular examples and stories. Clues are provided, but their implications aren't usually spelt out; metaphors abound, but it is up to the reader to unpack them.

Instead of chapters, Wittgenstein uses shorter numbered sections. The organisation of the book is not all due to Wittgenstein: it was published in 1953, two years after his death, and is based on a manuscript he was working on for a number of years.

RELATION TO *TRACTATUS LOGICO-PHILOSOPHICUS*

The only book of Wittgenstein's to be published during his lifetime was his *Tractatus Logico-Philosophicus,* which appeared in 1921. This austere series of numbered statements managed to combine a poetic style with a serious treatment of logic and the limits of human thought. It is most famous for the concluding pronouncement

'Whereof one cannot speak, thereof one must remain silent.' This wasn't a practical adage, but rather a summary of the views about the limits of thought. Most of what is important in human life lies outside the realm of what can be said meaningfully; it is inexpressible, but no less important for that. In many ways *Philosophical Investigations* is a critique of the views expressed in the *Tractatus*, and Wittgenstein even suggested that the *Tractatus* should be published as a preface to *Philosophical Investigations* to bring out what was distinctive about his more recent ideas.

THE NATURE OF PHILOSOPHY

In *Philosophical Investigations* Wittgenstein sees his role as letting the fly out of the fly-bottle. What he means by this is that philosophers buzz around trapped by their attempts to make language do what it cannot do. They are bewitched by language. As he puts it, 'Philosophical problems arise when language *goes on holiday*' (section 38). In other words, philosophical problems arise from using words in an inappropriate context.

Wittgenstein's approach is designed to dissolve such problems by attending to the actual use of language and thus letting the fly out of the fly-bottle. Hence his philosophical approach is often characterised as a therapeutic one: philosophy is the illness that needs to be cured. Philosophy examines 'bumps that the understanding has got from running up against the limits of language' (section 119). The cure is to look at how language actually functions, not how we imagine that it must function. But his analysis of actual uses of language is not an exercise in social anthropology. By mapping out some of the ways in which language is used Wittgenstein draws attention to the limits of thought and meaningfulness. A large part of this enterprise involved eliminating misleading theories about the nature of language. Another reason for focusing on particular uses of language was his belief that large-scale theorising is misguided in that it rests on the false assumption that we can discover the essence of the thing being investigated.

MEANING AS USE

A significant part of *Philosophical Investigations* is directed against what Wittgenstein thinks is a simplistic account of the nature of language. He takes Saint Augustine's account of language-learning by pointing to objects and naming them as representative of this view. Holders of this Augustinian picture of language believe that words are names of objects, and that combinations of words have the sole function of describing reality.

For example, on this view, in order to learn the meaning of the word 'apple' we present a child with an apple and say 'this is an apple'. This is called teaching by ostensive definition: pointing to the object that is named. Wittgenstein does not deny that such ostensive definition goes on, but draws attention to a number of difficulties with the view that this is the basis of all language-learning. For example, such ostensive definition requires a certain amount of stage-setting. The child might not understand the institution of pointing at an object, or else might think that you were pointing out the colour or the shape of the apple. Every case of ostensive definition allows for a variety of interpretations of what is being picked out. Furthermore, even if the child understands the particular case of ostensive definition, he or she might not be able to make the transition from this case to others like it.

Language is not simply a medium we use to represent the world. Rather it is more like a tool kit containing a wide range of implements which we use for different purposes. Or, to borrow another of Wittgenstein's metaphors, language is like the levers in the cabin of a locomotive. Words resemble each other, so we have a tendency to think that they all do the same sort of thing. However, like the levers in the locomotive the similarity is superficial: one lever operates a valve, another the brakes; one has only two positions, 'off' and 'on'; another can be moved continuously.

If we examine the nature of actual language, we very quickly find that the Augustinian picture is inaccurate. The meaning of words is given by their use rather than by what they might refer to. Language does not have an underlying essence, a common denominator, a unique function. Rather, if we examine language we find a pattern of overlapping functions which it serves in different contexts. Wittgenstein talks of 'language games'. He doesn't mean by this phrase that using language is a matter of being playful, but that there are many different rule-governed activities within which language functions. Language is embedded in our forms of life, the social conventions which have grown up around its various uses. The meanings of words are governed by how we happen to use them; isolated from a context of use, a form of life, they are meaningless.

FAMILY RESEMBLANCE TERMS

One common way of being bewitched by language is to assume that if we correctly use a word to refer to a range of cases, every case must have something in common with the others. We often assume that, for example, there is an essence of games, so that whenever we use the word 'game' we are alluding to the common feature that the activity in question shares with other games. Wittgenstein believes this to be a mistake. It is a mistake to assume that there *must* be an essence shared by all games as much as it is a mistake to assume that all language uses *must* have something in common.

Wittgenstein's defence of this view is based on an analogy with family resemblances. Blood relations often resemble each other. But that doesn't mean that every member of the family shares one or more common features: what usually occurs is that there is a pattern of overlapping resemblances rather than a single common feature found throughout. You might resemble your sister with respect to hair colour and your mother with respect to eye colour. Your sister and mother may have the same shaped nose. In this simple example no single feature is shared by all three members of the family, but this does not prevent there being a visible family resemblance. Similarly, there is no common essence shared by all the things we call 'games': board games, football, solitaire, throwing a ball against the wall, and so on. But we can nevertheless use the word 'game' meaningfully. Wittgenstein uses the phrase 'family resemblance' to refer to this sort of overlapping and criss-crossing resemblance.

THE PRIVATE LANGUAGE ARGUMENT

By far the most influential part of *Philosophical Investigations* is the group of comments and examples known as the Private Language Argument, although there is still some controversy about precisely what Wittgenstein meant by them. It is worth bearing in mind that Wittgenstein didn't use the phrase 'Private Language Argument', and it is only his commentators who have suggested that a series of his comments should be interpreted as a cumulative argument.

Nevertheless, it does seem reasonable to group his thoughts together in this way and to extract an argument from their progression. In order to begin to understand this argument, we need to get clear what Wittgenstein was attacking.

Most philosophers since Descartes have assumed that a proper study of the nature of the mind must begin from a consideration of the first-person case, that is, from one's own experience. I can be more certain that I am in pain, for example, than that you are. I have privileged access to the contents of my own mind that does not extend to the contents of yours. It is as if I have special access to a private cinema in which my thoughts and feelings are displayed; no one else has any idea of what happens within my private cinema. My experience is private to me, and yours to you. No one can really know my pain or my thoughts. I can describe my inner experience to myself, and no one else is able to judge whether or not my descriptions are accurate.

Wittgenstein's Private Language Argument undermines the view which props up the idea that my thoughts and feelings are fundamentally inaccessible to anyone else. The idea rests on a belief in the possibility of a private language. Wittgenstein shows that no such language is possible. By 'private language' he doesn't mean a private code, nor does he mean a language spoken by only one person, as, for instance, a Robinson Crusoe figure might devise to talk to himself about his life on a desert island. Rather, a private language, for Wittgenstein, is one that is in principle unshareable because it is used to refer to an individual's allegedly private experiences.

Someone who believes in the possibility of such a private language might argue that it would be possible for me to keep a diary recording my sensations. I have a particular sensation which I decide to call 'S'. I put an 'S' in my diary. The next time I have the same sort of sensation, I put another 'S' in the diary, and so on. Wittgenstein argues that this account is incoherent. There is 'no criterion of correctness' for the reidentification of my 'S' sensations, no way of proving that I was correct or incorrect in any case where I think I have reidentified a feeling of 'S'. It is like checking the time a train leaves by calling up your memory of the timetable, but with one important difference: there is no actual timetable out there in the world to serve as the touchstone of correctness. Where there is no possible way of checking up to see if I am correct in my application of a term, the term cannot have any meaning. Consequently, Wittgenstein's conclusion is that giving names to your private experiences by acts of private ostensive definition is a nonsensical notion. Language is public, and the criteria for the application and reapplication of words are public. No private language of the sort envisaged above is possible.

This is not, of course, to deny that people have sensations and experiences. However, from the point of view of the meaning of language, if these experiences were necessarily private, they would have no relevance. Imagine a situation in which everyone owned their own box with something in it which we call a 'beetle'. No one can look inside anyone else's box, and everyone claims to know what a beetle is by looking inside their own box. In this sort of case, Wittgenstein says, it wouldn't matter whether everyone had the same sort of thing in their box, or nothing at all. The thing in the box doesn't affect the meaning of 'beetle'.

The consequence of Wittgenstein's argument is that the picture of the mind suggested by Descartes is untenable. We don't each inhabit our own private cinema. Rather, language sets the limits of our thought, and language is an intrinsically public phenomenon. This argument also undermines the view of the mind presented in the empiricist tradition, including that given by Locke and Hume. Like Descartes, these philosophers implicitly assume the possibility of describing one's own sensations in a private language: in particular, Locke's view of language relies on the possibility of reidentifying privately labelled sensations.

Wittgenstein's Private Language Argument isn't entirely negative. In place of the traditional account of the relationship between our experiences and the language we use to describe them, he offers an alternative hypothesis. Perhaps words like 'pain' are not names of private sensations, but are rather part of our learnt pain-behaviour, with public criteria for their correct application. A child hurts herself and cries; adults teach the child to articulate the pain. What this means is that the child learns to speak about pain as a substitute for crying. Speaking about pain, however, is not simply a matter of describing a sensation. According to Wittgenstein, speaking about pain is another way of *expressing* pain.

SEEING ASPECTS

In the second part of *Philosophical Investigations* one topic which Wittgenstein discusses involves the familiar example of the duck-rabbit: a figure which can be interpreted as a drawing either of a duck or of a rabbit, but not both simultaneously. I look at the figure and see it as a duck; then, I see a new aspect of it: it looks like a rabbit. This change of aspect has not been brought about by any change in what is reflected on the back of my retina. Precisely the same visual stimuli give rise to my sense that I am looking at a picture of a duck as when I am seeing it as a rabbit. This seems paradoxical: the aspect changes when no line of the picture has been altered. It suggests that seeing involves a kind of judgement about what is being seen, and that this can be influenced by what we expect to see.

CRITICISMS OF *PHILOSOPHICAL INVESTIGATIONS*

Philosophical problems don't all dissolve

Many philosophers remain unconvinced that all philosophical problems arise when language 'goes on holiday'. For example, few contemporary philosophers of mind investigating the nature of human consciousness feel that all they need do is point to some of the ways we use language in order to rid ourselves for ever of the philosophical problem of how matter could give rise to thought and selfawareness. Wittgenstein's claims about letting the fly out of the fly-bottle are seductive; but traditional philosophical disputes continue to perplex and challenge philosophers, despite his attempts to explain them away as bewitchment by language. Wittgenstein, presumably, would respond to this by pointing out that the philosophers in question are still in thrall to the language they are trying to force into doing jobs that it just can't do.

Oracular pronouncements

A quite serious criticism of Wittgenstein's style in *Philosophical Investigations* is that it results in a book which is open to many conflicting interpretations. In many places it is not at all clear what the precise point of an example or parable is, nor is it always obvious that some of the views he seems to be attacking have ever been held. Often we seem to be getting just the tip of a submerged iceberg and are left to ourselves to work out what must lie beneath the surface of a remark. Although in recent years Wittgenstein's notebooks and his students' lecture notes have been made widely available, there is still fierce debate about some of his central doctrines.

Wittgenstein is surely responsible for the ambiguities and indeterminacies in his work, not all of which can be put down to the difficulty of presenting such radical and original ideas. Some of the difficulties stem directly from his piecemeal approach. There is no doubting the elegance and imaginative appeal of Wittgenstein's examples, but the lack of coherent argument or clarificatory passages leaves the reader with a great deal of work to do.

In Wittgenstein's defence, he was very open about his desire that his readers think for themselves rather than have views dished out to them by an authority. So in that sense contemporary disputes about interpretation are a tribute to his success, since they indicate that philosophers are having to think through what Wittgenstein could possibly have meant in order to make sense of the work at all.

Nevertheless, Wittgenstein's oblique and poetic style attracts discipleship. There has never been a shortage of ardent followers who cite paragraph numbers from *Philosophical Investigations* with all the enthusiasm of religious zealots. These followers for the most part are happy to get their ideas secondhand from the master, apparently unaware that that is precisely what he said he didn't want to happen. The oracular style of much of *Philosophical Investigations* seems to invite a reverential rather than critical approach, and so may undermine the aim of making its readers think for themselves.

Wittgenstein himself was never satisfied enough with his drafts of *Philosophical Investigations* to publish the book in his own lifetime. Perhaps, then, it is fairer to treat it as work in progress, rather than as his definitive views in the form he would have most liked them to have reached the world.

DATES

1889   born in Vienna.
1951   dies in Cambridge.
1953   *Philosophical Investigations* published posthumously.

GLOSSARY

duck-rabbit: a drawing which can be interpreted either as a duck or as a rabbit, but not both simultaneously. Wittgenstein uses this example to explain aspect-seeing.

essentialism: belief that, for example, all the things referred to by a particular word *must* have something in common.

family resemblance: a pattern of overlapping and criss-crossing resemblances with no common feature shared by all members of a family.

form of life: the culture and social conventions within which language games are embedded.

language game: a set of conventions about language use in a particular context.

ostensive definition: defining things by pointing to them and saying their name.

private language: for Wittgenstein, a language which necessarily cannot be understood by others. He thinks that such a language is an impossibility, but is nevertheless implied by some erroneous pictures of the mind.

FURTHER READING

A. C. Grayling *Wittgenstein* (Oxford: Oxford University Press, Past Masters series, 1988) gives a brief overview of Wittgenstein's philosophy.

Anthony Kenny *Wittgenstein* (Harmondsworth: Penguin, 1973) provides a more thorough and more sophisticated introduction.

Hans-Johann Glock *A Wittgenstein Dictionary* (Oxford: Blackwell, 1996) is an extremely useful guide which explains Wittgenstein's central ideas.

Ray Monk *Ludwig Wittgenstein: The Duty of Genius* (London: Vintage, 1991) is an excellent biography. It provides a compelling account of the personal life and thought of this unusual man.

27

JOHN RAWLS *A THEORY OF JUSTICE*

What kind of a society would you choose to live in if you didn't know the position you would occupy within it? John Rawls' *A Theory of Justice* provides the principles for constructing a fair and just society by imagining a reasonable person's response to this question. The book, first published in 1971, transformed political philosophy. It rejuvenated the social contract tradition established by Hobbes, Locke and Rousseau. Though a complex and in places rather dry book, it is one of the most widely read works of political philosophy of the twentieth century. Its most distinctive aspect is its use of the notion of the 'original position' to arrive at conclusions about fairness and justice and how we should achieve them in our social institutions.

THE ORIGINAL POSITION

If you were to choose the principles which should govern the best possible society you might be biased in various ways towards your own class, profession, sexual orientation, and so on. Rawls' way around this is to set up a thought experiment, a hypothetical situation in which all the facts about your self, and your particular desires, are hidden from you behind a veil of ignorance. You have to imagine not knowing whether or not you have a job, what sex you are, whether you have a family, where you live, how intelligent you are, whether you are an optimist, a pessimist, a drug addict. Yet at the same time you have a good grasp of politics and economics, the basis of social organisation and the laws of human psychology. You know that there are basic goods required for almost any lifestyle, and these include certain freedoms, opportunity, income and self-respect. Rawls calls this situation of ignorance about your own place in society 'the original position'.

In this hypothetical state of the original position, which principles would it be rational for someone to adopt for the organisation of society? The idea of asking this question is to eliminate all the non-relevant features of our actual lives which otherwise tend to intrude in our assessment of what sort of society there should be. Rawls assumes that principles rationally chosen under the conditions of the original position would have a special claim to being just ones, and that, other things being equal, we should adopt them.

The principles which emerge from this process should not be controversial since if we have carried out the thought experiment effectively, there should be no difference between any individuals engaging in it. This is because in the original position all the elements that distinguish us one from another should have been removed. The principles then, should be ones on which rational participants would agree. Carrying out this thought experiment, Rawls comes up with two basic principles, one concerned with liberty, the other with the just distribution of goods. These principles embody his basic political conclusions which are liberal and egalitarian.

Unlike some social contract theorists Rawls is not saying that we must all have implicitly agreed to these principles; rather he uses the thought experiment of the original position as a way of generating basic principles for the ordering of a just society and then compares these with pre-existing intuitions in order to make fine tunings. Rawls believes that the principles for ordering society that emerge together merit the name 'justice as fairness' since they have been arrived at by a rational and impartial process. The first of the two principles thus generated is the liberty principle.

THE LIBERTY PRINCIPLE

The liberty principle states that 'Each person is to have an equal right to the most extensive total system of equal basic liberties compatible with a similar system of liberty for all.' In other words, choosing behind a veil of ignorance a rational person would want everyone in the society to have the same right to basic liberties as anyone else. Otherwise that person might end up a victim of discrimination. For example, liberty of conscience, freedom to entertain whatever religious or secular beliefs you may find convincing, is a basic freedom that the state is not justified in curtailing. Only when your actions threaten others' liberties would state intervention be justified, since your liberty in this respect would not then be compatible with equal liberty for everyone else. Even the intolerant have a right to liberty up to the point at which they endanger the equal liberty of others. The rule of law is necessary to guarantee the various liberties which each member of a society has a right to.

Rawls stipulates that the principles he puts forward as the rational choices of anyone in the original position are ordered *lexically*. What this means is that they are ranked in such a way that the first principle has to be satisfied before considering the second; the second before moving on to the third and so on. Here this means that the right to equal liberty is the most basic principle in his theory, and always takes priority. The demands of this principle must be met first, and are more important than the demands of the second principle. Rawls' picture of a just society is, then, one in which a right to equal liberty for all is upheld and enforced by law.

THE FAIR EQUALITY OF OPPORTUNITY PRINCIPLE AND THE DIFFERENCE PRINCIPLE

Rawls' second principle, one concerned with the just distribution of primary goods, really consists of two principles: the fair equality of opportunity principle and the difference principle. As a whole, this second principle has lexical priority over any principles of efficiency. What this means is that justice is more important than utility.

The fair equality of opportunity principle states that any social or economic inequalities associated with particular offices or jobs can only exist if these offices or jobs are open to everyone under conditions of fair equality of opportunity. No one should be excluded from, for instance, the best-paid jobs, on non-relevant grounds such as sexual orientation or race. For Rawls equality of opportunity is more than mere anti-discrimination. It includes, for example, provision of education to allow all people to develop their talents. The equality of opportunity principle takes lexical priority over the other part of Rawls' second principle, the difference principle.

The difference principle insists that any social or economic inequalities should only be tolerated on condition that they bring the greatest benefits to the most disadvantaged members of society. This is an implementation of a strategy known as 'maximin'. Maximin is short for 'maximise the minimum', which means choose the option which gives the best deal for the worst case. This is probably easier to follow if we take the example of fair wages in a just society. Imagine two situations. In the first, most people earn a high wage, but ten per cent of the population can barely earn enough to survive. In the second case, although the average standard of living is far lower, the worst off ten per cent of the population have a reasonable standard of living. For someone choosing in the original position, Rawls claims, the second of the two situations is preferable because it guarantees that everyone in the society will be achieving a reasonable standard of living: the worst off aren't that badly off. In the first case, however, although there is a good chance of ending up quite well off, there is also a significant risk of being on a wage that barely allows you to survive. Adopting the maximin strategy, we should minimise the worst risks, and so should opt for the second case. It just isn't worth the gamble to risk living a life in abject poverty.

CRITICISMS OF *A THEORY OF JUSTICE*

The original position

A major criticism of the notion of the original position is that it is psychologically impossible to rid yourself of the knowledge of who and what you are, even in a thought experiment. Inevitably your prejudices evade the censor. Some critics of Rawls' approach have claimed that all Rawls has really done with the thought experiment of the original position is confirmed his pre-existing liberal prejudices and given them the aura of rationally chosen principles. It is unrealistic to think that you can simply imagine away what you know and what is so central to your individual existence.

In Rawls' defence it might be argued that all this shows is the difficulty of using the thought experiment effectively. It may yet be the best device we have for generating principles for ordering society, even if, because of features of human psychology, it is likely to be imperfect in many respects. Rawls never claimed that his method was infallible. But it is easy to see that it could eliminate some biased principles as obvious non-starters.

Nevertheless, the original position has built into it some basic assumptions. Rawls derives principles from it that present a vision of a liberal, tolerant society within which people can live side by side and pursue their own conception of what is good and right. The way the thought experiment is set up gives a high priority to autonomy, our capacity to make decisions for ourselves about how our lives should be led. Those from cultural or religious traditions which put a higher emphasis on hierarchy, tradition and obedience might see little reason for engaging in the thought experiment of the original position since it has this built-in bias towards a liberal and Kantian conception of what it is to be a rational moral agent.

Utilitarian objection

Utilitarians might object to Rawls' principles on the grounds that they don't necessarily maximise happiness. Utilitarians believe that the morally right action in any circumstance is the one that is most likely to produce the maximum amount of happiness. One of Rawls' main aims in writing *A Theory of Justice* was to develop a coherent alternative to this sort of utilitarian calculation. Defending a range of rights to freedom, and in particular implementing the difference principle, is unlikely to maximise happiness. A direct consequence of insisting that the only grounds for inequalities are that they benefit the worst off is that many social solutions which produce a far greater total or aggregate happiness will be ruled out.

Rawls' response to utilitarian approaches to society is that since you do not know what position in society you will occupy when you choose in the original position, the rational approach is to eliminate any risk of your leading an unpleasant life. Utilitarianism, at least in its simplest forms, doesn't safeguard basic human rights and liberties; it would not be rational for you to choose it in the original position. Rawls' approach emphasises that there can be more important goals than simply achieving the highest possible aggregate happiness.

Gambling versus playing safe

Adopting the maximin strategy is a way of playing safe. It guarantees that the worst off benefit from any inequalities built into social institutions. Yet many of us see the point in gambling, and will risk some discomfort for the chance of a substantial pay off. Why is it not rational in the original position to choose a society in which there is a high probability that I will do very well, even though I may in fact do badly? To a gambler this may seem preferable to the safe bet of the restricted inequalities that arise from application of the difference principle.

Rawls' response is that the gambler's strategy is too risky; but then the gambler thinks that Rawls' approach is too conservative.

Libertarian objection

Libertarian philosophers, such as Robert Nozick (1938–), have argued that beyond preserving some basic rights, the state should not be heavily involved in controlling social institutions. Nozick argues that only a minimal state is justified, one which protects individuals against theft and enforces contracts, but that any more extensive activity than this will violate some people's rights not to be coerced. Rawls' just society, in contrast, would, for example, tax property in a way that corrects the distribution of wealth.

Here Nozick assumes that the right not to be coerced is more fundamental than rights to equality of various kinds, and that rights such as property rights override any other considerations. Rawls makes different assumptions: he thinks that his principles, and in particular his principle of a right to equal liberty, are the bedrock of a just society. These represent two contrasting and incompatible approaches to political philosophy.

DATES

1921   John Rawls born.
1971   Publishes *A Theory of Justice*.
1993   Publishes *Political Liberalism* in which he further develops his theory of justice.

GLOSSARY

difference principle: the principle that any social or economic inequalities should only be tolerated on condition that they bring the greatest benefits to the most disadvantaged members of society.

libertarianism: a form of liberalism which stresses free choice above all. Libertarians oppose constraints on free choice imposed by political institutions and argue for a minimal state that simply protects against the use of force and theft.

maximin principle: short for 'maximise the minimum', which means choosing the option which gives the best deal in the worst case.

original position: the situation of ignorance about your place in society which is the starting point for Rawls' thought experiment.

primary goods: the basic requirements for a reasonable life, such as food and shelter, but also various freedoms, opportunities and self-respect.

utilitarianism: the view that the morally right action in any circumstance is the one which will maximise happiness.

veil of ignorance: in Rawls' thought experiment when we choose the kind of society we want we do not know what our position will be in that society: he uses the image of concealment with a veil.

FURTHER READING

Chandran Kukathas and Philip Petit *Rawls: A Theory of Justice and its Critics* (Cambridge: Polity, 1990) is a clear introduction to Rawls' work; it includes an assessment of some of his publications since *A Theory of Justice*.

Norman Daniels (ed.) *Reading Rawls: Critical Studies of A Theory of Justice* (Oxford: Blackwell, 1975) is a wide-ranging collection of articles, some quite difficult.

John Rawls *Political Liberalism* (1993) is Rawls' revision of his theory.

Ben Rogers outlines the salient features of John Rawls' life and also gives an overview of his philosophy in his article 'Behind the Veil: John Rawls and the Revival of Liberalism' in *Lingua Franca*, July/ August 1999, pp. 57–64.

INDEX

Philosophy:
The Basics, 4th edition

Nigel Warburton

Reviews of previous editions:

'An ideal introduction to the basics of philosophy for anyone approaching the subject for the first time. The book is beautifully written, admirably clear without being at all solemn, pretentious or patronising.' – *D.H. Mellor, University of Cambridge*

'I would strongly recommend this to sixth formers studying for A level Philosophy and also for those who are interested in learning something of the scope of philosophy.' – *Jennifer Trusted, Former Chief Examiner, Associated Examining Board*

'Simply and lucidly, does exactly what it says on the cover. An excellent way into the basics of philosophy, this book doesn't just instruct but tries to set the reader thinking as well.' – *Edward Craig, University of Cambridge*

'*Philosophy: The Basics* deservedly remains the most recommended introduction to philosophy on the market. Warburton is patient, accurate and, above all, clear. There is no better short introduction to philosophy.' – *Stephen Law*

Philosophy: The Basics is *the* book for anyone coming to philosophy for the first time. Nigel Warburton's best selling book gently eases the reader into the world of philosophy. Each chapter considers a key area of philosophy, explaining and exploring the basic ideas and themes.

ISBN10: 0–415–32772–5 (hbk)
ISBN10: 0–415–32773–3 (pbk)
ISBN13: 978–0–415–32772–5 (hbk)
ISBN13: 978–0–415–32773–2 (pbk)

Related titles from Routledge

Philosophy: Basic Readings

Nigel Warburton

Reviews of the First Edition

'Students will most likely find the readings understandable and interesting. Teachers will be happy to have so many fine readings from which to choose.' – *Harry Gensler, Times Higher Educational Supplement*

'The quality of Warburton's anthology is surely sufficient to silence the doubters who continue to believe philosophy cannot be popularised without being deformed. *Philosophy: Basic Readings* has filled a long-running vacancy for an introduction to philosophy that can be recommended without caveat or qualification.' – *Julian Baggini, Times Educational Supplement*

This is the ideal introduction to key philosophical texts for students. Nigel Warburton brings philosophy to life with an imaginative selection of philosophical writings on key topics. Each chapter considers a key area of philosophy, complementing the sections in *Philosophy: The Basics* with a selection of readings.

ISBN10: 0–415–33797–6 (hbk)
ISBN10: 0–415–33798–4 (pbk)
ISBN13: 978–0–415–33797–7 (hbk)
ISBN13: 978–0–415–33798–4 (pbk)

Available at all good bookshops
For ordering and further information please visit:
www.routledge.com

Related titles from Routledge

Philosophy:
The Essential Study Guide

Nigel Warburton

'Just what is needed. It is written in an easy style that makes it eminently clear and accessible to its intended audience . . . Drawing on my four decades of university teaching I don't think I could improve on the advice given.' – *Michael Clark, University of Nottingham*

Philosophy: The Essential Study Guide is a compact and straightforward guide to the skills needed to study philosophy, aimed at anyone coming to the subject for the first time or just looking to improve their performance. Nigel Warburton, bestselling author of *Philosophy: The Basics*, clarifies what is expected of students and offers strategies and guidance to help them make effective use of their study time and improve their marks. The four main skills covered by the book are:

- **READING** philosophy – both skimming and in-depth analysis of historical and contemporary work, understanding the examples and terminology used
- **LISTENING** to philosophy – formal lectures and informal classroom teaching, preparation, picking up on arguments used, note taking
- **DISCUSSING** philosophy – arguing and exploring, asking questions, communicating in concise and understandable ways
- **WRITING** philosophy – planning and researching essays and other written tasks, thinking up original examples, avoiding plagiarism.

Written in Nigel Warburton's customary student-friendly style and filled with sound advice and top tips, *Philosophy: The Essential Study Guide* is an indispensable guide for anyone getting to grips with their first philosophy course.

ISBN10: 0–415–34179–5 (hbk)
ISBN10: 0–415–34180–9 (pbk)

ISBN13: 978–0–415–34179–0 (hbk)
ISBN13: 978–0–415–34180–6 (pbk)

Available at all good bookshops
For ordering and further information please visit:
www.routledge.com